SYSTEMS, INSTITUTIONS, AND VALUES IN EAST AND WEST

SYSTEMS, INSTITUTIONS, AND VALUES IN EAST AND WEST

Engaging with János Kornai's Scholarship

Edited by
Dóra Piroska and Miklós Rosta

CEU PRESS

Central European University Press
Budapest–New York

Published in 2020 by
Central European University Press

Nádor utca 9, H-1051 Budapest, Hungary
Tel: +36-1-327-3138 or 327-3000
E-mail: ceupress@press.ceu.edu
Website: www.ceupress.com

224 West 57th Street, New York NY 10019, USA

ISBN 978-963-386-373-2 cloth

Library of Congress Cataloging-in-Publication Data

Names: Piroska, Dóra, editor. | Rosta, Miklós, editor.
Title: Systems, institutions, and values in East and West : engaging with János Kornai's scholarship / edited by Dóra Piroska and Miklós Rosta.

Description: New York : Central European University Press, 2020. | Includes bibliographical references and index.
Identifiers: LCCN 2020007798 (print) | LCCN 2020007799 (ebook) | ISBN 9789633863732 (hardback) | ISBN 9789633863725 (adobe pdf)
Subjects: LCSH: Central planning. | Economic policy. | Post-communism. | Mixed economy. | Kornai, János.
Classification: LCC HD87 .S97 2020 (print) | LCC HD87 (ebook) | DDC 338.9—dc23
LC record available at https://lccn.loc.gov/2020007798
LC ebook record available at https://lccn.loc.gov/2020007799

Printed in Hungary

Table of Contents

János Kornai
Photo by Katalin London

Engaging with János Kornai's Scholarship

Systems, Institutions, and Values

Dóra Piroska and Miklós Rosta

A remarkable feature of János Kornai's scholarship is its potential to stir up the academic community. His insights, tools, and analyses have invited researchers of various fields to conceptually argue, empirically question, and methodologically engage with his observations. This volume is a testament to the ability of Kornai's scholarship to engage researchers today. In this volume, leading social scientists, empirical analysts, and policy practitioners demonstrate the various ways in which Kornai's insights have permeated academic discussions on contemporary institutional change. In this way, this volume's editors and contributors come together to celebrate János Kornai.

Taken together, the various contributions collected here provide a review of Kornai's scholarship from several points of view. The various authors explore Kornai's ideas about socialism, capitalism, and post-socialist transition, as well as those about different economic sectors, including health economics, fiscal rules, and independent fiscal institutions. In addition, the various chapters look at the conditions for balanced economic growth, the process of European integration from a systemic approach, and the importance of democracy versus economic growth in post-socialist experiences. The analyses are conducted at various levels, ranging across the macro-, meso-, and micro-levels. Each of Kornai's principal concepts—e.g., soft budget constraints, rush versus harmonic growth, non-Walrasian equilibrium, the normal state of an economic system, the systemic approach, bureaucratic coordination, the undividable power of the communist party, property rights, institutionalism, surplus versus shortage economy—are covered by different authors.

As numerous scholars have observed, Kornai's conceptual tools cannot be easily linked to any one dominant school or approach, neither in economics narrowly defined or in the social sciences more broadly understood. Kornai, for example, is at the same time a hard-to-define political economist,[1] a lax institutional economist,[2] as well as a transition economist pursuing the never-ending quest of understanding economies in transition from one stage to the next.[3] In fact, Kornai is one of the best examples of how to be an independent thinker. His work is testimony to the fact that it is not necessary for a scholar to be part of any school of thought. His background and history, coming from socialist Hungary, and the marked changes in his interest in research and methods—which were, as Mihály Laki has observed,[4] not independent from each other—have made him a very-hard-to-categorize person in Western academia.

As a consequence, Kornai has never been part of a particular school in the field of economics. He did not have the intention to join a school of thought, nor to create one of his own. Nevertheless, he made a lasting impact in the broad field of economics and beyond. Independence has been his strength. Following from this observation, this volume does not attempt to place Kornai's work within any existing, or tempting, school of thought. Instead, this volume puts Kornai's rich offer of conceptual innovations into the center of its own analysis and invites readers to engage with these ideas on their own term.

The essays included in this volume investigate Kornai's conceptual innovations at three distinct points of entry into Kornai's scholarship: *systems*, *institutions*, and *values*. In fact, these three concepts represent more profound intellectual categories in Kornai's work. For Kornai, a *system* is a conceptu-

---

1 See Stephan Haggard, "Jánosl Kornai as Political Economist," *Acta Oeconomica* 68, no. 1 (March 2018): 9–25.

2 See Geoffrey M. Hodgson and J. W. Stoelhorst, "Introduction to the Special Issue on the Future of Institutional and Evolutionary Economics," *Journal of Institutional Economics* 10, no. 4 (December 2014): 513–40.

3 See Katharina Pistor, "Towards a New Transition Economics: Comments on Konstantin Sonin's 'The End of Economic Transition,'" *Economics of Transition and Institutional Change* 21, no. 1 (January 2013): 11–16.

4 See Mihály Laki, "Kornai János a kapitalizmusról, 1953–1989," *Korall: Társadalomtörténeti Folyóirat* no. 72 (2018): 117–136.

ally and uniquely defined lens through which to look at the functioning of a society; *institutions* are worth studying not only for their own unique characteristics, but also as building blocks of larger systems; *values* stand as the choices of researchers that, although they stay, implicitly, in the background of research questions and methods, nevertheless serve as guides during the conduct of their research. Taken together, systems, institutions, and values serve as rewarding conceptual guides for the quest to better understand how a society functions.

In the first part of this volume, *systems*—Kornai's core analytical category—and their varieties, such as socialism, capitalism, and systemic transformations, are analyzed by leading social scientists. In the first essay, Iván Szelényi revisits Kornai's three themes of socialism. Szelényi looks at the core of Kornai's definition of socialism as a system and engages the readers to reconsider the basic building blocks put down by Kornai. In the second essay, Gérard Roland turns to Kornai's concept of capitalism with the intention to develop his own understanding of capitalism. Next, Péter Mihályi invites readers to a re-reading of Kornai's work on economic growth together with Ferenc Jánossy's work in order to distill commonalities and differences between the two authors. Finally, Geoffrey Hodgson takes the opportunity to elaborate on Kornai's observations on the widespread and problematic stretching of the concept of 'market' in order to suggest minimal conditions for the existence of a market that can help researchers establish where markets do not exist. These four theoretical essays taken together offer readers a variety of ways in which to rethink Kornai's observations on systems and reconsider their applicability in their own research.

The second section of the volume puts *institutions* at the meso- and micro-level into the focus of analysis. Here, a policy analyst, a policy practitioner, a business analyst, and a policy advocate join forces to engage with Kornai's post-financial crisis analysis of European and national institutional change. Applying systemic analysis to institutional change, first, Bruno Dallago looks at Kornai's contribution to systemic analysis, stressing the importance of a complex view and reads the fundamental documents of Eurozone integration through Kornai's concept of systemic paradigm. Next, László Jankovics engages with Kornai's remarks on the importance of setting limits on the apolitical application of fiscal rules and independent fiscal institutions (IFIs). Jankovics points out that IFIs have the potential to increase the transparency and accountability of fiscal policy; however, in case of an overly extensive mandate, IFIs also have the potential to undermine the scope of democratic policymaking. In the following essay, Éva Krenyácz demonstrates empirically that Kornai's notion of soft budget constraint (SBC) is still an excellent tool to depict management problems that arise in the healthcare sector, while evaluating the performance of the Orbán government's recent effort to reform the Hungarian healthcare sector. Finally, József Péter Martin uses Kornai's revisited system paradigm, which describes the current Hungarian polity as autocracy, as an inspiration to develop a typology of forms of resource allocation mechanisms in the Hungarian crony system beyond the widely discussed public procurements.

Nevertheless, perhaps the most valuable part of this volume is the inclusion of the concluding remarks made by Kornai himself, in which Kornai emphasized, not for the first time, the indispensability of *values* when conducting social scientific research. Kornai's speech is remarkable both for its academic content as well as for the advice he gave to future generations of economists.

First, János Kornai drew up a general overview of his long intellectual journey (from his PhD thesis, "Over-centralization," written in 1956, to the present) and gave his perspective on the way his work might be extended and deepened in the future by new generations of economists. Furthermore, there are some theoretical points on which Kornai took positions for the first time. For example, he made a remark that Nobel Prize winner Eric Maskin's game-theoretical model does not capture all the richness of the soft budget constraint concept. He also underlined the importance of non-Walrasian equilibrium and suggested a research program combining chronic disequilibrium with soft budget constraints.

Second, the selected contributions take seriously Kornai's advice, given in this speech, that "even if you are working in other fields of economic analysis, at least in your way of thinking don't become apolitical. At least in the back of our minds, all of us should be political economists. And in that capacity, it is our never-ending task to think about the complex dilemmas of choosing fundamental values."[5] These suggestions are ever more pressing in Eastern Europe in general, but most notably in Hungary. Kornai, in particular, points out the importance of values such as "freedom, liberties, liberty of speech, liberty of free expression of thoughts, liberty of the press, autonomy for the individual and for voluntary communities, democracy, state of law."

[5] See János Kornai's concluding essay in this volume.

As Kornai aptly describes it, "everyone who is not Eastern European should study the recent Eastern European experience, should study what is going on in Hungary, what is going on in Poland. These are two remarkable countries, which could serve as laboratories demonstrating the procedure for liquidating the great achievements of democracy." Therefore, this volume, in addition to engaging with Kornai's scholarship, also engages with his heartfelt request for taking values seriously while doing academic research. This volume presents a selection of authors who do not recoil from the task of building on Kornai's recommendations in their study of the Hungarian political economy. This task, we must note, is increasingly problematic in contemporary Hungary.

Kornai's impact on economic research has been assessed by a number of earlier works. An earlier selection of articles dedicated to the Kornai70 conference was published by Maskin and Simonovits in 2000.[6] That volume collected essays from contributors coming from Kornai's two intellectual homes: Harvard and the Hungarian Academy of Sciences. The papers, nevertheless, come from within one discipline—economics—only: the contributors were some of the best-known economists writing about comparative economics and the problems of transition. Instead, in this volume, world-leading experts—not from the field of mainstream economics, but from a variety of fields including sociology (Iván Szelényi), institutional economics (Geoffrey Hodgson) and development economics (Gérard Roland)—demonstrate the various ways in which Kornai's scholarship informs broad fields of research. Moreover, it is quite clear that, twenty years ago, a major goal of Kornai's followers was to horn the analytical precision of Kornai's concepts while applying them in formal modelling. Today, none of the contributors to this volume use formal models. Instead, they all take advantage of the conceptual richness of Kornai's developed tools and put them to use for their own research interests. Moreover, there is a marked shift in the interests of researchers compared to twenty years *ante*. The Maskin and Simonovits volume organized sections along three issues of institutional change, such as "planning," "shortage," and "transformations." Our volume has a broader theoretical interest. It goes beyond institutions alone; we therefore included a section on systems. Finally, this volume, following Kornai's advice, takes values seriously, a task that was not so markedly important twenty years ago.

[6] Eric Maskin and András Simonovits, eds., *Planning, Shortage, and Transformation: Essays in Honor of János Kornai* (Cambridge, MA: The MIT Press, 2000).

This shift in focus reflects changes in academic interest in general, but also that of Kornai himself over time. In sum, our volume not only shows changes in interest in Kornai's work over the past twenty years, but demonstrates that Kornai clearly stepped out of the disciplinary boundaries of economics theoretically and moved forward in his empirical interests: from the transition from socialism to capitalism to the pressing political and economic transformations of the European Union and Hungary, that he called elsewhere the "U-Turn."[7]

The latest publication that includes a wide-ranging selection of contributions that variously deal with Kornai's insights was published in 2016, edited by Miklós Rosta and Balázs Hámor. The contributions to that collection had a very specific focus and thus narrowed the possible scope of engagement with Kornai's rich collection of analytical tools. That volume exclusive dealt with "the forces driving development and the constraints hindering progress in economic systems and subsystems."[8] The present volume is richer in two senses: it includes a number of theoretical engagements with Kornai's conceptional tools and it includes empirical analysis at the macro-, meso-, and micro-levels of institutional change. All three sections of this volume are interesting for two very different kinds of audiences. One—and in all likelihood the larger audience—is interested in Kornai's work and seeks advice in dealing with his concepts from leading social scientists, established scholars, and practitioners. However, because our contributors are leaders in their own fields, another audience will seek out this volume because of their interest in the contributors' take on Kornai's concepts.

The content of this edited volume is based on the Kornai90 conference organized in February 2018 at the Corvinus University of Budapest to honor János Kornai's ninetieth birthday.[9] The purpose of the conference was to bring together scholars from around the world who currently work with the themes that Kornai tackled throughout his long career, broadly understood. The large number of participants and the large varieties of research presented con-

[7] János Kornai, "Hungary's U-Turn," *Capitalism and Society* 10, no. 1, article 2 (2015).

[8] Balázs Hámori and Miklós Rosta, eds., "Introduction," *Constraints and Driving Forces in Economic Systems: Studies in Honor of János Kornai* (Newcastle upon Tyne: Cambridge Scholars Publishing, 2016), 6.

[9] See more information about the conference Ádám Kerényi, "Kornai-láz a Közgázon. Beszámoló a Kornai János 90. születésnapja alkalmából szervezett eseménysorozatról," *Közgazdasági Szemle* 65, no. 6 (2018): 667–676.

firmed the organizers' perception that Kornai's oeuvre is as influential today as it has been for decades.

There is an important limitation to this volume: the lack of articles on Kornai's influence on contemporary research in the political economy of China. The Kornai90 conference included a number of important presentations from the greatest followers and students of Kornai's, such as Yingyi Qian (Dean, Tsinghua University's School of Economics and Management), whose presentation was titled "Surplus, Innovation and the System"; David Daokui Li (Director of the Center for China at Tsinghua University's School of Economics and Management), whose presentation was titled "The Chinese Ideology"; Chenggang Xu, (Professor of Economics, Cheung Kong Graduate School of Business) who gave a speech titled "Analyzing Political Economic Regime Changes in China"; Yijiang Wang, (Associate Dean, Cheung Kong Graduate School of Business) who gave a presentation on "War, Peace, and the Making of the State: A Theory of Social Order"; and finally Chong-en Ba, (Executive Associate Dean, Tsinghua University's School of Economics and Management) who presented a speech on the "Selective Helping Hand." As these presentations were specifically prepared for the Kornai90 conference, quite understandably, no written version was available for inclusion in this volume. However, videos of the talks are available at http://www.kornai90.hu/conference-videos/.

As a final word, we would like to thank others who made this edited volume possible. We are grateful to all the contributors to this edited volume for their excellent work. The recommendations of two reviewers of this volume have substantially increased the quality of the work. We would also like to acknowledge the invaluable assistance of the members of the Kornai90 conference organizing committee. This volume could not have been realized without their dedicated work. We are especially grateful for the various kinds of help provided by Tamás Balog, Katalin Bereczky, Renáta Borbély, Réka Csaba, Rita Fancsovits, Diána Horváth, Tünde Horváth, Márton Katona, Ádám Kerényi, Erzsébet Kovács, Mihály Laki, Péter Mihályi, András Olivér Németh, Tamás Nyisztor, Dóra Papp, Andrea Reményi, and András Simonovits. Finally, we are indebted to OTP Bank for providing financial support to the Kornai90 conference.

The organization of the volume

In this volume's first section, leading contemporary theorists engage with Kornai's most fundamental concepts and themes. Iván Szelényi revisits Kornai's three themes of socialism that together make up his concept of socialism. Kornai defined socialism with three characteristics: it eliminated private ownership, replaced markets with bureaucratic coordination, and it is a system ruled by one party legitimated by Marxism-Leninism. Szelényi offers variations on these three basic themes.

In turn, Gérard Roland surveys János Kornai's thinking on the capitalist system, from *Anti-Equilibrium* to his most recent work. For Kornai, Roland argues, the capitalist system is one of constant excess supply generated by the dominance of private property, market coordination, and hard budget constraints. He puts forward some elements of his own thinking on capitalism, many of them inspired by insights from Marx, Schumpeter, Hayek, and Kornai. Roland emphasizes three additional issues for the better understanding of capitalism: the role of democracy for the survival of capitalism, the political sustainability of capitalism, and the role of culture.

In the next chapter, Péter Mihályi revisits two books of two economists, Ferenc Jánossy's *The End of the Economic Miracle* (1966) and Kornai' s *Rush versus Harmonic Growth* (1972). This chapter shows that the two concepts of growth and the similar conclusions pertaining to the "too high" pace of the contemporary Hungarian growth rate rested on different theoretical bases. Jánossy was a Marxist, and the labor theory of value was his starting point. Kornai, by contrast, broke with Marxism well before he wrote the cited book. However, Mihályi demonstrates that there was a common moral point of the two authors: they both had the courage and the energy to think through scrupulously and comprehensively the pros and cons of the classical model of the planned economy.

In the last contribution to the first section, Geoffrey Hodgson argues that much of the work of János Kornai has addressed the structural and institutional differences between planned and market economies. Kornai insisted on the importance of understanding "the real market" and its capacity to promote dynamism and innovation. While market and planned economies have some things in common, they also have important features that are not shared. This is sometimes overlooked, argues Hodgson, particularly by those that use the term market non-metaphorically to describe a very wide variety of arrangements or processes in the real world. In the next step, Hodgson establishes some minimal necessary features of a market, to show that some particular arrangements are not markets. He also demonstrates that by reducing politics to a form of "market" economics, market universalism corrodes the conceptual separation of civil society from the state.

In the second section of the volume, first, Bruno Dallago argues that the careful definition and development of a consistent Eurozone system paradigm and economic system were disregarded and remained undeveloped during the process of European integration. For Dallago, this is due to the fact that the integration effort was concentrated on finding compromises among member states and in pursuing the formal convergence of economies to the advantage of financial stability. This disregard, Dallago reveals, has caused serious problems for integration among different countries. In particular, he argues that what is good for the advancement of stability may lead to negative effects for individual countries, in particular to diverging performance between countries with different economic systems and dissimilar economic and financial conditions and situations. Dallago concludes by considering proposals and changes that European and national authorities are submitting in order to fix these problems and strengthen Eurozone resilience.

Next, László Jankovics looks at independent fiscal institutions (IFIs), a new set of public institutions, in order to evaluate their potential in the scales set up by János Kornai. Fiscal rules and independent fiscal institutions have recently emerged as complementary institutions to address deficit bias and pro-cyclicality. Through continuous monitoring of numerical rules, IFIs are expected to promote transparency and accountability in fiscal policy. János Kornai emphasized the importance of limiting the mandate of IFIs to positive economics, and refrain from assigning normative tasks or veto rights, as these latter functions would necessarily involve value judgment, which should be left for elected politicians. Jankovics analyzes the extent to which existing IFIs in EU member states match the advice of Kornai in terms of their key design features and operational role in national budgetary processes. Jankovics concludes with a number of potential ideas for strengthening IFIs to the benefit of sound fiscal policymaking.

In the following chapter, Éva Krenyácz looks at the recent attempt of the Orbán government to stabilize the healthcare sector through centralization and nationalization. At an organizational level, these phenomena would require better management support systems and devices. Building on Kornai's recent analysis of the healthcare system, Krenyácz shows that the environment of centralized healthcare affects the decision support systems at hospitals and has the ability to modify the attitude of management. Krenyácz's research results show that the top management of Hungarian healthcare organizations face unique challenges caused by (under)financing, performance volume limitation, debt accumulation, and centralization/nationalization. These elements have a significant impact on the internal systems of hospitals and on the interests of stakeholders. Taken together, these environmental factors amount to the impact of Kornai's notion of soft budget constraint (SBC). The result is that a financial perspective becomes dominant in the thinking of top hospital managers with the expected adverse effect; they try to achieve economic stability by monitoring liquidity and lobbying for bailout.

In the last chapter, József Péter Martin reveals some manifestations of recent resource reallocation in Hungary, and constructs a simple scheme of the interplay among institutions, economic policy, perceptions, and economic performance. Martin argues that, after 2010, the Hungarian government started to build a new regime that instrumentalized most public institutions and distorted resource allocation mechanisms in favor of clients. He suggests a typology of the different manifestation forms of cronyism beyond the widely discussed public procurement system. Hungarian specificities of policy failures, state capture, and elite moves are discussed in a regional context. Martin concludes that in the current Hungarian regime, corruption has become centralized and the collusion of officials and oligarchs provides both groups with undue benefits. This further undermines the level playing field, but reduces the transaction costs of corruption and may improve the economic performance in the short run. In longer term, however, it could have negative impacts on the country's economy performance.

References

Haggard, Stephen. "János Kornai as Political Economist." *Acta Oeconomica* 68, no. 1 (March 2018): 9–25.

Hámori, Balázs, and Miklós Rosta, eds. *Constraints and Driving Forces in Economic Systems: Studies in Honor of János Kornai*. Newcastle upon Tyne: Cambridge Scholars Publishing, 2016.

Hodgson, Geoffrey M., and J. W. Stoelhorst. "Introduction to the Special Issue on the Future of Institutional and Evolutionary Economics." *Journal of Institutional Economics* 10, no. 4 (December 2014): 513–40.

Kerényi Ádám, "Kornai-láz a Közgázon. Beszámoló a Kornai János 90. Születésnapja alkalmából szervezett eseménysorozatról," *Közgazdasági Szemle* 65, no. 6 (2018): 667–676.

Kornai, János. "Hungary's U-Turn." *Capitalism and Society* 10, no. 1, article 2 (2015).

Laki, Mihály. "Kornai János a kapitalizmusról, 1953–1989." *KORALL: Társadalomtörténeti Folyóirat* no. 72 (2018): 117–136.

Maskin, Eric, and András Simonovits, eds. *Planning, Shortage, and Transformation: Essays in Honor of János Kornai.* Cambridge, MA: The MIT Press, 2000.

Pistor, Katharina. "Towards a New Transition Economics: Comments on Konstantin Sonin's 'The End of Economic Transition.'" *Economics of Transition and Institutional Change* 21, no. 1 (January 2013): 11–16.

János Kornai's Theory of Socialism

Iván Szelényi

Introduction

I decided to write a "verbal sonata" in three movements, on themes by János Kornai. In the large literature on what is/was socialism, Kornai, with his brilliantly clear mind, made a sharp definition—based on three pillars—of the characteristics of socialism.[1] Each of his definitions (or movements) can be interpreted and expanded, modified in different ways, and so I use his definitions as musicians often used "themes" from "old masters" to write "variations" on these themes.

Property relations

Here is the first theme: the elimination of private property.

MOVEMENT 1

Allegro vivace (the "vigorous passage" from feudalism/capitalism to socialism). Kornai's first thesis is that socialist countries outlawed private ownership of the means of production and that all those means became

[1] János Kornai, *The Socialist System* (Princeton: Princeton University Press, 1992), 33–109.

government (that is, publicly) owned. This indeed was a rather "vigorous passage," and in the process a few eggs were broken—as is necessary, as we know from Anarchism 101—for any revolution.

VARIATION 1

Kornai is quite right: all actually existing socialist countries made a (rather) dramatic (hence "*allegro vivace*") effort to eliminate private ownership of the means of production. But let's not forget that Marx, in his early formulation, saw state ownership as "crude communism" rather than real socialism, which would establish the ownership of the means of production by direct producers.[2]

In fact, Marx, in his debate with Bakunin,[3] found himself on the defensive. In 1872, Bakunin accused Marx of being a "statist," and substituting the dictatorship of the proletariat with the dictatorship of the [statist] "socialist scholars." Bakunin arrived at the formulation that "Marx is the Bismarck of Socialism." Marx tried to ignore Bakunin's criticism, and the difficult task of refutation was left to Engels, who, in his *Anti-Dühring*,[4] introduced the phrase "withering away of the state"—a variation on this theme then repeated and elaborated by Lenin in *The State and Revolution*.[5] Engels had to accept that initially socialism can only proceed by nationalizing private property, but he believed this was just one step in a long process that would eventually lead to the "withering away" of the state. Lenin went a step further, arguing that with the "proletarian revolution" the working class had "smashed the bourgeois" state. Yet, he did not quite explain what the future of the new proletarian state would be and how it would "wither away." Stalin went one step further than Lenin in his essay "The Possibility of Building Socialism in One Country."[6]

---

[2] Karl Marx, *The Economic and Philosophic Manuscripts of 1844*, in Karl Marx and Friedrich Engels, *Collected Works*, vol. 5 (London: Lawrence and Wishart, 1975), 294–295.

[3] Mikhail Bakunin, "Marx the Bismarck of Socialism (1870)," in *Patterns of Anarchy*, ed. L. Krimmermann and L. Perry (New York: Anchors, 1966), 882–83.

[4] Friedrich Engels, *Ani-Dühring* [1877], in Karl Marx and Friedrich Engels, *Collected Works*, vol. 25 (London: Lawrence and Wishart, 1987), 5–309.

[5] Vladimir Ilich Lenin, *The State and Revolution* (Whitefish, MT: Kessinger Publishing, 2004 [1918]).

[6] Josef V. Stalin, "The Possibility of Building Socialism in One Country," in *Collected Works*, vol. 8 (Moscow: Foreign Language Publishing House, 1954 [1926]), 101–104.

Since socialism had now been built in one country, Soviet Russia, and was now surrounded by enemies, it required the strengthening of the state. The "withering away" is a dialectical process: the state will wither away, but it must be strengthened first. Indeed, this vision (or tone, sure, and only the first step in this dialectical process) was the reality of the Stalinist version of socialism.

It was not only anarchists like Bakunin who were uncomfortable with this "statist vision" of socialism. Kautsky, as early as 1920, defined the emerging Soviet state as "state capitalist" rather than socialist.[7] Leon Trotsky,[8] once exiled, accepted that the nationalization of private ownership had completed the "economic revolution," but this was politically betrayed, for the USSR under Stalin was a "deformed worker's state" in need of a "political revolution." It was socialist all right, but to become "genuine" socialism it needed an anti-bureaucratic revolution. (This was very much on the minds of the reform communists behind the 1956 Hungarian Revolution, as well as the reformers of the Prague Spring, who never considered the privatization of public goods.)

After the Hitler-Stalin Pact, the "deformed worker's state" was not a precise enough description of the USSR for many followers of Trotsky. As far as property relations were concerned, the emphasis was then put on "control by the direct producers," hence state ownership was defined as a "collective private ownership by the bureaucracy," and therefore the USSR was regarded either as a state capitalist[9] or a bureaucratic collectivist[10] system.

The bottom line: Marx, and even Engels, hesitated to say whether state ownership of the means of the production is either a necessary or sufficient condition of socialism. Later Marxists often tended to identify state ownership with bureaucratic control, antithetical to the socialist project.

7 Karl Kautsky, *Terrorism and Communism: A Contribution to the Natural History of the Revolution* (London: Allen and Unwin, 1920).

8 Leon Trotsky, *The Revolution Betrayed: What is the Soviet Union and Where is it Going?* (New York: Pathfinder, 1962 [1937]).

9 Tony Cliff, *State Capitalism in Russia* (London: Pluto Press, 1974 [1955]).

10 Antonio Carlo, "The Socio-economic Nature of the USSR," *Telos* 21 (1974): 2–86; Cornelius Castoriadis, "The Social Regime in Russia," *Telos* 38 (1978): 212–48. The bureaucratic collectivist view deeply influenced Ferenc Fehér, Ágnes Heller, and György Márkus as well. See Ferenc Fehér, Ágnes Heller, and György Márkus, *Dictatorship Over Needs* (Oxford: Blackwell, 1983).

VARIATION 2

The distinction between socialism and capitalism. Marx, in his later work, most forcefully in the "Critique of the Gotha Program,"[11] distinguishes two distinct phases of transition from capitalism to communism. The first is called variably as "socialism" or the "revolutionary dictatorship of the proletariat"; the second, communism. In the first phase, a strong state is required, the dictatorship of the majority over a minority of capitalists, and people are regarded according to their contribution to the collective good. The second phase will be control over the means of production by direct producers, the state then withering away, and people rewarded according to their needs.

This distinction came in handy in the USSR, and even contemporary China, where the parties are called "Communist," but the societies are described as being in a transition stage, socialism, where dictatorial means and state ownership are necessary until the social and material base of an egalitarian communist society is established.

It can be, on the other hand, debated whether "state capitalism" or "state socialism" is indeed a step forward from free-market capitalism, or it is more a step backward, to a society based on rank rather than merit (and class). Thomas Piketty,[12] for instance, foreshadows the raise of "patrimonial capitalism." Unfortunately, in Piketty's work the concept of "patrimonial capitalism" is not clearly defined. In my interpretation, it is a rent-seeking economic system in which either big capital captures the state—what Donald Trump seems to try to do in the US—or what Putin's Russia or Orbán's Hungary are good approximations of, namely "market capture by the state." In both cases, it is a "statist version" of capitalism. Some commentators see re-nationalization in Russia or in Hungary as a "restoration of communism," but it is probably better called "state capitalism," that is, a step backward to feudalism.

[11] Karl Marx, *Critique of the Gotha Program*, in Karl Marx and Friedrich Engels, *Selected Works*, volume 3 (Moscow: Progress Publishers, 1970 [1875]), 13–30.

[12] Thomas Piketty, *Capitalism in the Twenty-First Century* (Cambridge, MA: Harvard University Press, 2013).

VARIATION 3

The property form also varied under most actually existing socialist societies. A distinction was made between "state ownership" and "cooperative ownership."[13] Whether this difference was consequential, and even which form was more "progressive," was debated. The official Soviet doctrine regarded the *kolkhoz* (agricultural cooperative) as a temporarily surviving remnant of the Russian village commune, which would eventually turn into more advanced state ownership (in agriculture, these were called *sovkhozy*). Critics of the communist system often argued that under socialism only pseudo-cooperatives existed—they were not genuine collectives.

All of this can be debated. Even in rigid socialist systems, cooperatives had some unique features. Members of cooperatives typically received only an "advance payment" on their annual earnings, and at the end of the financial year they received their "share," while in state-owned enterprises monthly wages were paid. Co-op leadership was often—at least formally—elected rather than appointed. What is even more interesting is that, in the last stages of communism, in some former communist countries, like in Hungary, cooperatives gained more autonomy. Even within state firms, the bureaucratic organization was complemented by sorts of cooperative associations of workers.[14] In such state-owned enterprises, workers formed sort of semi-private work organizations, used the firm's facilities, but stayed after working hours and continued production, though in a sort of profit-sharing arrangement. As communism was collapsing between 1988 and 1990, some theorists saw an opportunity to pass ownership to workers rather than privatize firms: one may say even some kind of Proudhonian socialism[15] appeared as a distinct possibility out of state socialism.[16]

---

[13] Frank Ellis, *Peasant Economics* (Cambridge: Cambridge University Press, 1993).

[14] David Stark, "Coexisting Organizational Forms in Hungary's Emerging Mixed Economies," in *Remaking the Economic Institutions of Socialism*, ed. Victor Nee and David Stark (Stanford: Stanford University Press, 1989), 137–68.

[15] Proudhon wanted to generalize property rather than eliminate it. Passing state ownership to post-communist firms to workers through vouchers is consistent with Proudhon's initial ideas of "mutualism." See Pierre-Joseph Proudhon, *What is Property*, eds. Donald R. Kelly and Bonnie G. Smith (Cambridge: Cambridge University Press, 1994 [1866]).

[16] Erzsébet Szalai, *Gazdaság és Hatalom* (Budapest: Aula Kiadó, 1989), 177–97.

Mechanisms of economic coordination

The second major theme of Kornai's theory of socialism focuses on economic coordinating mechanisms.

MOVEMENT 2

Minuetto (dances around market and redistribution). Kornai's second thesis is that socialism replaced the market coordination of the economy with bureaucratic coordination (it was also called a command economy, centrally planned economy, or redistributive economy). Indeed, all "actually existing socialist societies" tried to eliminate or at least reduce the operation of markets. Hence Kornai is right on the dot.

VARIATION 1

How "bureaucratic" were socialist societies? Weber believed that bureaucracy is the purest form of legal-rational authority. If socialism was a "command economy" as many analysts believed it was,[17] it inevitably was the opposite of the Weberian notion of bureaucracy. Command economy assumes that a central authority has absolute power to issue commands, which will be carried out along the line of command. Weber understood bureaucracy as an organization,[18] which is bound by pre-established rules, where activities are carried out by qualified people—experts—where there is a channel of appeal against decisions, where members of the staff have no property rights (including the rights of disposal), and which is operated on the grounds of formal rationality. Socialist economies are a far cry from such a bureaucratic organization.

Some theorists question the description of state socialism as "command economy" (they argued a great deal of "plan-bargain" occurs at various levels), but few question that these economies operated on substantive rather than on formal rationality. The staff is appropriated at least certain rights of disposal.

---

[17] Gregory Grossman, "Notes for a Theory of Command Economy," *Soviet Studies* 15, no. 4 (1963): 101–23.

[18] Max Weber, *Economy and Society*, vol. 1 (Berkeley: University of California Press, 1978 [1920]), 217–20.

VARIATION 2

Ironically, it appears that the Weberian ideal type of bureaucracy seems to be operating within capitalist market economies. Oliver Williamson[19] pointed out that too much uncertainty in competitive markets demands hierarchical (bureaucratic) organization within firms. If uncertainties on the market impose costs that are too high, the firm will incorporate such activities within its own organization. Vertical integration of economic activities within the same firm has its costs, and when those costs become too high, activities will be subcontracted to other business organizations in market transactions. Hence a balance is created between market transactions of hierarchical organizations depending on transaction costs. A smart firm will not rely on an external supplier if the risk of untimely delivery of materials or goods by that supplier is too high. Rather, the firms will produce those goods within its own hierarchy. If the supervision of such sub-organization activities becomes too expensive, the alternative would be to use another firm as a contractor. Markets and hierarchies (that is, bureaucracies) do not contradict each other; they complement each other.

VARIATION 3

Given the above-mentioned imprecisions of the term "bureaucracy," I prefer to use a concept borrowed from Polanyi—"redistribution"—to describe the nature of the socialist economy. Polanyi used the term "redistribution" to characterize the economic integration of early imperial economies, where one central hand concentrated the means available for expanded reproduction and redistributed it according to one central will (or, occasionally, local needs).[20]

Ancient China, with its extensive irrigation system, which required a central authority to build and maintain such a system covering large areas and multiple communities, was a classical empire. Polanyi never used the concept of redistribution systematically for Soviet-type economies, but I found this concept adaptable (certainly better than bureaucracy, central planning, or command economy). In actually existing socialist economies, central authorities appropriated all surplus from the production organiza-

---

[19] Oliver Williamson, *Markets and Hierarchies* (New York: The Free Press, 1975).

[20] Karl Polanyi, ed., *Trade and Market in Early Empires* (New York: Free Press, 1957).

tion and, through a complex bargaining process with regional- and firm-level authorities, redistributed it. It would be misleading to regard the central hand as an all-powerful "command center." It had to make compromises with lower-level organizations. Planning, or central planning, is also a misleading term, since it assumes a well-conceived, pre-established aim for the action of the central hand, when it often resulted from the outcomes of political compromises, which may have contradicted the initial intentions of the "central hand." Kornai brilliantly showed[21] that such bargaining with various levels of economic actors systematically produced shortages. The central hand was a good patron, tried to please all of its clients, and hence redistributed its resources thinly, which inevitably ran out. This resulted in a great volume of incomplete, unproductive investments. Socialist economies entered a stage of crisis: given the shortages of resources, they had to freeze some investment projects. Once the selected few were completed, the economy moved from crisis into a new boom. While market capitalist economies were driven by the tendency of over-production, socialist economies were driven by crisis of acute shortages.[22] David Stark called this type of analysis "mirrored comparison."[23] Both capitalist and socialist systems are driven by "business cycles," but the causes of the cycles are the opposite. Ironically, when a redistributive economy entered a severe crisis of shortages, socialist economies began to rely on market forces to compensate for the chronic shortages.[24] While market capitalist economies use welfare redistribution to fight crisis caused by overproduction, socialist economies rely on markets to compensates for chronic shortages.

VARIATION 4

The ghost of "market socialism" haunted socialist ideologues early on. Michael Kalecki was one of the first Marxist theorists who considered, in responding to the inefficiencies of centrally planned economies in some of his essays of the 1930s and early 1940s, the need of market mechanisms for

[21] See János Kornai, *Economics of Shortage* (Amsterdam: North Holland, 1980).

[22] János Kornai, *A Hiány* (Budapest: Közgazdasági és Jogi Kiadó, 1982), 224–29.

[23] David Stark, "Recombinant Property in East European Capitalism," *The American Journal of Sociology* 101, no. 4 (1996): 993–1027.

[24] Iván Szelényi, "Social Inequalities in State Socialist Redistributive Economies," *International Journal of Comparative Sociology*, no. 1–2 (1978): 63–87.

properly functioning socialist economies.[25] Oskar Lange, as early as 1936,[26] suggested a market socialist model and the idea became quite fashionable during the reform years of the 1960s and 1970s in former socialist societies. Tibor Liska went as far as to suggest that the existence of a proper market economy was impossible with private property.[27] For Liska, private ownership, and especially inherited wealth, is a limitation of free markets, so genuine free markets are only possible under socialism.

In contrast, János Kornai, in a brilliant paper delivered during the mid-1980s at a conference in Moscow, pointed out that there is an "elective affinity" between forms of ownership and coordinating mechanisms: the free market presumes the existence of private ownership.[28] If Kornai is right, "market socialism" is not possible—it is contradiction of terms.

VARIATION 5

China, since the mid-1980s, put the concept of "market socialism" back on the agenda. Kornai himself hesitated for a while to decide whether China is, as of the late twentieth and early twenty-first centuries, socialist or capitalist.

Ideologues of late twentieth-, early twenty-first-century China insist it is still a socialist country on its way to capitalism, but that it is a market economy.[29] China undoubtedly applied a great deal of market forces after 1978, and after the late 1990s even started the privatization (at least formally—who became the "real" owners is disputed) of public firms. Nevertheless, the Chinese Communist Party has retained its power monopoly, and the ownership of large Chinese corporations looks rather like "recombinant property rights," to use David Stark's term, and the Chinese government interferes in multiple ways (especially through the banking system) into the functioning

25 See Michal Kalecki, *Selected Essays in Economic Planning* (Cambridge: Cambridge University Press, 2011), which contains his early essays.

26 Oskar Lange, "On the Economic Theory of Socialism," *Review of Economic Theory* 4, no. 1 (1936): 53–71.

27 Tibor Liska, *Ökonosztát* (Budapest: Közgazdasági és Jogi Könyvkiadó, 1988).

28 János Kornai, "The Affinity between Ownership Forms and Coordinating Mechanisms," *The Journal of Economic Perspectives* 4, no. 3 (1990): 131–47.

29 For a fuller discussion, see Iván Szelényi, "Capitalism in China? Comparative Perspectives," in *Chinese Capitalisms*, ed. Yin-wah Chu (Hong Kong: Palgrave Macmillan, 2010), 199–223.

of the economy. Victor Nee called the Chinese economy a "hybrid one."[30] For world-systems theorists, this is not much of a challenge. At least in his early work, Immanuel Wallerstein,[31] and many of his disciples, saw even the USSR, after interacting with the world market—and by implication, China entering the world economy—as "capitalist," since they became integral parts of the "world system." Only those countries like North Korea in the 1970s and 1980s, which did break the logic of the world market, remained genuinely socialist according to orthodox world-systems theorists (including in the early works of Wallerstein himself). For some Marxists, this grossly overemphasizes the role of the market, instead of property and class relations, in the definition of capitalism, hence Wallerstein was accused of committing the crime of "Smithian Marxism."[32] The world-system theorist's position is debatable: actually existing socialist societies usually depended on—to use Karl Polanyi's terminology—"ports of trade" (i.e., foreign trade companies that adjust world market prices to domestic prices), and to some extent keep the pressures of the world market off of domestic economies. Even at the time of the oil boom, its impact was greatly limited on the satellites of the USSR, since the USSR was not a member of OPEC and adjusted its oil export prices to world market prices only gradually or not at all.

Political system

Kornai's third thesis centers on the nature of the political system under socialism. It is important to see that, for Kornai's theory, the socialist system is a "set menu" and not *à la carte*. You either have all three components of the system or none.

[30] Victor Nee, "Organizational Dynamics of Market Transition: Hybrid Forms, Property Rights, and Mixed Economy in China," *Administrative Science Quarterly* 37, no. 1 (1992): 1–27.

[31] Immanuel Wallerstein, *The Modern World System* (Berkeley: University of California Press, 1974).

[32] Robert Brenner, "The Origins of Capitalist Development: a Critique of Neo-Smithian Marxism," *New Left Review* 25 (July 1977): 25–94.

MOVEMENT 3

Finale presto (the dramatic end of Communist Party rule).

The third thesis of Kornai is that socialist countries are ruled by one party, which legitimates itself by the ideology of Marxism-Leninism (or Maoism). Kornai is, of course, right. All "actually existing socialist societies" were one-party states and they tried to legitimate themselves with reference to Marxist-Leninism (or some further elaboration of the classical doctrine).

VARIATION 1

But is it conceivable by "true" Marxists to establish socialist systems at the periphery of the word system? Classical Marxism without any doubt believed that socialism would emerge at the very core of capitalist systems, once the "relations of production" no longer allow the development of the "forces of production." This is Marxism 101 from *The German Ideology*. Socialism was supposed to emerge in England, or to put it in twentieth-century terminology, in Scandinavia, but certainly not in backward Russia, rural China, or in Cuba. It was Lenin's great contribution to Marxism (Marx might have felt unconformable with this "innovation") that the revolution should start at the "weakest chains in the capitalist system."[33] Mao Zedong further added to this theory by emphasizing that peasant masses are more capable to carry out the proletarian revolution than (the practically hardly existing) industrial proletariat in the China of the late 1940s. So is it really Marxist, that which attempts to implement the Marxian project in a mostly backward, peasant country? Can the system thus created be called "socialism" at all?

VARIATION 2

Socialism in one country. Marx and Engels anticipated a world-wide proletarian revolution and even Lenin, and following him, Trotsky, saw the Russian Revolution as just the beginning of a world-wide revolution. As communism won the civil war and established itself in the USSR, Stalin developed the concept of "socialism in one country."[34] This was, of course, a major deviation

---

[33] Lenin, *State and Revolution*.

[34] Stalin, "The Possibility of Building Socialism in one Country."

from the original project of Marx and Engels, and was met with vehement criticism by Leon Trotsky and the Fourth International. They always insisted that socialism can only be conceived as a word-wide system. Can a party that gives up the ideals of internationalism be called "Communist" at all?

Let me allow for a little personal anecdotal digression. In 1986–88, I was the chair of the doctoral program in Sociology at the City University of New York, which, at that time, was located on 42nd Street in Manhattan. My predecessor was Bogdan Denitch, who was active in the so-called Democratic Socialist Movement (DSM), which played some role in the New York City of the 1980s. Bogdan appointed only those people to the faculty who were members of his movement, and admitted only those students who were affiliated with the movement. Sociology occupied the thirteenth floor of the building. When I took over Bogdan's job, some of my colleagues jokingly asked: "Will you keep building socialism on the 13th floor?" Well, I assured them that I would not, and my first appointment—which was highly controversial, eventually leading to my resignation and transfer to UCLA—was a good statistician.

VARIATION 3

After the possibility of socialism in one country was accepted, the question was occasionally posed—not without reason—whether these parties were communist or nationalist. During the Second World War, the USSR was not fighting for international revolution, but was engaged in a "Great Patriotic War." While Mao was fighting Confucius during post-communist times, some principles of Confucius were adapted to "communist" China, so a young American political scientist half-jokingly recommended that the Chinese Communist Party should be renamed as the Chinese Confucian Party, so it could keep its acronym.[35] Yugoslavia followed its "national" model of socialism, and that idea was greatly appealing to various countries, from Albania to Hungary, from Poland to North Korea, and so on. Were these countries communist at all?

[35] Daniel Bell, *China's New Confucianism* (Princeton: Princeton University Press, 2008).

MOVEMENT 4 AND FINAL VARIATION

Marxist parties—OK. But which Marxism? Marx once famously said about himself (in a letter written to Bernstein in 1882): "I am not a Marxist." And indeed Marx changed over his lifetime from the *Paris Manuscripts* of 1844 (the "voluntarist" or Hegelian Marxist phase) to the "scientific Marxism" of 1867's *Das Kapital.*

Karl Korsch, in his wonderful *Marxism and Philosophy*, applied the Marxist method to Marxism and demonstrated a great deal of varieties within Marxism.[36] Yes, Kornai is absolutely right—all actually existing socialist societies legitimated themselves on some sort of Marxist grounds. But did they interpret the Marx of the *Paris Manuscripts* (none did!), or from the Marx of *Das Kapital* to Stalin's innovative piece on socialism in one country. So, one-party rule by all means. But which party—if any—was "Marxist"?

Kornai is, again, right: the disintegration of communist parties is the most dramatic end of "socialism as we know it" (hence, the *Finale Presto*). So, the question "What was socialism?" has not been resolved. Kornai's lucid definition gives us a great starting point, but what the final answer is—or will be, if there ever will be a final answer—remains the subject of social struggles. More interesting: We can still debate *if* socialism "was," or whether "real socialism" will just occur sometime in the future, given the position that so far it never really existed. This is a conversation to continue. The critical question, however, remains: shall we use the term "socialism" only in sentences of the past tense? Or is socialism still a "potentiality," unrealized by systems that called themselves by this name?

References

Bakunin, Mikhail. "Marx the Bismarck of Socialism (1870)." In *Patterns of Anarchy*, ed. L. Krimmermann and L. Perry. New York: Anchors, 1966.

Bell, Daniel. *China's New Confucianism*. Princeton: Princeton University Press, 2008.

Brenner, Robert. "The Origins of Capitalist Development: A Critique of Neo-Smithian Marxism." *New Left Review* 25 (July 1977): 25–94.

Carlo, Antonio. "The Socio-economic Nature of the USSR." *Telos* 21 (1974): 2–86.

Castoriadis, Cornelius. "The Social Regime in Russia." *Telos* 38 (1978): 212–48.

Cliff, Tony. *State Capitalism in Russia*. London: Pluto Press, 1974.

[36] Karl Korsch, *Marxism and Philosophy* (London: New Left Books, 1972 [1923]).

Ellis, Frank. *Peasant Economics*. Cambridge: Cambridge University Press, 1993.
Engels, Friedrich. *Anti-Dühring*. In Karl Marx and Friedrich Engels, *Collected Works*, vol. 25. London: Lawrence and Wishart, 1987.
Fehér, Ferenc, Ágnes Heller, and György Márkus. *Dictatorship Over Needs*. Oxford: Blackwell, 1983.
Grossman, Gregory. "Notes for a Theory of Command Economy." *Soviet Studies* 15, no. 4 (1963):101–23.
Kalecki, Michal. *Selected Essays in Economic Planning*. Cambridge: Cambridge University Press, 2011.
Kautsky, Karl. *Terrorism and Communism: A Contribution to the Natural History of the Revolution*. London: Allen and Unwin, 1920.
Kornai, János. *A Hiány*. Budapest: Közgazdasági és Jogi Kiadó, 1982.
———. *Economics of Shortage*. Amsterdam: North Holland, 1980.
———. "The Affinity between Ownership Forms and Coordinating Mechanisms." *The Journal of Economic Perspectives* 4, no. 3 (1990): 131–47.
———. *The Socialist System*. Princeton: Princeton University Press, 1992.
Korsch, Karl. *Marxism and Philosophy*. London: New Left Books, 1972.
Lange, Oskar. "On the Economic Theory of Socialism." *Review of Economic Theory* 4, no. 1 (1936): 53–71.
Lenin, Vladimir Ilich. *The State and Revolution*. Whitefish, MT: Kessinger Publishing, 2004.
Liska Tibor. *Ökonosztát*. Budapest: Közgazdasági és Jogi Könyvkiadó, 1988.
Marx, Karl. *Critique of the Gotha Program*. In Karl Marx and Friedrich Engels, *Selected Works*, vol. 3. Moscow: Progress Publishers, 1970.
Marx, Karl. *The Economic and Philosophic Manuscripts of 1844*. In Karl Marx and Friedrich Engels, *Collected Works*, vol. 5. London: Lawrence and Wishart, 1975.
Nee, Victor. "Organizational Dynamics of Market Transition: Hybrid Forms, Property Rights, and Mixed Economy in China." *Administrative Science Quarterly* 37, no. 1 (1992): 1–27.
Piketty, Thomas. *Capitalism in the Twenty-First Century*. Cambridge, MA: Harvard University Press, 2013.
Polanyi, Karl. ed. *Trade and Market in Early Empires*. New York: Free Press, 1957.
Proudhon, Pierre-Joseph. *What is Property*. Edited by Donald R. Kelly and Bonnie G. Smith. Cambridge: Cambridge University Press, [1866] 1994.
Stalin, Josef V. "The Possibility of Building Socialism in One Country." In *Collected Works*, vol. 8. Moscow: Foreign Language Publishing House, 1954.
Stark, David. "Coexisting Organizational Forms in Hungary's Emerging Mixed Economies." In *Remaking the Economic Institutions of Socialism*, edited by Victor Nee and David Stark, 137–68. Stanford: Stanford University Press, 1989.
———. "Recombinant Property in East European Capitalism." *The American Journal of Sociology* 101, no. 4 (1996): 993–1027.
Szalai, Erzsébet. *Gazdaság és hatalom*. Budapest: Aula Kiadó, 1989.
Szelényi, Iván. "Capitalism in China? Comparative Perspectives." In *Chinese Capitalisms*, edited by Yin-wah Chu, 199–233. Hong Kong: Palgrave Macmillan, 2010.
———. "Social Inequalities in State Socialist Redistributive Economies." *International Journal of Comparative Sociology*, no. 1–2 (1978): 63–87.

Trotsky, Leon. *The Revolution Betrayed: What is the Soviet Union and Where is it Going?* New York: Pathfinder, 1962.

Wallerstein, Immanuel. *The Modern World System*. Berkeley: University of California Press, 1974.

Weber, Max. *Economy and Society*, vol. 1. Berkeley: University of California Press, 1978.

Williamson, Oliver. *Markets and Hierarchies*. New York: The Free Press, 1975.

Thinking Capitalism with János Kornai

Gerard Roland

1. Introduction

János Kornai produced the most comprehensive theory of "actually existing socialism" in *Economics of Shortage* (1980) and *The Socialist System* (1992). This work has been widely cited in economics and social sciences more generally, and stands as an intellectual monument for all those who want to understand how the socialist economic system really worked. While producing his theory of the socialist economic system, Kornai's comparative approach, since *Anti-Equilibrium* (1971), has also given us a "mirror vision" of capitalism as an economic system. That is the object of this paper: to discuss János Kornai's vision of capitalism as it emerges through his writings.

It is not a surprise that one may get a clearer view of capitalism when analyzing non-capitalist systems. Indeed, the strength of the comparative approach is that it helps highlight essential differences between different economic systems, which helps to better understand both. It is no coincidence that some of the best insights produced by economists on the nature of capitalism were related to the "capitalism-socialism" debates of the twentieth century. It is well known that general equilibrium theory benefited greatly from the central planning debate.[1] In fact, the central planning debate gener-

[1] Among others, see Enrico Barone, "The Ministry of Production in the Collectivist State (1908)," in *Collectivist Economic Planning: Critical Studies on the Possibility of Socialism*, ed. Friedrich Hayek (London: Routledge, 1935), 245–90; Ludwig von Mises, "Economic Calculation in the Socialist Commonwealth (1920)," in ibid.,

ated mathematical models in its aftermath that were very similar to general equilibrium models, but were rather models of planning, generating its own literature (the "Economics of Planning") in the sixties and seventies. One piece of Kornai's early work, developed in collaboration with Tamás Lipták,[2] produced one of the most noted models in that literature. Whereas general equilibrium theory focused mostly on proving the existence of equilibria, planning models focused more on generating optimizing models that could be fed into computers and produce a solution. Duality theorems and the two theorems of general equilibrium theory showed the intellectual proximity between the analysis of the interaction of many markets under perfect competition (general equilibrium theory) and the elaboration of models of planning, solving for supply-demand interactions between different goods and sectors. In a way, the central planning debate forced those like Oskar Lange, who favored central planning, to respond to the objections of von Mises and others and build models of planning that could be compared to models of the market economy. After the first spurt of models of planning—focusing mostly on algorithms and computational convergence of planning models—incentive theory, and what later became mechanism design theory, started to be developed in connection with the economics of planning literature, in particular the notion of incentive compatibility developed by Leonid Hurwicz (1973). Indeed, Hurwicz's concept of incentive compatibility started with the simple question of whether agents in the planning process (e.g., enterprise managers) would have an incentive to reveal their true supply and demand plans when given prices by the planner. It is generally acknowledged that incentive issues were a major problem in actually existing socialism. Kornai's famous concept of the soft budget constraint is the most famous incentive issue analyzed in the context of socialist economies.

Despite major advances in economic theory (be it in general equilibrium theory or incentive theory) being produced in relation to questions about central planning, and their comparison with market economies, it is fair to say that neither price theory (general equilibrium theory is essentially

87–103; Oskar Lange, "On the Economic Theory of Socialism," pts. 1 and 2, *Review of Economic Studies* 4, no. 1 (1935): 53–71; ibid., no. 2 (1935): 123–42; and Friedrich Hayek, "The Use of Knowledge in Society," *American Economic Review* 35, no. 4 (1945): 519–30.

[2] János Kornai and Tamás Lipták, "Two-Level Planning," *Econometrica* 33, no. 1 (1965): 141–69.

a theory of price formation) nor incentive (i.e., contract) theory pretend to be theories of an economic system.

The field of comparative economics, especially the work developed by John Montias and others in the seventies,[3] attempted to build theories of comparative economic systems using abstract mathematical models. These theoretical constructions were very abstract in design, in the spirit of the times (social choice theory seems, in my view, the closest in terms of abstraction and intellectual ambition), but often did not have enough "bite" on reality, in the sense of delivering specific enough predictions that were at the same time sufficiently close to reality.

Kornai's work, starting with *Anti-Equilibrium*, was more ambitious and comprehensive than models of general equilibrium or mechanism design as it aimed at understanding both capitalism and socialism as economic systems. It was also much more specific in its predictions than other models of comparative systems. When rereading *Anti-Equilibrium* today, one will find that, although it is long on concepts, notations, and definitions, it delivers a number of important insights (e.g., on the role of information or of bargaining) and provides an innovative, original, and extremely relevant comparative systems analysis on "Pressure and Suction" (part three of the book).

In section 2, I ask why it is interesting to think of capitalism as a system. In section 3, I briefly discuss some mistakes to avoid when doing comparative systems analysis. In section 4, I present some of the most important views of Marx, Schumpeter, and Hayek on the capitalist system. In section 5, I discuss Kornai's views on capitalism since *Anti-Equilibrium*. In section 6, I present my own views of capitalism. In section 7, I discuss the specificities of Chinese capitalism. Section 8 concludes.

2. Why think about capitalism as a system?

While scholars in comparative economics find it natural to think that we need a theory of the capitalist system, this may not be obvious to the economics profession at large. Why would we need to think about capitalism as a system?

[3] John M. Montias, *The Structure of Economic Systems* (New Haven, CT: Yale University Press, 1976); see also Egon Neuberger and William J. Duffy, *Comparative Economic Systems: A Decision-Making Approach* (Boston, MA: Allyn and Bacon, 1976).

Attempts in the twentieth century to establish a socialist alternative to capitalism, and their spectacular failure, would seem to force one to think of the difference between the capitalist and socialist *systems*. Those not interested in non-capitalist systems have usually little interest in understanding capitalism as a system. A large part of the economics profession thinks students should never learn about socialism since it has disappeared. A similar feeling exists among many economists about history in general.

Upon further thinking, it would appear that mainstream economic theory is not really interested in understanding capitalism as a system. General equilibrium theory, though framed as theory of markets, is essentially a theory about price movements across sectors in response to exogenous shocks in demand and supply. While general equilibrium theory helps analyze all interactions between markets, its focus of analysis is still partial compared to what one might expect from a theory about capitalism as a system. Disequilibrium theory was seen as very promising in the seventies, partly because it could provide a common framework to understand capitalism and socialism, but mostly because prices are in reality downwardly rigid. Understanding the macroeconomy in a world where prices are downwardly rigid is fundamental to grasp the business cycle properties of capitalism. Despite its promises, disequilibrium theory was focusing mainly on the analysis of spillovers of excess demand and supply from one market onto other markets. Even though it took prices as fixed, its focus was still pretty much similar to price theory. Essentially, it still took supply and demand curves as the basis of economic analysis.

All in all, it would seem to be a paradox that it is in political science, and not in economics, with the "varieties of capitalism" literature, that patterns in institutional variations of capitalist systems have been studied. Even though mainstream economic analysis has put in little effort to understand capitalism as a system, it seems obvious that this intellectual endeavor is fundamental not only for intellectual purposes, but also for practical policy purposes. In particular, it seems fundamental to know which elements of capitalism are necessary to its existence and which elements can be changed, and possibly could be changed from a normative perspective. Hayek, who was prophetic in his analysis of the socialist economy,[4] thought that the introduction of the welfare state after WWII would mean the end of capitalism. His famous book,

---

[4] See Friedrich Hayek, "The Use of Knowledge in Society," *American Economic Review* 35, no. 4 (1945): 519–30.

The Road to Serfdom (1944),[5] is mostly about how the introduction of the welfare state in post-WWII Britain would lead to the end of capitalism. In reality, capitalism adapted very well to the introduction of the welfare state. Today, similarly to debates about the welfare state seventy years ago, questions are raised about the link between the introduction of a universal basic income and capitalism. Are they compatible or not? What would capitalism look like under a universal basic income? Who would have thought capitalism could survive the high tax burdens one has observed since second half of the twentieth century? Kornai's comparative systems analysis, for example, sheds light on the inevitability of unemployment in the capitalist economy, raising important questions about the place of social welfare.

Reflecting on this, an economic system is not just about the economy in a narrow sense, but also about the institutions of that system. For example, it has been established that central planning is incompatible with democracy.[6] Similarly, there are many interactions of the economy with the capitalist system's political and legal institutions as well as with existing cultural values and beliefs. Marx and Weber have given a lot of thought, albeit different answers, to the link between capitalism, its "superstructure," and the prevailing culture.

3. Mistakes to avoid in comparative systems analysis

If one is convinced that a comparative approach can deliver rich insights in comparative systems analysis, there are nevertheless a number of mistakes that one should best avoid in performing such an analysis.

There is no space in this article to list all these mistakes. I just want to point to the most important one. This is what I call the "negative mirror image" mistake. By negative mirror image, I mean the attempt to characterize an economic system by listing characteristics of one system that are absent in the other system. It is useful to give a few examples. Characterizing central planning by the "absence of markets" and the associated efficiency issues is not wrong, but it does not help analyzing central planning. Similarly, Marxist descriptions of capitalism as market chaos and absence of the "visible hand" of a central planner do not help much to understand capitalism. A similar mistake is often also made

5 Friedrich Hayek, *The Road to Serfdom* (London: Routledge, 1944).
6 See e.g. János Kornai, *Dynamism, Rivalry and the Surplus Economy: Two Essays on the Nature of Capitalism* (Oxford: Oxford University Press, 2014).

in the study of autocratic political systems, as compared with democracies. One thus tends to define and characterize autocracies not in terms of how they really work, but in terms of absence of characteristics of democracies.

The "negative mirror image" suffers at least from two problems. First, it does not deliver interesting insights into how a system works as its characteristics are defined in terms of absence of characteristics that are present in another system. Second, these negative mirror image comparisons are usually done with a theoretical system. Thus, central planning is compared with a theoretical capitalist system, autocracy is compared with a theoretical democratic system. Since some of those theories may be wide off the mark, in terms of how well they describe reality, the "negative mirror image" framework compares an existing system by the absence of characteristics of another system as described by a particular theory. Therefore, not only does it not provide useful real comparative analysis, but the comparison of a negative mirror image with a theoretical system may be completely misleading in the comparison of systems itself.

4. Marx, Schumpeter, and Hayek on capitalism

Before talking about Kornai's view of capitalism, it is useful to be reminded of the main visions of capitalism by some of the big thinkers who were interested in understanding it as a system. I cannot be complete in this article, and will mention only the ideas of Marx, Schumpeter, and Hayek. Even then, what follows will necessarily be very schematic and incomplete.

Marx saw capitalism as driven by greed (i.e., the material interests of the bourgeoisie).[7] Greed was at the center of his analysis of the difference between the "commodity relation" (trade in the formation of one's consumption bundle) and the "capital relation" (investment of capital with the goal of increasing one's wealth). Greed was, in his view, insatiable, leading to a formidable process of capital accumulation to finance profit-maximizing technology. Marx saw the capitalist "superstructure" (e.g., formal legal and political institutions, culture) as driven by the class interests of the bourgeoisie, and together they formed a system.

Marx saw capitalism as doomed by its internal contradictions, mainly what he saw as the main contradiction between the global connectedness of

[7] Karl Marx, *Das Kapital* (Hamburg: Otto Meissner, 1867).

production and the private character of asset property. This kind of reasoning is based on Hegelian dialectics, characterized by its logical vagueness and rhetorical crispness, and does not appear convincing in its logical consequences. That being said, it would be foolish to deny that private capitalist interests in many cases are in conflict with the interests of society at large.

Schumpeter's view was certainly influenced by Marx, despite being one of the main intellectual proponents of capitalism. Schumpeter paid less attention to markets, in contrast to classical and neo-classical economists. He emphasized the fundamental role of entrepreneurship, innovation and creative destruction in generating growth. The themes of innovation and creative destruction have been taken over by many economists, in particular Baumol, Aghion, and Howitt, among others.

It is less well known, at least among mainstream economists, that Schumpeter, despite being an ardent defender of capitalism, was also pessimistic about its future. In *Capitalism, Socialism and Democracy*,[8] he predicted that capitalism was about to become more and more bureaucratic and was doomed to choke on the bureaucratization of large corporations and government agencies.

Hayek is a major thinker of capitalism as a system. He strongly emphasized the importance of law (a constitutional order and common law) and the rule of law to protect individual freedom as a basis for economic progress.[9] Hayek also strongly emphasized individual responsibility in conjunction with freedom. We will come back to this when discussing Kornai's concept of capitalism. According to Hayek, society evolves best as a spontaneous order where the role of government should be limited as its actions may often be counterproductive.

Hayek's insights on central planning were truly prophetic. In "The Use of Knowledge in Society," Hayek argued that central planning was doomed to fail because of the numerous informational issues that would plague the necessary centralization of information required in a central planning system, and which are otherwise solved in a decentralized way in a spontaneous market order.[10] As a classical liberal, Hayek emphasized the danger of overly

[8] Joseph Schumpeter, *Capitalism, Socialism and Democracy* (London: Allen and Unwin, 1943).

[9] Friedrich Hayek, *The Constitution of Liberty* (Chicago: University of Chicago Press, 1960).

[10] Friedrich Hayek, "The Use of Knowledge in Society," *American Economic Review* 35, no. 4 (1945): 519–30.

large government encroaching on individual liberties. He insisted on the importance of fighting to preserve freedom and the rule of law.

5. Kornai's views on capitalism since *Anti-Equilibrium*

Kornai's *Anti-Equilibrium* represented a big breakthrough in comparative economics and our understanding of capitalism through the systematic analysis of "pressure" (buyer's markets, surplus) and "suction" (seller's markets, shortage), its origins, and its effects. His insights on capitalism were derived from comparison with the socialist shortage economy.

One of Kornai's fundamental conclusions from *Anti-Equilibrium*'s analysis of capitalism is that surplus (excess supply) in capitalist economies is the normal state of affairs, not just a feature of business cycles. In contrast, shortage (excess demand) is the normal state of affairs in the centrally planned socialist economy. Surplus produces competition between producers. This competition leads in turn to better product quality, a drive for innovation, advertising to convince consumers to buy one's products, as well as price reductions and discounts. Kornai stated that surplus is a fundamental cause of competition, partly independent of market forces, at least in contrast with shortage, which creates monopoly positions for producers, and where competition is among buyers.

Kornai's theory emphasizes mostly the reproduction of surplus and shortage. Among the causes of surplus versus shortage, he identifies the dominant ownership form in society (i.e., private versus state ownership) as well as the political power structure favoring either.

Here, I emphasized Kornai's main originality in understanding capitalism in *Anti-Equilibrium*, but the book contains many other originalities.

First of all, in the book, he takes the transaction as the unit of analysis, not the market. This is extremely insightful, as the institutionalist school—with Douglass North[11] and especially Oliver Williamson[12]—argued that transactions should be the main unit of economic analysis, since this would help economists understand transaction costs and improve our understanding

[11] Douglass North, *Institutions, Institutional Change and Economic Performance* (Cambridge: Cambridge University Press, 1990).

[12] Oliver E. Williamson, *Markets and Hierarchies: Analysis and Antitrust Implications: A Study in the Economics of Internal Organization* (New York: Free Press, 1975).

of how institutions either helped to reduce transaction costs or, instead, increased them.

Second, Kornai introduced the importance of aspirations in determining economic behavior as well as adjustments of aspirations to environment. This is closely related to themes of behavioral economics that analyze how people determine their choices. In connection with this, Kornai writes about the role of conventions and rules of thumb, an element that would be analyzed later, for example, by Andrew Schotter.[13] In that context, he made the distinction between routine responses in particular situations and larger adaptations to a more changing environment. These are themes that one finds for example in the works of Herbert Simon[14] or Richard Nelson and Sidney Winter.[15]

Third, Kornai emphasizes the importance of bargaining in transactions. His analysis is very close to what would later be called "Nash bargaining," but he emphasizes how bargaining power is affected by the fundamentals of the economic system (pressure or suction, i.e., situations of excess supply or excess demand).

After *Anti-Equilibrium*, Kornai deepened his analysis of the socialist system in his two major works, *Economics of Shortage* and *The Socialist System*. His major innovation, though not the only one, is the concept of soft budget constraint.

The introduction of the concept of the soft budget constraint and the analysis of its consequences and its causes (i.e., the communist regime and dominant state ownership) was a major breakthrough in understanding generalized shortage, its reproduction and its short-, medium- and long-term consequences for the socialist economy. The emphasis is on a disaggregated approach in order to avoid the pitfalls of aggregation of surpluses and shortages. Those two books provided the most comprehensive analysis of the socialist system so far. They also paved the way for an analysis of the capitalist system in contrast to the socialist system.

The two essays that comprise Kornai's *Dynamism, Rivalry and the Surplus Economy* provide the most advanced thinking of János Kornai on capitalism

---

13 See Andrew Schotter, *The Economic Theory of Social Institutions* (Cambridge: Cambridge University Press, 1981).

14 Herbert A. Simon, *Administrative Behavior: A Study of Decision-Making Processes in Administrative Organization* (New York: Free Press, 1947).

15 Richard Nelson and Sidney Winter, *An Evolutionary Theory of Economic Change* (Cambridge, MA: Belknap Economic Press, 1982).

as a system.[16] The first essay emphasizes the fundamental role of innovation under capitalism and lack thereof in the socialist economy. (Stanislaw Gomulka had already approached the subject in his *Growth, Innovation and Reform in Eastern Europe*.[17]) Much of comparative systems analysis focuses on issues of allocative efficiency. When it comes, however, to dynamic efficiency, the capacity of an economic system to deliver innovation is of first order importance. Here, it is quite clear that capitalism is very good at delivering innovation while socialism is not. Creative destruction and endogenous obsolescence of capital play a key role in the growth process. Endogenous growth theory[18] provides the analytical tools to understand the power of growth compared to static efficiency. It also contains technological optimism about capitalism since the main variable that creates growth is the stock of knowledge. So, growth can continue as long as scientific and technological knowledge continues to grow.

Kornai's second essay provides his most complete analysis so far on the building blocks of the capitalist system as a system of chronic excess supply. Chronic excess supply is incompatible with supply-demand equilibrium of price theory. The closest formal models that can be used to understand chronic excess supply are search models, but they have not really been used for comparative systems analysis so far. The main innovation, compared to *Anti-Equilibrium*, is not only the emphasis on the dominance of private property and market coordination in capitalism, leading to entrepreneurship, innovation and supply drive. Now, hard budget constraints play a key role in the analysis. Hard budget constraints play a key role in capitalism in curbing demand so that the economy stays in a state of excess supply. Moreover, hard budget constraints play a fundamental role in making the process of firm exit work properly. Firm exit is indeed a key ingredient in the process of creative destruction, as it frees resources for new entrants with higher productivity. Downward price and wage stickiness reinforce the effects of hard budget constraints on excess supply, keeping the latter always at a positive level since higher than equilibrium prices maintain a high level of supply and a lower

16 János Kornai, *Dynamism, Rivalry and the Surplus Economy.*

17 Stanislaw Gomulka, *Growth, Innovation and Reform in Eastern Europe* (New York: St. Martin's Press, 1986).

18 See Paul M. Romer, "Endogenous Technological Change," *Journal of Political Economy* 98, no. 5 (1990): 71–102; as well as Philippe Aghion and Peter Howitt, *Endogenous Growth Theory* (Cambridge, MA: The MIT Press, 1997).

level of market demand. Kornai mentions efficiency wages as a cause of downward wage rigidity, but downward price rigidity and the speed of upward price adjustment are still not totally well understood by economists.

When comparing Kornai's analysis with other analyses of capitalism, hard budget constraints are very close to Hayek's emphasis on the role of responsibility in a free society. Responsibility is the flipside of freedom. If we are free to choose our actions, we must also take responsibility for them, according to Hayek. Kornai does not use that kind of terminology or reasoning, but his analysis implies that private property means risk-taking, and thus acceptance of the downside risks.

To sum up, for Kornai, excess supply is the norm under capitalism. The dominance of private ownership and market coordination—together with hard budget constraints implied by private ownership—lead to innovation, competition, and creative destruction, generating growth via innovation.

6. My own views on capitalism

My own views on capitalism were strongly influenced by Kornai when I was a student in the eighties. As a scholar of the transition process, I was forced to think about the capitalist system in a serious way. Rereading Kornai's views on capitalism throughout his career has forced me to think more systematically about my own views on capitalism, admittedly very partial ones. Moreover, apart from Kornai, there are a whole series of thinkers who have influenced me.

Since my research on transition, summed up in *Transition and Economics. Politics, Markets and Firms*, I was strongly influenced by the institutionalist school. Here are some fundamental ideas I got from the institutionalist school. First, transactions, not markets or supply and demand, are the basis of the analysis. This is a key insight I understood when analyzing the output fall in Eastern Europe. It cannot be explained by general equilibrium or price theory and the models that explain the output fall take the transaction as unit of analysis.[19] A key insight of institutionalism is that legal institutions affect transactions, while political institutions affect the rule of law and the protection

[19] See Olivier Blanchard and Michael Kremer, "Disorganization," *Quarterly Journal of Economics* 112, no. 4 (1996): 1091–1126; as well as Gerard Roland and Thierry Verdier, "Transition and the Output Fall," *Economics of Transition* 7, no. 1 (March 1999): 1–28.

of private property rights. Moreover, liberal democracy, separation of powers, and press freedom are fundamental to protect freedoms and human rights.[20] Many of these institutions are under attack today in the world. The outcome of these attacks may well determine the future of capitalism.

I realize that many of my ideas about capitalism are also directly or indirectly influenced by Marx's analysis of capitalism that I read carefully more than thirty years ago when writing a book on use value.[21] A key insight, nearly trivial in its truth, that I got from Marx is the importance of greed and its related drive for capital accumulation. Kornai calls this the "expansion drive." Marx emphasized the role of capital accumulation in realizing aspirations derived from greed. He analyzed the role of "primitive capital accumulation" in generating the individual capital needed to reach a certain threshold that allows one to benefit from the economies of scale described by Adam Smith. Marx also vividly described greed-driven innovation and unbridled expansion towards new inventions, new products, and new territories. Some of this improves welfare and living standards, but capitalist expansion also depletes resources on the planet. It also tends to destroy primitive and more traditional societies once they come in contact with capitalism. Marx did not, at the time, insist on the environmental consequences of capital accumulation, but their analysis fits well in the Marxian logic of how capitalism operates.

Another idea I took from Marx is that unbridled capitalist expansion favors tendencies towards monopoly that need to be counteracted. This was true in the nineteenth century and is still true in the twenty-first, particularly with the advent of the so-called FANGs (Facebook, Amazon, Netflix, Google). Monopolies also use their political power to oppose anti-trust measures that would hurt their profits. Another idea that was present in Marx's writing, but which is very much debated today, is that the dynamics of capitalism cannot assure a stable and decent life for workers in the long run whose role is essentially that of a commodity. The welfare state was introduced to counteract this tendency, and discussions these days on universal basic income relate to this fundamental problem faced by capitalism.

---

20 See Torsten Persson, Gerard Roland, and Guido Tabellini, "Separation of Powers and Political Accountability," *Quarterly Journal of Economics* 112, no. 4 (1997): 1163–1202; as well as idem., "Comparative Politics and Public Finance," *Journal of Political Economy* 108, no. 6 (2000): 1121–1161.

21 Gerard Roland, *La valeur d'usage chez Karl Marx* (Brussels: Éditions de l'Université de Bruxelles, 1985).

The tendency towards increases in inequality, à la Piketty, and towards the development of a plutocracy benefiting from this increase in inequality, are a fundamental feature of capitalism.

A theme present in Marx is the recurrence of global financial crises. These crises have the potential to become ever more severe with the higher interconnectedness of firms and financial markets. The occurrence of these crises relates to the hardness of budget constraints, but also to mass psychology. Fortunately, the Great Depression produced Keynesian macroeconomics, whose insights proved already extremely helpful in the Great Recession of 2008. Nevertheless, financial instability and the occurrence of big crises are a big vulnerability of capitalism. Even the Great Recession of 2008, despite good monetary and fiscal policy, in the US at least, led to major losses of jobs and housing for millions, and to other social and political consequences that we are only starting to grasp.

Another important idea present in Marx is the importance of class interests in politics. Government in capitalism is not a social welfare maximizer like in Pigovian public economics, but it is also not the Leviathan of public choice theory. In my view, the best way to think about government under capitalism is that it is a locus of influence activities by class interests and special interests. In many policy areas, special interests manage to defend monopoly positions and special interests of particular capitalist groups. Worker interests are also defended, in particular via trade unions. Democracy, with the principle of "one man, one vote" (that is, one *person*, one vote) has helped the majority of poor correct income inequalities via the political system. Universal suffrage inexorably led to the introduction of the welfare state.

Where Marx was wrong, of course, was to think socialism and central planning could solve the problems of capitalism. The failures of socialism and central planning have helped us recognize that capitalism is necessary to obtain growth and prosperity. These failures have left us with the difficulty to grapple with the trade-off between preserving the dynamic properties of capitalism and simultaneously making progress in social welfare. Globalization with rule of law at the international level, together with democracy at the country level, can help keep that balance, but there are several caveats. First of all, the international rule of law is still fragile, which means that the global economic order is vulnerable to disruptive shocks. Misguided protectionist tendencies, which are becoming stronger by the day in advanced industrial economies, are difficult to counteract. There is also no institutional mechanism to protect people from capitalism's destruction of the planet's resources.

Schumpeter has, of course, also been an important source of inspiration for my thinking about capitalism. As a student of the socialist system, I became acutely aware of its failure to generate innovations, and, *mutatis mutandis*, of the importance of innovation and entrepreneurship in generating growth—key ideas expressed by Schumpeter.

These themes are well known. One idea that is less well known was Schumpeter's pessimism about the future of capitalism. In *Capitalism, Socialism and Democracy*, he pointed to the bureaucratization process that was taking place both inside large corporations and government agencies. He thought that this bureaucratization process was inevitable and would destroy the positive elements of capitalism, especially the dynamics of innovation and creative destruction.

Schumpeter saw this as a slow and irreversible process towards socialism. In hindsight, he was blatantly wrong, but it is nevertheless worthwhile discussing some of Schumpeter's ideas. The progress in the development of technology and the greater diversity of products and services associated with economic development substantially increase the informational requirements of coordination within firms, between firms, within government agencies and across governments.

Too little attention is paid to this. It is generally known that the increasing complexity of economic relations became the Achilles' heel of the socialist economy,[22] vindicating Hayek, who had predicted the socialist economy would experience a problem of information overload. Too little attention has, however, been paid to the issue of complexity in advanced market economies. Take international trade agreements. The text of such agreements has become increasingly long over time. The same can be said of legislation in advanced democracies. Brexit made it clear that (1) divorce from the EU is complex and (2) so is the negotiation of a new relationship between the UK and the EU. The issue of complexity is easy to understand. For every new product, the number of informational links necessary to manage becomes ever larger as the economy develops. These links are usually managed in a decentralized "Hayekian" way, but, to the extent that any new informational link in the economy involves a management cost, however small, these informational

---

22 See Alec Nove, *The Soviet Economic System* (London: Allen and Unwin, 1977); as well as Gerard Roland, *Economie Politique du Système Soviétique* (Paris: L'Harmattan, 1989); and idem., "Complexity, Bounded Rationality and Equilibrium: The Soviet-Type Case," *Journal of Comparative Economics* 14, no. 3 (1990): 401–24.

costs should grow exponentially with the level of economic development. This should reduce marginal returns significantly. Inside government, the issue of complexity is even more severe as governments must manage a large amount of informational links with the economy. Think only of financial regulation. The 2008 crisis made policy-makers and the general public acutely aware of the need for financial regulation. Nevertheless, there is no consensus among experts about what optimal regulation should look like. To a large extent, that is due to the fact that financial regulation issues are very complex. In a celebrated book,[23] Richard Gordon has documented the growth of total factor productivity over time in different economies and found that the IT revolution did not increase total factor productivity (TFP) as much as the technological revolutions of the early twentieth century. If this is indeed the case, it is quite possible that the IT revolution has substantially decreased the costs of informational links, while not decreasing complexity.

I have mentioned above how my thinking about capitalism was influenced by great economists. Let me mention some more personal insights that I have developed in recent years.

A first insight is about the importance of democracy for the survival of capitalism. I am aware that this is controversial, but I became more and more convinced of it over time. Democracy not only protects freedom, of fundamental value in itself, but is also in the interest of successful economic growth. It also helps collective action of the majority of poor to correct the inequalities of capitalism. This is a property that may not be seen as desirable by many. Nevertheless, it is in my view not only important for its intrinsic value (i.e., the reduction of inequality) but also more generally for the political sustainability of capitalism, a point to which I come below.

A point that has not, in my view, been made sufficiently is the positive role of democracy in mitigating the capital levy problem. The capital levy problem itself has not been given enough attention in economics (see, for example, the work of Torsten Persson and Guido Tabellini[24]). The problem is related to the issue of lack of government commitment. Before an investment has been made, the *ex ante* elasticity of capital to taxation is very high. At that stage, capital has not yet been transformed into physical capital and it is

---

[23] Robert J. Gordon, *The Rise and Fall of American Growth: The U.S. Standard of Living since the Civil War* (Princeton: Princeton University Press, 2016).

[24] Torsten Persson and Guido Tabellini, "Representative Democracy and Capital Taxation," *Journal of Public Economics* 55, no. 1 (September 1994): 53–70.

very sensitive to variation in tax rates on capital in particular countries. Based on public economics, the tax rate should be low on tax bases that are highly mobile. Once a capital investment has been made, its elasticity to taxation becomes essentially zero as the capital investment is now a sunk cost. If the government lacks commitment, it should promise a low tax rate *ex ante*, but will be tempted to charge high tax rates once investments have been sunk. As a consequence, lack of government commitment should lead investors to shy away from investing despite *ex ante* promises of low tax rates. Autocratic governments have, in general, commitment issues, and the capital levy problem should have negative effects on investment in autocracies unless autocratic governments are able to come up with credible mechanisms for commitment to avoid predatory behavior. Democracies tend to solve this commitment problem much better than autocracies. Tax rates may change in democracies, but this happens only as the result of a legislative process. So, even if the executive branch of government is strongly tempted to tax investments that have been sunk, only the legislative branch of government can make those decisions. The separation of powers inherent to democracies thus provides a strong institutional protection against the capital levy problem.

A second insight relates to modern political economy: how to assure the political sustainability of capitalism? This is an important question that, in my view, has been given too little attention. There is no foolproof solution to the political sustainability issue, but it is reasonable to argue that the dividends of growth need to be redistributed in order to minimize the number of losers. In other words, a sustainable capitalism needs to be inclusive.

A third insight relates to the role of culture in capitalism. Research I have done on the topic suggests that capitalism has fared best in countries with an individualist culture fed by centuries of market development, improvements in protection of property rights, protection from state encroachment, as well as social stratification. The individualist culture emphasizes citizenship, equality before the law, and freedom, while social prestige is associated with one standing out from others. The social prestige motivation gives a cultural motive for innovation that dynamically dominates efficiency advantages from collectivist culture in terms of coordination of production.[25]

[25] Yuriy Gorodnichenko and Gerard Roland, "Culture, Institutions and the Wealth of Nations," *The Review of Economics and Statistics* 99, no. 3 (2017): 402–16.

Individualist culture, citizenship, and equality before the law are also congruent with the institutions of democracy. We found that democratization tends to occur earlier in individualist countries as collectivist cultures may keep "efficient autocracies" for very long periods.[26] Taking culture into account leads one to reject the unilinear trend towards democracy implied by modernization theory.[27]

Individualist culture is also a good antidote to nationalism, as it emphasizes individual citizenship and the universality of human rights, in contrast to national, ethnic, or tribal loyalties. Individualist culture, on the other hand, makes collective action more difficult, because the free-rider problem is more acute under an individualist culture. Collective action problems have been ubiquitous in countries with an individualist culture, be it with the Dutch Republic between the sixteenth and eighteenth century, with the European Union, or within international organizations set up to provide public goods at the international level, be it peace, trade, health, or protection against climate change.

7. How to think about Chinese capitalism?

This is a special question that needs to be raised, given the unique institutional setup of contemporary Chinese capitalism. China is a capitalist economy with a communist political regime emphasizing the leading role of the party. China has had a collectivist culture for thousands of years. Politically, censorship and lack of property rights protections are not good for innovation in the long run. China's autocratic political regime deprives citizens of certain freedoms and human rights. All these characteristics contradict some of the elements I put forward in the previous section, as important conditions for the success of capitalism. On the other hand, China's autocratic system is very stable, as it has solved most problems of government: succession, information, and taxation.

[26] Yuriy Gorodnichenko and Gerard Roland, "Culture, Institutions and Democratization," NBER Working Paper 21117, National Bureau of Economic Research, Cambridge, MA, 2015.

[27] Seymour M. Lipset, "Some Social Requisites of Democracy: Economic Development and Political Legitimacy," *American Political Science Review* 53, no. 1 (March 1959): 69–105.

Rules for succession were set up after Mao's death. Mostly, mandatory retirement ensures rotation of leadership at the highest level. Since Deng Xiaoping, a leader used to nominate his successor's successor. Deng thus nominated Hu Jintao, Zhiang Zemin nominated Xi Jinping and Hu Jintao nominated Hu Chunhua. Xi Jinping, however, appears to have thrown away that rule together with the rule of two term limits for president of the Republic. It is too early to tell what will happen to rules for leader succession in China.

Informational problems were a big problem under Mao Zedong. The vertical communication channels did not function during the Great Leap Forward when provincial leaders did not dare tell Mao about the famine that was developing for fear of retaliation if bringing bad news. Instead, they falsified information about the "successes" of the Great Leap Forward. Since that terrible experience, leaders have learned to use alternative communication channels. This is why they tolerate both local protest actions and limit censorship of social media, because they provide alternative communication channels in case the vertical channels do not work properly. During the SARS epidemic, for example, whistleblowers played a role in ensuring the diffusion of information.

Taxation is not a problem in China given the large state capacity. The government can afford to charge low tax rates as it commands large control over resources of the large state sector.[28] The leaders of the Chinese Communist Party also have an instrument that is generally absent in advanced democracies, namely large campaign mobilizations, in case of an earthquake or a national catastrophe.

China's collectivist culture is a disadvantage for innovation, as I argued in the previous section, but it is an advantage in terms of coordination. This is probably one of the reasons the collectivist countries from East Asia have, taken together, become the manufacturing hub of the world. China still has much scope for economic catch up, but given its cultural disadvantage in terms of fundamental innovation, it is doubtful that it will overtake the richest countries of the world in terms of GDP per capita.

The Chinese system has been, so far, quite inclusive—even though it is not a democracy—since poorer segments of the population have benefited strongly from the past forty years of fast growth.

---

[28] See Roger Gordon and Wei Li, "Tax Structures in Developing Countries: Many Puzzles and a Possible Explanation," *Journal of Public Economics* 93, no. 7–8 (2009): 855–66.

What about the capital levy problem? As argued above, this is a weakness of non-democracies. In China, nevertheless, specific institutional solutions have been found, such as the combination of meritocracy within the hierarchy (e.g., promotion based on economic performance) and rotation of cadres.[29]

China, as a market economy, has become very dependent on the world economy for its growth. Without competition from the world economy, Chinese economic dynamism, based mostly on export promotion, would likely fade away and the state sector might, once again, take the dominant role in the economy. In contrast to twentieth-century communism, China needs strong integration in the world economy and Chinese leaders therefore have no interest in dominating the world. Differences in cultures and political regime with the rest of the world, and especially with advanced Western democracies, will nevertheless undoubtedly lead to frictions that must be managed peacefully

8. Conclusion

In building a comprehensive theory of the socialist economy, János Kornai's comparative analytical approach has also provided many elements for a comprehensive theory of the capitalist system. In reviewing Kornai's thinking about the capitalist system, I have also provided some elements of my own thinking, emphasizing the importance of democracy for capitalism to survive, the issue of political sustainability of capitalism, and the role of individualist culture in the capitalist system.

References

Aghion, Philippe, and Peter Howitt. *Endogenous Growth Theory*. Cambridge, MA: The MIT Press, 1997.

Barone, Enrico. "The Ministry of Production in the Collectivist State (1908)." In *Collectivist Economic Planning: Critical Studies on the Possibility of Socialism*, edited by Friedrich Hayek, 245–90. London: Routledge, 1935.

Blanchard, Olivier, and Michael Kremer. "Disorganization." *Quarterly Journal of Economics* 112, no. 4 (1996): 1091–1126.

[29] Weijia Li, "Rotation, Performance Rewards, and Property Rights," Monash University working paper, February 2019.

Gomulka, Stanislaw. *Growth, Innovation and Reform in Eastern Europe*. New York: St. Martin's Press, 1986.

Gordon, Robert J. *The Rise and Fall of American Growth: The U.S. Standard of Living since the Civil War*. Princeton: Princeton University Press, 2016.

Gordon, Roger, and Wei Li. "Tax Structures in Developing Countries: Many Puzzles and a Possible Explanation." *Journal of Public Economics* 93, no. 7–8 (2009): 855–66.

Gorodnichenko, Yuriy, and Gerard Roland. "Culture, Institutions and Democratization." NBER Working Paper 21117, National Bureau of Economic Research, Cambridge, MA, 2015.

———. "Culture, Institutions and the Wealth of Nations." *The Review of Economics and Statistics* 99, no. 3 (2017): 402–16.

Hayek, Friedrich. *The Constitution of Liberty*. Chicago: University of Chicago Press, 1960.

———. *The Road to Serfdom*. London: Routledge, 1944.

———. "The Use of Knowledge in Society." *American Economic Review* 35, no. 4 (1945): 519–30.

Hurwicz, Leonid. "The Design of Mechanisms for Resource Allocation." *American Economic Review* 63, no. 2 (1973): 1–30.

Kornai, János. *Anti-Equilibrium*. Amsterdam: North Holland, 1971.

———. *Dynamism, Rivalry and the Surplus Economy: Two Essays on the Nature of Capitalism*. Oxford: Oxford University Press, 2014.

———. *Economics of Shortage*. Amsterdam: North Holland, 1980.

———. *The Socialist System*. Oxford: Oxford University Press, 1992.

———. *Dynamism, Rivalry and the Surplus Economy: Two Essays on the Nature of Capitalism*. Oxford: Oxford University Press, 2014.

———, and Tamás Lipták. "Two-Level Planning." *Econometrica* 33, no. 1 (1965): 141–69.

Lange, Oskar. "On the Economic Theory of Socialism." Pts. 1 and 2. *Review of Economic Studies* 4, no. 1 (1935): 53–71; no. 2 (1935):123–42.

Li, Weijia. "Rotation, Performance Rewards, and Property Rights." Monash University working paper, February 2019.

Marx, Karl. *Das Kapital*. Hamburg: Otto Meissner, 1867.

von Mises, Ludwig. "Economic Calculation in the Socialist Commonwealth (1920)." In *Collectivist Economic Planning: Critical Studies on the Possibility of Socialism*, edited by Friedrich Hayek, 87–103. London: Routledge, 1935.

Montias, John M. *The Structure of Economic Systems*. New Haven, CT: Yale University Press, 1976.

Nelson, Richard, and Sidney Winter. *An Evolutionary Theory of Economic Change*. Cambridge, MA: Belknap Economic Press, 1982.

Neuberger, Egon, and William J. Duffy. *Comparative Economic Systems: A Decision-Making Approach*. Boston, MA: Allyn and Bacon, 1976.

North, Douglass. *Institutions, Institutional Change and Economic Performance*. Cambridge: Cambridge University Press, 1990.

Nove, Alec. *The Soviet Economic System*. London: Allen and Unwin, 1977.

Persson, Torsten, and Guido Tabellini. "Representative Democracy and Capital Taxation." *Journal of Public Economics* 55, no. 1 (September 1994): 53–70.

Persson, Torsten, Gerard Roland, and Guido Tabellini. "Comparative Politics and Public Finance." *Journal of Political Economy* 108, no. 6 (2000): 1121–1161.

———. "Separation of Powers and Political Accountability." *Quarterly Journal of Economics* 112, no. 4 (1997): 1163–1202.

Roland, Gerard. "Complexity, Bounded Rationality and Equilibrium: The Soviet-Type Case." *Journal of Comparative Economics* 14, no. 3 (1990): 401–24.

———. *Economie Politique du Système Soviétique.* Paris: L'Harmattan, 1989.

———. *La valeur d'usage chez Karl Marx.* Brussels: Éditions de l'Université de Bruxelles, 1985.

———. *Transition and Economics. Politics, Markets and Firms.* Cambridge, MA: The MIT Press, 2000.

———, and Thierry Verdier, "Transition and the Output Fall." *Economics of Transition* 7, no. 1 (March 1999): 1–28.

Romer, Paul M. "Endogenous Technological Change." *Journal of Political Economy* 98, no. 5 (1990): 71–102.

Schotter, Andrew. *The Economic Theory of Social Institutions.* Cambridge: Cambridge University Press, 1981.

Schumpeter, Joseph. *Capitalism, Socialism and Democracy.* London: Allen and Unwin, 1943.

Simon, Herbert A. *Administrative Behavior: A Study of Decision-Making Processes in Administrative Organization.* New York: Free Press, 1947.

Williamson, Oliver E. *Markets and Hierarchies: Analysis and Antitrust Implications: A Study in the Economics of Internal Organization.* New York: Free Press, 1975.

The Theories of János Kornai and a Less-known Hungarian Economist, Ferenc Jánossy, on Unbalanced Economic Growth*

Péter Mihályi

Introduction

Although it may sound surprising today, the pace of growth in Hungary during the 1960s appeared to be *too high* to at least two far-sighted theoretical economists. This happened at a time when it was considered a trivial fact by virtually all economists that the higher the growth rate, the better it was for everyone. The two main heroes of the present paper, János Kornai (b. 1928) and Ferenc Jánossy (1914–1997), were then about the same age and knew each other. They were both fairly renowned in academic circles, but both of them belonged to the "politically tolerated" category of intellectuals in Hungary. This meant that they were allowed to work in middle-level research positions, could travel to the West if they were invited, and could openly publish their writings both at home and abroad. But their influence on policymaking was indirect at best and—just like everybody else working in the social sciences—they were obliged to exercise self-censorship in their domestic publications. When their two books were published, neither Jánossy nor Kornai were allowed to teach at the Karl Marx University of Economics, the flagship higher education institution in Hungary at that time. Kornai doesn't need any personal introduction—especially not in the current volume, which is entirely devoted to his *oeuvre*. But Jánossy was less prominent and is

* Paper prepared for the conference "The Importance of Kornai's Research Today," organized to celebrate János Kornai's ninetieth birthday at the School of Economics, Corvinus University of Budapest.

hardly known among Hungarian economists of the younger generation today. This is what readers need to know about him.

Jánossy was the stepson of the internationally well-known Marxist philosopher, Georg Lukács (1885–1971). Jánossy's mother, Gertrúd Bortstieber was Lukács's second wife. He grew up with his parents and siblings in Austria and Germany, then worked and completed his engineering studies in the Soviet Union between 1933–46 as a communist *émigré*. Between 1942–45, he was interned in a Soviet Gulag based on false accusations. He returned to his native Hungary in 1946, that is, after World War II. For biographic reasons, German remained Jánossy's first language throughout his life; therefore everything he wrote in German had to be translated "back" into Hungarian. His most original idea, which made him widely known at the time, was that the main driver of the great post-war boom in Germany, Italy, and Japan, as well as in Central and Eastern Europe, was the reconstruction character of their economies. These countries merely returned to what he called the pre-war "trendline."[1] Focusing on industrial production, he demonstrated that all post-war economic "miracles" lasted only until production achieved the output that should have been reached if there had been no war.

The works of our two authors were written and published at roughly the same time. Jánossy's book, *The End of the Economic Miracle*, came out in its first Hungarian edition in 1966, while Kornai's book, *Rush versus Harmonic Growth*, appeared in its first published form as a series of lectures given in the Netherlands during the spring of 1971.[2] In Kornai's work, Jánossy's important publications were duly referenced and quoted in the spirit of full agreement. Subsequently, Jánossy's book was re-written for a second Hungarian edition in 1975 (this is the version I am using in this paper), while Kornai's manuscript received its final book form in 1972. It is important to note that these two books had exceptional careers outside of Hungary as well. Within a decade of its first publication, Jánossy's book was published in German (1966), Czech (1969), English (1971), French (1972), and Spanish (1974) translations.[3] Kor-

[1] For a recent, English language study on Jánossy's post-war reconstruction theory, see Tamás Vonyó, "Post-war Reconstruction and the Golden Age of Economic Growth," *European Review of Economic History* 12, no. 2 (August 2008): 221–241.

[2] Kornai was invited to lecture at the annual F. de Vries Foundation seminar series in Rotterdam to honour the memory of the renowned Dutch economist who died in 1958.

[3] I have found indirect references to a possible Japanese translation as well, but I have failed to confirm whether it actually exists.

nai's work was translated into English (1972) and then into Czech and Spanish (1977). I cannot think of any other Hungarian economists—dead or living—that have achieved anything close to this level international reputation and presence.

Rush versus Harmonic Growth

Kornai's story started with a descriptive narrative. At the beginning of *Rush versus Harmonic Growth*, he quoted the official figure of the Hungarian Central Statistical Office (CSO) published in 1971, according to which the rate of economic growth on average was more or less "steady" in the "two previous decades," meaning the years from 1950 to 1969.[4] For obvious reasons, the closing year of the analysis was pre-determined: there were no later figures available at the time he wrote the book. The starting year, 1950, was both a statistical convenience (there were no official CSO figures for the 1945–49 period), and an analytical tool. The planned economic system in Hungary, based on Marxist doctrines and emulating Soviet practice, had consolidated its shape at about that time. In a later work, *The Socialist System*, Kornai extensively argued why it makes sense for him to label this period as the "classical period of socialism" in Hungary, which ended in 1968 with the introduction of important and very ambitious reform measures initiated by the Hungarian party-state: the New Economic Mechanism (*Új gazdasági mechanizmus*). The precise figure, which was starting point of Kornai's analysis, was 5.7%. If we go back to the original CSO publication, one realizes that Kornai used the national income time series at constant prices, and the rate of growth was calculated as the average annual rate of change between the two extreme years (see Graph 1). In other words, short-term fluctuations in growth were simply disregarded. Using a simple trend-fitting function in an Excel spreadsheet (a tool that didn't exist in 1972), at first we can only agree with Kornai: the trend carries his interesting story, and not the numerous upward and downward deviations from it.

[4] János Kornai, *Rush versus Harmonic Growth: Meditation on the Theory and on the Policies of Economic Growth* (Amsterdam–London: North-Holland Publishing Company, 1972), 5.

Graph 1: The growth of national income in Hungary, 1950–1969 (Volume indices, 1950 = 100)

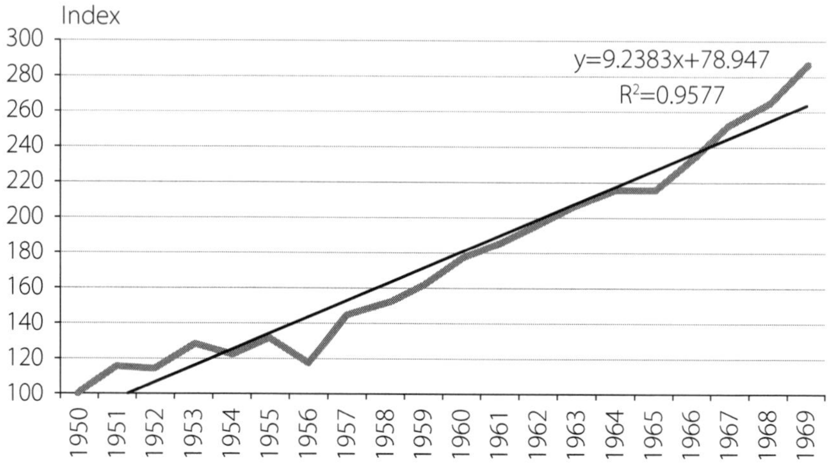

Method and source: Author's calculations. Constant price data are taken from official CSO data.

Evaluating the 5.7% growth rate, this is what Kornai had to say:

> Apart from minor fluctuations, the growth rate was stable in the past two decades. [...] This is not a bad performance in itself, but growth is faster in many other countries. From among the socialist countries, the rate of growth is higher in Rumania or Poland; from among the capitalist countries, however, it is higher not only in Japan, recently also in Spain or Greece.[5]

With the benefit of hindsight, however, we can only regret that Kornai didn't think of helping his readers with a visual presentation of the issue from another angle. In a very important way, the impressive overall 5.7% growth rate hid something: the "minor fluctuations" were not negligible at all. In fact, they were alarmingly large (Graph 2).[6]

---

5 Kornai, *Rush versus Harmonic Growth*, 5–6.

6 It is worth noting that another Hungarian economist and contemporary of Kornai and Jánossy, András Bródy, was already working on the "cycle" problem, but the most valuable research results of his were born only in the second half of the 1970s. For Bródy's work on this topic, see András Bródy, "Zur Feinstruktur der Investitionen" [On the fine structure of investments], unpublished manuscript, 1972; idem.,

Graph 2: The annual change of national income in Hungary, 1951–1969

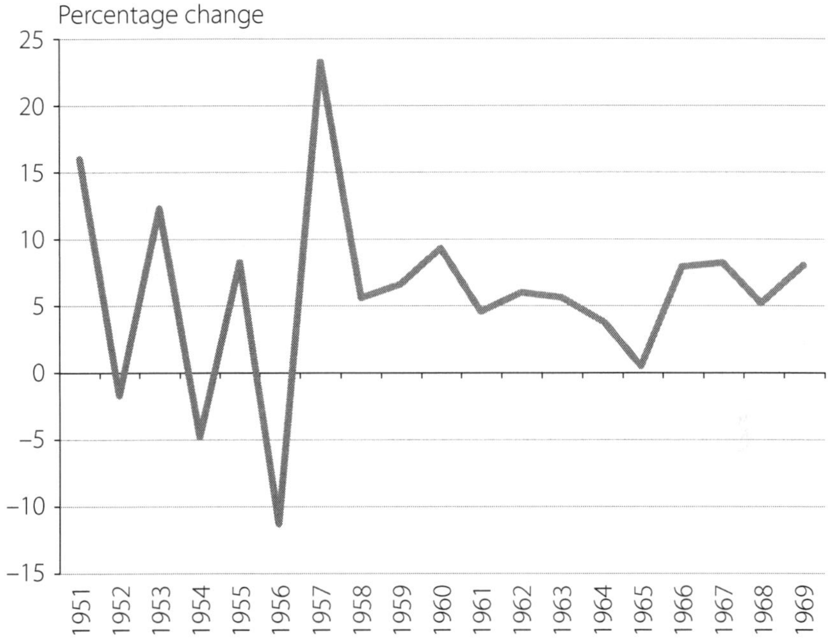

Method and source: See Figure 1.

But Kornai's main concern in *Rush versus Harmonic Growth* was something else. As a Hungarian citizen, living in the country and experiencing the quickly changing living conditions, and—also importantly—as an active participant in the medium-term planning works under the control of the National Planning Office, he saw an intrinsic contradiction between the relatively high ("not bad") rate of growth on the one hand, and the annoying shortcomings of the classical model of the planned economy system on the

"About Investment Cycles and Their Attenuation," *Acta Oeconomica* 31, no. 1–2 (1983): 37–51. In addition, see Tamás Bauer, "Investment Cycles in Planned Economies," *Acta Oeconomica* 21, no. 3 (1978): 243–60; Mária Lackó, "Cumulating and Easing of Tensions (A Simple Model of the Cyclical Development of Investments in Hungary)," *Acta Oeconomica* 24, no. 3–4 (1980): 357–77; and Károly Attila Soós and George Hajdu, "Causes of Investment Fluctuations in the Hungarian Economy," *Eastern European Economics* 14, no. 2 (Winter 1975–76): 25–36. For a detailed overview of this literature, see Péter Mihályi, *Socialist Investment Cycles: Analysis is Retrospect* (Dordrecht–Boston–London: Kluwer Academic Publishers, 1992).

other. He interpreted this contradiction with a metaphor, characterizing the "soul" of the central planners. On the one hand, planners tried to do everything in order to maximize the rate of growth of production in the short-term, but at the same time, they had to take into account other needs serving growth only in the long-term. Without stating them explicitly, Kornai's main conclusions were clear for his sufficiently sophisticated Hungarian readers:

1 The everyday problems of the Hungarian economy, which annoyed and infuriated the men of the street (above all the shortages and the poor quality of consumer goods), were not caused by mistakes in the central planning process or by the improper execution of the plans. These problems were inherently "coded" into the system as such and they would not disappear automatically with time as many contemporary politicians and ordinary communist party members honestly believed.

2. Kornai showed, through many examples and statistical facts, that the earlier "not bad" rate of growth (the often quoted 5.7%) was not sustainable in the long term, therefore the Hungarian economy was liable to slow down in the 1970s and the decades after that.[7]

3. With a few cautious references to the experience of other contemporary socialist economies, Kornai demonstrated that the likely slowdown is not a unique Hungarian phenomenon—the same danger threatens the other socialist countries. Thus, if the average past and present growth rates are not sustainable in the long-term in any of the socialist planned economies, the promised catching up of the "socialist camp" with the capitalist world will not materialize, as it had been solemnly promised by Soviet leaders.[8]

[7] In fact, the English language edition contains a short comparison between the first and second decade of the planned economy in Hungary—a sentence missing from the Hungarian edition. According to this, the average growth was 5.9% in 1950–59 and 5.5% in the 1960–69 period. Thus, the first sign of the slowdown was already noticed by Kornai.

[8] As it was widely publicized in all socialist countries, even the date of the "catching-up" was known. Outperforming America so possessed Khrushchev that, defying prudence, he included it as the main economic task in the party program adopted in 1961 by the last party congress, the 22nd, that he controlled. There, he even stated the exact year—1980—when this goal would be achieved, and when the USSR, as the program stated, "will have left the USA far behind."

Cutting a long story short, in this slim book (eighty-six pages in the original Hungarian edition), Kornai elaborated a twelve-point list of requirements serving the long-term growth process and showed that—*ceteris paribus*—the investments necessary to achieve these objectives would dampen the growth of national income in the short term. In fact, this contradiction—or using a well-known technical term in the economics profession, the "trade-off"—was reflected in the title of the book: *Rush versus Harmonic Growth*. If you "rush," you can run faster from point A to point B. However, if you are concerned about tomorrow and the years and decades to come, you have to make sure that you create the conditions for sustainable growth for future generations as well.

Table 1, below, summarizes a long list of goals constituting the framework for a harmonic (or balanced) path formulated and discussed in Kornai's book. For the sake of brevity, I summarized them into twelve headings, although in Table 3 of the book, these twelve goals are further broken down to sub-goals, and thus the total number tallies to twenty-three.

Table 1: The most important requirements for balanced growth

1	Continuous rise of consumption	7	Structural proportionality in the noncompetitive productivity
2	Proportionate satisfaction of consumer needs (elimination os shortages)	8	Up-to-dateness of production technologies
3	Incentive and equitable distribution of income	9	Equilibrium of trade and balance of payments
4	Social protection (full employment, health and pensions, public safety)	10	Careful maintanence of reproducible of physical capital
5	Care about the next generation	11	Protection of environment and nature
6	Fast development of education	12	High levels of state reserves

Source: Author's compilation based on Table 3 in Kornai (1972).

Kornai's main concern was that the country had to pay a high price during the first two decades of socialist central planning for the ambitious rate of growth dictated by the central planners in the form of (a) direct sacrifice, (b) indefinite postponement, and (c) neglect.

In Kornai's argument, the rapid industrialization of the Hungarian economy simply didn't leave room for the proportionate satisfaction of consumer needs. In the sphere of retail trade, recurrent shortages meant that buyers had to give up their personal preferences in favor of what was actually available (sacrifice). If there was meat in the shop at all, customers had to queue for a long time. If urban families wanted to rent an apartment from the state, they had to wait for many years. If they wanted to buy a passenger car, they couldn't because the Ministry of Foreign Trade was unwilling to import (indefinite postponement).[9] Since planners' main preference was to build more and more new factories, not enough resources remained to maintain existing production capacities, to keep roads, bridges, and other pieces of infrastructure in good shape, etc.

With the benefit of (better) hindsight, we can identify one more negative consequence of the forced growth/industrialization policies of the 1950s and 1960s. From memoirs and archives we have access to today, the 5.7% steady growth rate was partly financed from brutally expensive hard currency loans provided by Western private banks. Although the country's indebtedness was very small by the standards of today, they were dangerously high if compared to the country's hard currency generating capacity of those decades.[10] For the contemporary analysts, the relevant data were inaccessible. This was the reason why Kornai did not mention this problem.

Toward the very end of this short book, Kornai draws the readers' attention to his "recently" written book, *Anti-Equilibrium*, and the theoretical links between the two books. "Rush is a possible path of economic growth," he explains, but with such a policy path shortages are prevalent in many parts of the economy:

> Rush claims great investments. Its financing takes place partly in an inflationary manner: purchasing power swells. On the other hand, government price control puts a brake on the rise in prices. Repressed inflation then leads to excess demand, to 'suction' [or shortage—P.M.]. [...] As long as in major fields investment tension, suction, disequilibrium persist, we [in Hungary] are at most halfway between forcing the

---

9 For a detailed description of the contemporary Hungarian automobile market, see Kapitány et al. (1984).

10 See Péter Mihályi, *A magyar gazdaság útja az adósságválságba, 1945–2013* [The road of the Hungarian economy into the debt crisis, 1945–2013] (Budapest: Corvina Kiadó, 2013).

rate of growth and harmony, but we have not yet consistently taken the path to harmonic growth.[11]

The end of the economic miracle

As we already outlined in the introduction to this paper, the starting point of Ferenc Jánossy's narrative was not Hungary, but West Germany and other fast-growing post-war economies (including the Soviet Union). Both for cultural and economic reasons, the case of the Federal Republic of Germany was the most interesting reference country for Hungary. In the 1950s and the 1960s, the West German economy displayed similarly steady and even higher growth rates than Hungary (Graph 3).

Graph 3: The growth of per capita GDP in West Germany and Hungary, 1950–1969

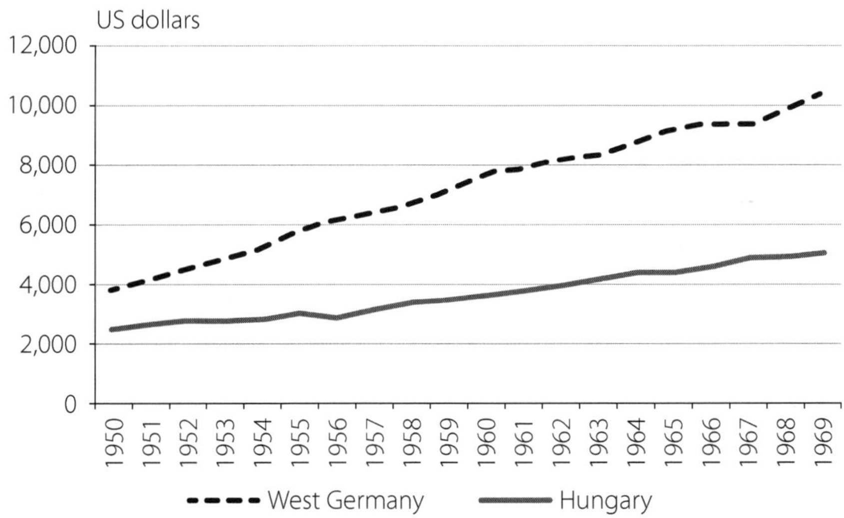

Method and source: Author's compilation, based on Angus Maddison's 2010 database, entitled "Historical Statistics of the World Economy, 1–2008 AD," expressed in 1990 International Geary-Khamis US dollars. Graph 1 and Graph 3 cannot be directly compared because the underlying data were calculated differently in more than one aspect (national income vs. GDP; volume indices vs. 1990 constant prices at PPP parities; output vs. output per head; etc.).

---

11 Kornai, *Rush versus Harmonic Growth*, 133–35.

Jánossy's main contention was that the recorded high average growth rates could not be sustained—neither in Germany, nor in Italy, nor in Japan. As noted above, Jánossy was a Marxist. For him, the ultimate source of economic growth was human capital, more precisely the rise in labor productivity, which in turn was driven by the qualitative improvement of average working skills. In every year, a certain number of old workers left the labor market, while new, younger, and more productive workers entered the market at the same time. On the basis of past statistical data, Jánossy's estimate for average long-term growth arising from the change of generations was on the order of 2% per annum. This is what he called the "trendline" of growth. If the average growth rate was higher than 2% for a longer period of time (as indeed it was in Germany and Japan in the first fifteen years of the post-war period), this must have been attributable to special, temporary factors, such as the process of post-war reconstruction. Post-war reconstruction is relatively easy and "cheap," Jánossy asserted, since existent but partially broken or dismembered machines and buildings could be repaired with relatively little investment. Plus, those workers who survived the war could return to normal production and use their *previously* acquired skills without any further education or training.

Graph 4: Jánossy's trendline of growth during post-war reconstruction—an illustration

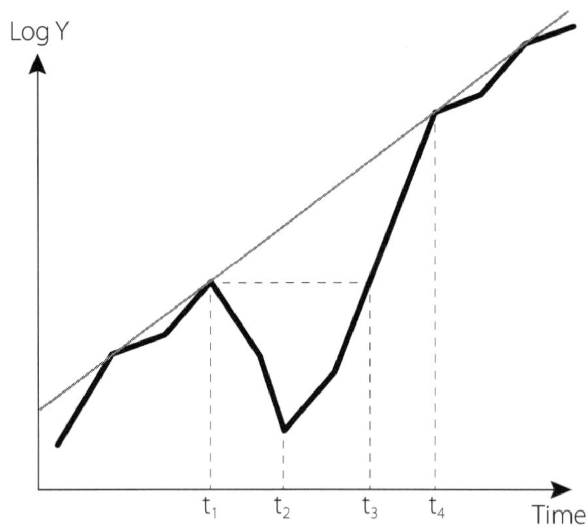

Comments and source: On the vertical axis log Y notes the logarithmic value of output in a model post-war economy. The illustration comes from Nagy (2000).

For Jánossy, as well as for many contemporary economists, the most challenging question was whether the long-term average growth rate could be increased with some kind of "smart" economic policies *above* the 2% "trend-line." He considered three seemingly trivial options.

More investments? One theoretical possibility—which was actually tried by the central planners in Hungary—was forced industrialization, keeping the share of investments high in the proportion of national income. "Rush," to use Kornai's terminology. In Jánossy's formulation, the dilemma was this: in the manufacturing sector, forced industrialization usually evolves through loss-making investments, because it takes years for the newly built factories to produce high-quality products. To pursue such a policy may make sense, Jánossy said, only if and when the loss-making investments help significantly in the training and upgrading of the work force in the enterprise concerned. In fact, the internationally well-known concept of "learning by doing" was discovered by Jánossy independently from Kenneth Arrow. More importantly, his own formulation—learning from the machine—was more illuminating than Arrow's.[12] As Jánossy wrote:

> [C]utting can only be learned at a lathe, crushing at a milling machine, and driving at the wheel of the car. [...] This transfer of knowledge through the means of production is of particular interest ... because this is precisely what causes the misleading impression that perfection of machinery is the primary factor of economic development.[13]

Due to this important link, there is no real substitution between capital and labor. Both of them are needed simultaneously at a given point in historical time and in more or less fixed proportions.

The example of the Soviet industrialization drive in the 1930s proved that such policies were indeed sustainable for quite some time. Between 1928 and 1940, the Russian economy grew by 3.8% annually, much faster than

---

[12] See Kenneth J. Arrow, "The Economic Implications of Learning by Doing," *The Review of Economic Studies* 29, no. 3 (June 1962): 155–173.

[13] Ferenc Jánossy, *The End of the Economic Miracle. Appearance and Reality in Economic Development* (White Plains, NY: International Arts and Science Press, Inc., 1966), 209.

Germany (2.3%) or the United States (0.5%) over the same period.[14] Millions of peasants were brought into the newly built industrial towns, and factories were equipped with imported machinery. The investment decisions were largely based on military and ideological considerations; profitability and the rate of return on the investments were of very little importance. But there were two painful by-products of such a policy based on the presumption that the allocative efficiency of assets doesn't count. Firstly, to maintain such a system, the state needed a large and brutal oppressing apparatus because these loss-making investments were financed to the detriment of consumption. Secondly, the slow growth of consumption slowed down the qualitative improvement of the labor force. Widespread knowledge of driving supposes private ownership of passenger cars; clean working hands, the existence of bathrooms at home. Knowledge of foreign languages cannot be imagined without mass tourism, etc.

In an essay published in *Acta Oeconomica* in 1969, entitled "Widersprüche in der ungarischen Wirtschaftsstruktur" (Contradictions in the Hungarian economic structure), Jánossy introduced the concept of "quasi-development."[15] As he argued almost fifty years ago now, when a country tries to accelerate economic growth in general, and develop its manufacturing industry with protectionist trade policies and the artificial manipulation of the exchange rate, etc., there is a danger that the emulation will be successful only in a statistical sense. The volume of production will increase, but the quality of goods coming off of the conveyor belts of the newly created factories will be hopelessly inferior to the products of advanced market economies. Many socialist countries went through this bitter experience. Perhaps the most telling illustration of this scheme is the fate of the Soviet Lada passenger cars produced during the 1970s and 1980s, originally copied from a 1966 model of the Italian car manufacturer Fiat. Millions of these cars were manufactured, but they were outmoded from Day One, and the factory made financial losses on the Western exports of these cars.

---

14 Growth rates were calculated by the author from data retrieved from the database "Historical Statistics of the World Economy, 1–2008 AD," compiled by Angus Maddison (2010), expressed in expressed in 1990 International Geary-Khamis dollars.

15 See Ferenc Jánossy, "Widersprüche in der ungarischen Wirtschaftsstruktur—wie sind sie entstanden und wie können sie überwunden werden" [Contradictions in the Hungarian economic structure—how they arose and how they can be overcome], *Acta Oeconomica* 4, no. 4 (1969): 351–77.

Can research and development accelerate growth? Jánossy, who spent many years in the Hungarian Planning Office during the 1960s, warned his contemporary socialist planners not to try to accelerate economic growth through radically increased research and development (R&D) expenditures, either. Although it is not easy to comprehend at first hearing, innovation, the output of research, does not generate welfare directly. Innovation is merely a "recipe" that shows how the structure of production needs to be modified in order to increase the productivity of labor.[16] Whether the conditions to implement the prescribed restructuring of production are present, in a given country and a given industry, depends on the quality of the labor force at large, and not on the quality of the researchers. It doesn't help if R&D activity runs far ahead of the quality of the labor force. If this happens, it can only lead to massive societal waste.

Aggressive spending on schooling? It follows from Jánossy's development concept that economic growth cannot be accelerated by the forced expansion of schooling, either. Let us illustrate this point first with present-day pair-wise comparisons. Take Poland and Germany. According to standardized OECD data, the share of persons in the labor force with a tertiary education degree is exactly the same in both countries (28%), while productivity[17] is more than 2.1 times higher in Germany. We can take another, even more shocking example. 54% of Russian workers in the 25–64 age group had some kind of tertiary education, which is much higher than the corresponding American, Japanese, or Israeli figures (all between 45–50%), let alone the comparable Danish figure (37%). In terms of productivity, however, the American level is 2.5 times higher than in Russia.

Similar differences can be identified when the least educated population is compared (*primary education*). The share of Hungarians in the labor force with no more than eight years spent in school is just 1%, while in Portugal this indicator stands at 32%. On the basis of this strikingly large difference, one would assume that the Hungarian economy must display higher productivity levels. But the contrary is the case: output per hours worked is 10% higher in Portugal than in Hungary.[18] It is worthwhile to cite old cross-

16 Jánossy, *The End of the Economic Miracle*, 117.

17 The figure measured as output per hour worked in international US dollars (converted to the 2016 price level with updated 2011 PPPs).

18 The source of education and productivity data are OECD.Stat, Educational attainment and labour-force status (accessed August 30, 2017), https://stats.oecd.org/Index.aspx?DataSetCode=EAG_NEAC; and The Conference Board (2016). All data refer to 2015.

country comparisons, as well. In 1910, the percentage of illiterates in Hungary amounted 15% and the country's GDP was estimated by Angus Maddison at $2000/person.[19] By contrast, in Italy and Belgium, where the illiteracy rates were 38% and 25%, respectively, the GDP per capita figures were $2332 and $4064 dollars—i.e., both higher—especially in Belgium—than in Hungary.

Cross-country studies equipped with rigorous econometric tools lead to a similar conclusion, too. In Pritchett's 2006 study, the lack of econometric evidence for the quantitative "knowledge gap" is explained by the fact that schooling at all levels (from primary to tertiary) has expanded massively on all continents over the last fifty years, while there has been a historical and continued divergence in output per capita.[20] Hence the cross-national dispersion of schooling per worker and the dispersion of output per head have moved strongly in opposite directions. Thus, the fact that the level and growth of aggregated schooling per worker can only, at best, modestly explain the growth of output per worker only confirms Jánossy's assertion born in the 1960s.

As another Hungarian economist, István Polónyi, already noted in 2010,[21] this "over-education" is not a unique Hungarian phenomenon. It holds for all the post-socialist countries that the population's formal educational level is higher than in market economy countries with similar levels of economic development. Quite clearly, this over-education drive was—to a very great extent—driven by the absence of tuition-fees during the decades of socialism. As Mária Holló and Jánossy (1975), who worked together, showed,[22] the extensive growth strategy in general and in the educational sector, in particular, leads to quasi-development and over-education, or simply waste—if we allow for ourselves to use such a brutal term. Later research upheld this speculative finding. In a 2010 study, covering more than 60 countries with comparable PISA-test results, McKinsey & Company, the consulting firm, found that in low- and middle-income countries, "systems

---

19 GDP per capita data constant with the value of the US dollar in 1990.

20 See Lant Pritchett, "Does Learnind to Add up Add up? The Returns to Schooling in Aggregate Data," in *Handbook of the Economics of Education*, vol. 1, ed. Erik Hanushek and Finis Welch (North Holland: Elsevier, 2006), 635–95.

21 István Polónyi, "A mitikus oktatás," in *Felsőoktatási intézmények és az innováció*, ed. Ágnes Kotsis and István Polónyi (Debrecen: Debreceni Egyetem, Közgazdaság- és Gazdaságtudományi Kar, 2010), 143–63.

22 See Mária Holló, *Technika és társadalom* [Technology and society] (Budapest: Kossuth Kiadó, 1974); and Ferenc Jánossy, *A gazdasági fejlődés trendvonaláról* [On the trendline of economic development] (Budapest: Magvető Könyvkiadó, 1975).

with similar education spending have widely varying levels of performance—until the USD 6,000 spend per student (PPP) mark is reached, system performance spans the full spectrum of poor, fair, good, and great."[23] Simply put, better schools do not necessarily lead to more growth.[24]

Conclusions: The resistance to change

Jánossy showed with simple argumentation that fast economic progress is not easy at all, since people—for good reasons—resist change in the ways they work and live:

> For if no great resistance would stand in the way of the diffusion of new achievements and of greater labor productivity, there would be no people left who carry drinking water home in earthen vessels on their heads from the well, no nomad tents, and even no steam locomotives, the last specimens of which would already stand in museums next to waterwheels and hand looms.[25]

In Jánossy's growth concept, it didn't matter whether, in a given country, the means of production are privately or collectively owned. In either case, resistance to change in the structure of production and accustomed-to technology is generated by the intrinsic conservatism of the workers themselves on the one hand and the similar conservatism of the consumers on the other. The low levels of readiness to learn new production methods are affected by the widespread belief that you can't teach an old dog new tricks, so to speak. But the same rule applies to a certain extent on the side of demand as well: people insist on buying the same goods and services for long times. Thus, his final conclusion is that it does not matter whether a given country is capitalist or socialist—the growth rate of a modern, industrialized economy simply cannot surpass the 2% trendline rate for a prolonged period of time.

---

23 Mona Mourshed, Chinezi Chijioke, and Michael Barber, *How the World's Most Improved School Systems Keep Getting Better* (McKinsey & Company, 2010), 14–15.

24 See Eric A. Hanushek and Ludger Woessmann, "Do Better Schools Lead to More Growth? Cognitive Skills, Economic Outcomes, and Causation," *Journal of Economic Growth* 17, no. 4 (2012): 267–321.

25 Jánossy, *The End of the Economic Miracle*, 135.

In Kornai's concept, growth, ownership, and the ways in and means by which markets function have always played a crucial role in his work since the beginning of his professional economic career. In 1971, his reading of the recent past—i.e., the 1950s and 1960s—was that planners do possess the means to keep the growth rate high, but this is not desirable from a societal point of view. His central contention is that harmonic growth—where planners look ahead for fifteen years at least, give autonomy to enterprises, and allow price mechanisms, profits, and market processes in general to play a bigger role—is preferable, and would be particularly better for his own country, Hungary.

References

Arrow, Kenneth J. "The Economic Implications of Learning by Doing." *The Review of Economic Studies* 29, no. 3 (June 1962): 155–73.

Bauer, Tamás. "Investment Cycles in Planned Economies." *Acta Oeconomica* 21, no. 3 (1978): 243–60.

Bródy, András. "Zur Feinstruktur der Investitionen." Unpublished manuscript, 1972.

———. "About Investment Cycles and Their Attenuation." *Acta Oeconomica* 31, no. 1–2 (1983): 37–51.

Hanushek, Eric A., and Ludger Woessmann. "Do Better Schools Lead to More Growth? Cognitive Skills, Economic Outcomes, and Causation." *Journal of Economic Growth* 17, no. 4 (2012): 267–321.

Holló, Mária. *Technika és társadalom* [Technology and society]. Budapest: Kossuth Kiadó, 1974.

Jánossy, Ferenc, *A gazdasági fejlődés trendvonaláról* [On the trendline of economic development] Budapest: Magvető Könyvkiadó, 1975.

———. *The End of the Economic Miracle: Appearance and Reality in Economic Development.* White Plains, NY: International Arts and Science Press, Inc., 1966.

———. "Widersprüche in der ungarischen Wirtschaftsstruktur—wie sind sie entstanden und wie können sie überwunden werden." *Acta Oeconomica* 4, no. 4 (1969): 351–77.

Joffe, Michael. "Evidence and the Micro-foundations of Economic Growth." *Economics and Business Review* 17, no. 3 (2017): 52–79.

Kapitány, Zsuzsa, János Kornai and Judit Szabó. "Reproduction of Shortage on the Hungarian Car Market." *Soviet Studies* 36, no. 2 (April 1984): 236–256.

Kornai, János. *Rush versus Harmonic Growth: Meditation on the Theory and on the Policies of Economic Growth.* Amsterdam–London: North-Holland Publishing Company, 1972.

Lackó Mária. "Cumulating and Easing of Tensions (A Simple Model of the Cyclical Development of Investments in Hungary)." *Acta Oeconomica* 24, no. 3–4 (1980): 357–77.

Maddison, Angus. "Historical Statistics of the World Economy: 1–2008 AD." Last modified August 3, 2008. http://www.ggdc.net/maddison/Historical_Statistics/horizontal-file_02-2010.xls.

Mihályi, Péter. *Socialist Investment Cycles: Analysis is Retrospect*. Dordrecht–Boston–London: Kluwer Academic Publishers, 1992.

———. *A magyar gazdaság útja az adósságválságba, 1945-2013* [The road of the Hungarian economy into the debt crisis, 1945–2013]. Budapest: Corvina Kiadó, 2013.

Mourshed, Mona, Chinezi Chijioke, and Michael Barber. *How the World's Most Improved School Systems Keep Getting Better*. McKinsey & Company, 2010.

Nagy, András. "Jánossy Ferenc trendjei a Magyar gazdaságban" [The trends of Ferenc Jánossy in the Hungarian economy]. *Eszmélet*, October 2001.

Polónyi, István. "A mitikus oktatás." In *Felsőoktatási intézmények és az innováció*, edited by Ágnes Kotsis and István Polónyi, 143–63. Debrecen: Debreceni Egyetem, Közgazdaság- és Gazdaságtudományi Kar, 2010.

Pritchett, Lant. "Does Learning to Add up Add up? The Returns to Schooling in Aggregate Data." In *Handbook of the Economics of Education*, vol. 1, edited by Erik Hanushek and Finis Welch, 635–95. North Holland: Elsevier, 2006.

Soós, Károly Attila, and George Hajdu. "Causes of Investment Fluctuations in the Hungarian Economy." *Eastern European Economics* 14, no. 2 (Winter 1975–76): 25–36.

The Conference Board. 2016. The Conference Board Total Economy Database™ (Adjusted version), November 2016, http://www.conference-board.org/data/economydatabase/.

Vonyó, Tamás. "Post-war Reconstruction and the Golden Age of Economic Growth." *European Review of Economic History* 12, no. 2 (August 2008): 221–41.

Mistaking Markets

Seeing Markets Where They Do Not Exist[*]

Geoffrey M. Hodgson

Introduction

A strong and enduring theme in the work of János Kornai is a stress on the importance of understanding the mechanisms that govern the flow of information in any complex economy. This means addressing *all* information signals, and not market prices alone.[1]

This insistence on the difference between price and non-price information signals implies a meaningful analytical distinction between market and non-market allocation mechanisms. Such a distinction was necessary to have a fruitful discussion, which Kornai was always trying to engender, concerning the respective, and potentially complementary roles, of markets and state

[*] The author is very grateful to Zoltán Ádám, Richie Adelstein, Jens Beckert, Fred Block, Hulya Dagdeviren, Matthias Klaes, János Kornai, Richard Langlois, Richard Lipsey, Deirdre McCloskey, Károly Mike, Philip Mirowski, Richard Nelson, John O'Neill, Martin Ricketts, Viktor Vanberg and others for discussions on the theme of this paper. It makes use of material from Geoffrey M. Hodgson, "How Mythical Markets Mislead Analysis: An Institutionalist Critique of Market Universalism," *Socio-Economic Review*, published online, 2019.

[1] János Kornai, *By Force of Thought: Irregular Memoirs of an Intellectual Journey* (Cambridge, MA: MIT Press, 2006), 188. See also idem., "Mathematical Programming as a Tool of Socialist Economic Planning (1965)," in *Socialist Economics*, edited by Alec Nove and D. M. Nuti, 475–88 (Harmondsworth: Penguin, 1972); idem., *Anti-Equilibrium: On Economic Systems Theory and the Tasks of Research* (Amsterdam: North Holland, 1971).

intervention. Hence, Kornai wrote of the status of Western economics as it was at around the time of the publication of his book *Anti-Equilibrium*:

> I found two typical errors [...] One was the tendency to idealize the market without impressing on economists sufficiently the need for state action and other auxiliary regulatory mechanisms. The other was its failure to point to the true advantage of the real market and the forces propelling capitalism [...] Its picture of the market was at the same time too rosy and not rosy enough.[2]

Later Kornai encountered a related problem among mainstream economists. When his book *The Socialist System* appeared, it was met with a number of highly positive reviews.[3] An exception was a scathing reaction by the Czech economists and rising politicians Václav Klaus and Dušán Tříska.[4] As Kornai noted in response:

> They had not a good word to say about my book. The main objection [...] was that I had diverged unnecessarily from the tried methodology and conceptual framework of mainstream economics. [...] The communist system did not show a single feature that could not be examined in the customary way, with optimization models and the arsenal of conventional micro- and macroeconomics. [...] The role of the public sphere, in their view, could be clarified fully in terms of public choice theory, which stated with general validity that a politician displayed behavior tending to maximize his or her power or material interests. [...] University departments of political science, if they took this review to heart, would immediately dissolve and let their members retrain as neoclassical economists.[5]

There are at least two major issues at stake here. The first is the long ideological dispute between socialism and capitalism, between public and private

---

[2] Kornai, *By Force of Thought*, 190.

[3] János Kornai, *The Socialist System: The Political Economy of Communism* (Oxford: Clarendon Press, 1992).

[4] Václav Klaus and Dušán Tříska, review of János Kornai, *The Socialist System*, in Václav Klaus, *Renaissance: The Rebirth of Liberty in the Heart of Europe* (Washington, DC: Cato Institute, 1997), 163–9.

[5] Kornai, *By Force of Thought*, 340.

ownership, and between planning and markets. Kornai has recognized the virtues of both markets and some state intervention and takes a pragmatic view of their efficacy in given circumstances.

A second question is less obvious, but it is quite different and equally important. It is the question of the actual distinction between a market and a non-market mechanism. Do we have the conceptual tools to recognize the difference? Kornai's work has very much been about the development of analytical criteria, not only to recognize the difference, but also to understand reasons for divergences in outcomes.

Kornai has also suggested that markets are a special case of what might be described as *decentralized coordination mechanisms*.[6] Because of the impossibility of planning an entire economy from the center—due to problems of complexity, dispersed knowledge, and so on—even socialist economies must rely on numerous mechanisms for decentralized coordination, including in some cases the market. But other decentralized coordination mechanisms exist, including direct communication between decentralized units. The ubiquity of the problem of decentralized coordination may account in part for the over-application of the term *market* to mechanisms that lack explicit prices or contractual exchanges. Yet Kornai himself has always been clear about the differences between market and non-market mechanisms.

If we unable to understand the difference between what is and what is not a market, then we cannot compare market and non-market mechanisms of information transmission. We also cannot appreciate fully the virtues of the market as well as its vices: the market is "too rosy and not rosy enough."

Accordingly, in their reaction to Kornai's work, Klaus and Tříska adopted a theoretical framework that passed without substantive amendment from socialism to capitalism, and from markets to politics. This conceptual framework is blind to major substantive differences between the different spheres, which may require domain-specific analytical tools. It lacks adequate historical or institutional specificity.[7]

---

[6] See Kornai, *The Socialist System*. In an email of April 17, 2018, to the author, Kornai suggested the term "decentralized coordination mechanism," indicating that they may be universal in human societies, while markets are not. I have sometimes replaced "mechanism" by "system."

[7] Geoffrey M. Hodgson, *How Economics Forgot History: The Problem of Historical Specificity in Social Science* (London and New York: Routledge, 2001).

This paper is not about the virtues or vices of markets. It is about the need to identify markets and to distinguish them from other mechanisms of information processing and resource allocation. Market fundamentalism is typically defined (mostly by its critics)[8] as the belief that unfettered markets bestow welfare and prosperity, and that state interference with market processes generally decreases human well-being. Market fundamentalism typically involves normative claims concerning the economic or moral superiority of free markets. This paper offers neither a critique nor a defence of market fundamentalism; it is neither a critique nor a defence of a market economy. Instead it is about seeing the difference between markets and other mechanisms.

This essay focuses on the prolific, non-metaphorical use of the term *market* to describe a large number of varied arrangements or processes in the real world. It suggests that markets are ubiquitous, or nearly so, as if they were the universal essence of unhindered human interaction. The term *market universalism* is used here to refer the non-metaphorical tendency to use the term *market* to describe a wide variety of arrangements or processes in the real world.

Karl Polanyi rightly pointed out that "equating the human economy in general with its market form" was a serious error.[9] He explained that phenomena such as reciprocity and gift-giving are different from market relations. Against this, some authors describe political elections as *markets*, and perceive *markets* for ideas, laws, marriages, and much else. Margaret Radin noted the tendency toward "universal commodification" in both language

[8] See George Soros, *The Crisis of Global Capitalism: Open Society Endangered* (New York: Public Affairs, 1998); idem., *The New Paradigm for Financial Markets: The Credit Crisis of 2008 and What It Means* (New York: Public Affairs, 2008); Jospeh E. Stiglitz, "Stiglitz: The Fall of Wall Street Is to Market Fundamentalism What the Fall of the Berlin Wall Was to Communism," by Nathan Gardels, *The Huffington Post*, September 16, 2008. http://www.huffingtonpost.com/nathan-gardels/stiglitz-the-fall-of-wall_b_126911.html, accessed July 10, 2017; as well as Fred Block and Margaret Somers, *The Power of Market Fundamentalism: Karl Polanyi's Critique* (Cambridge MA: Harvard University Press, 2014).

[9] Karl Polanyi, *The Livelihood of Man*, ed. Harry W. Pearson (New York: Academic Press, 1977), 6, 10. Despite its importance, Karl Polanyi's attempt to argue that there are limits to markets in *The Great Transformation* (New York: Rinehart, 1944) has major problems and inconsistencies. See Geoffrey M. Hodgson, "Karl Polanyi on Economy and Society: A Critical Analysis of Core Concepts," *Review of Social Economy* 75, no. 1 (March 2017): 1–25.

and reality.[10] Market universalists misuse the term *market* to describe some arrangements which, by reasonable minimal criteria, are not really markets at all: they are *mythical markets*.

Note that one can advocate markets fervently without positing them as already universal. If markets are already omnipresent then their promotion loses much ideological potency. If the word *market* is used too liberally, then it is difficult to identify adequately any non-market processes or arrangements. For example, writers such as Peter Boettke and his co-authors rightly emphasize that markets vary in their natures and institutional structures. But these scholars open the door to market universalism by their three-times repetition of the claim that "markets are ubiquitous," adding: "… like weeds they crop up wherever the opportunity arises … markets are omnipresent."[11] But they do not tell us clearly what kinds of arrangements or processes are *not* markets. This is a frequent omission by market universalists.

Any normative case for markets needs to identify more clearly the instances of their absence, instead of merely pointing to impediments or restraints. If anyone wishes to identify spheres where markets should be excluded, then they need to explain what a market is, and what might take its place.

Some market universalists identify exchange with choice and markets with competition. But competition likewise covers any contest, including sports or games. Clearly, not all choice or competition involves exchange or markets. We need additional criteria, particularly to identify what are *not* markets.

The following section first distinguishes metaphorical from non-metaphorical uses of the term *market*. It then establishes some minimal institutionalist conditions for the existence of markets. Section three gives prominent examples where the term market has been attached to phenomena that are not really markets by these minimal criteria. Section four discusses some analytic outcomes, particularly the neglect of missing markets and their consequences. Section five examines some dangers in the dissolution of the political into the economic sphere. Section six concludes the essay.

10 See Margaret Jane Radin, *Contested Commodities: Trouble with Trade in Sex, Children, Body Parts and Other Things* (Cambridge, MA: Harvard University Press, 1996).

11 Peter J. Boettke, Christopher J. Coyne, and Peter T. Leeson, "The Many Faces of the Market," *Journal des Economistes et des Etudes Humaines* 14, no. 2 (2004): 71, 73, 74, 83.

The slippery idea of the market—pinning down minimal conditions

Metaphor is legitimate and unavoidable in science. Much use of the word *market* may be metaphorical. But some highly influential uses of this term are not with warnings that these terms are intended to be merely metaphorical. Instead, their authors suggest that what are described as markets really are markets.

Of course, there have been attempts to increase the role of markets in the economy, including the extension of genuine markets for intellectual property, and so on. There has also been a market rise in the use of contracted services—by lobbyists, advisors, consultants and others—in the political sphere. Hence, to a degree, rising usages of these terms may reflect real-world phenomena. But it is still the case that highly influential usages of these terms are not confined to these cases where genuine markets or contracts are involved.

Something may, or may not be, a market. This paper is concerned solely with phenomena that are *not* markets. If a phenomenon is described a market, then that description may be intended as literal or metaphorical. This paper is concerned solely with literal (non-metaphorical and false) descriptions of non-market phenomena as markets. For effective rebuttal of such false claims, two conditions must be satisfied. First, it must be shown that there is no sign of metaphorical intent. Second, it must be shown that phenomenon does *not* qualify as a market by minimal criteria. All that are required are some minimal (that is, necessary but not sufficient) criteria for a market. It is unnecessary here to provide a full definition. The following section outlines such minimal criteria.

Nobel Laureate Douglass North noted perceptively: "It is a peculiar fact that the literature on economics and economic history contains so little discussion of the central institution that underlies neo-classical economics—the market."[12] Similarly, Nobel Laureate Ronald Coase observed that "in modern economic theory the market itself has an even more shadowy role than the firm."[13] Even when it is defined, there are typically further problems and ambiguities.

---

[12] Douglass C. North, "Markets and Other Allocation Systems in History: The Challenge of Karl Polanyi," *Journal of European Economic History* 6, no. 3 (Winter 1977): 710.

[13] Ronald H. Coase, *The Firm, the Market, and the Law* (Chicago: University of Chicago Press, 1988), 7.

In ordinary language, a market typically refers to a place where commodities of a particular type or types are regularly traded. As Karl Polanyi wrote: "A market is a meeting place for the purpose of barter or buying or selling."[14] With the Internet, this "place" may be virtual, as with eBay or Amazon. Such a narrow definition can distinguish markets from trade in general and from "relational exchange."[15]

By contrast, many economists propose a broader definition, where *market* implies any form of trade, not simply trade organized in one place. Trade is much older than organized markets.[16] As an example of a more inclusive definition, William Stanley Jevons wrote of the term *market* being "generalized, so as to mean any body of persons who are on intimate business relations and carry on extensive transactions in any commodity."[17] Much later, in a prominent textbook, Hugh Gravelle and Ray Rees declared that "a market exists whenever two or more individuals are prepared to enter into an exchange transaction."[18]

The terms "transaction" and "exchange" also require definition in these formulations. Such terms also have broader versus narrower meanings. Economists are often vague on the issue. In sociology, the extremely broad and general "exchange theory" of George Homans[19] and Peter Blau[20] proposes that a wide range of activities—including gift-giving and interpersonal communications—are "exchanges." In modern social science, basic concepts such as *exchange*, *contract*, and *transaction* cannot be taken for granted. Ambiguities and multiple usages allow for further slippages in connotation, affecting the meaning of the term *market* itself.

Sometimes, broader and inclusive definitions are driven by a desire to make foundational concepts as general as possible. But if "markets" become

---

14 Polanyi, *The Great Transformation*, 56.

15 See Victor P. Goldberg, "Relational Exchange: Economics and Complex Contracts," *American Behavioral Scientist* 23, no. 3 (1980): 337–52.

16 Geoffrey M. Hodgson, "Commodity Exchange and Markets," chap. 5 in *Conceptualizing Capitalism: Institutions, Evolution, Future* (Chicago: University of Chicago Press, 2015).

17 William Stanley Jevons, *The Theory of Political Economy*, 3rd ed. (London: Macmillan, 1888), 84.

18 Hugh Gravelle and Ray Rees, *Microeconomics*, 2nd ed. (Harlow: Longman, 1992), 3.

19 George C. Homans, *Social Behaviour: Its Elementary Form* (London: Routledge and Kegan Paul, 1961).

20 Peter J. Blau, *Exchange and Power in Social Life* (New York: Wiley, 1964).

ubiquitous, then the door is opened to the treatment of almost everything as a market.

In this vein, von Mises saw all action, even by an isolated individual, as "exchange"—as a "rational" attempt to swap inferior for superior circumstances.[21] But, when he struggled alone to survive on his island, with whom did Robinson Crusoe "exchange" rights to property? Who ensured that the agreement was enforced? By exchange, Mises meant *any situation involving choice*, even when one sole individual is involved.

In 1907, the sociologist Georg Simmel described production as an "exchange with nature."[22] One wonders who negotiates on nature's behalf, and whether she is satisfied with the deal. Again, a view of exchange was implied that could involve one human agent alone.

Douglas Allen defined transaction costs as "the costs of establishing and maintaining economic property rights,"[23] where property rights were defined simply as "the ability to freely exercise a choice." This suggests that a "transaction" can simply be a matter of the choice and control by one individual over an object. As with Mises' definition of "exchange," such a strange "transaction" need not involve more than one person.[24]

We need to pin down some minimal elements. The requirement is not to define a market, but to establish some of the rudimentary conditions required

---

[21] Ludwig von Mises, *Human Action: A Treatise on Economics*, 1st ed. (London and New Haven: William Hodge and Yale University Press, 1949), 97.

[22] Georg Simmel, *The Philosophy of Money*, trans. Tom Bottomore and David Frisby (London and New York: Routledge, 2004), 81.

[23] Douglas W. Allen, "The Coase Theorem: Coherent, Logical, and not Disproved," *Journal of Institutional Economics* 11, no. 2 (June 2015): 383.

[24] Leading economists of property rights regard property simply as control or possession. See Armen A. Alchian, "Some Economics of Property Rights," *Il Politico* 30, no. 4 (1965): 816–829; and Yoram Barzel, *Economic Analysis of Property Rights* (Cambridge: Cambridge University Press, 1989). For contrasting views, see John R. Commons, *Legal Foundations of Capitalism* (New York: Macmillan, 1924); Daniel H. Cole and Peter Z. Grossman, "The Meaning of Property Rights: Law versus Economics?" *Land Economics* 78, no. 3 (August 2002): 317–330; Gunnar Heinsohn and Otto Steiger, *Ownership Economics: On the Foundations of Interest, Money, Markets, Business Cycles and Economic Development*, trans. Frank Decker (London and New York: Routledge, 2013); Hodgson, *Conceptualizing Capitalism*; idem., "Much of the 'Economics of Property Rights' Devalues Property and Legal Rights," *Journal of Institutional Economics* 11, no. 4 (December 2015): 683–709; and Simon Deakin et al., "Legal Institutionalism: Capitalism and the Constitutive Role of Law," *Journal of Comparative Economics* 45, no. 1 (February 2017):188–200.

We need to pin down some minimal elements. The requirement is not to define a market, but to establish some of the rudimentary conditions required for markets to exist. These minimal conditions help identify phenomena that are *not* markets.

A full and precise definition of a market would immediately become controversial because of the clash between broad and narrow definitions in the literature, as noted above. There is no attempt to posit a full definition of a market here.[25] For the purposes of this essay, agreement on an adequate definition is unnecessary. Required instead is the establishment of some minimal, necessary characteristics to identify what are *not* markets.

A key precondition of a (broadly-conceived) market is the existence of multiple traders who are interacting and communicating with some shared understandings. The traders are capable of entering into agreements with others to supply assets or services in exchange for money or other assets. But (even with illegal markets) there need to be shared rules to determine what constitutes a mutually validated agreement.[26]

These rules do not have to be written down and they do not need to be laws. It is accepted that there can be illegal as well as legal markets. With legal markets, a combination of law and custom may determine the essential rules. With illegal markets, the rules may be those of a mafia or a criminal gang.[27]

and Simon Deakin et al., "Legal Institutionalism: Capitalism and the Constitutive Role of Law," *Journal of Comparative Economics* 45, no. 1 (February 2017):188–200.

25 See Geoffrey M. Hodgson, "Markets," in *New Palgrave Dictionary of Economics*, 2nd ed. (Basingstoke: Macmillan, 2008); idem., *Conceptualizing Capitalism*; idem., "Taxonomic Definitions in Social Science, with Firms, Markets and Institutions as Case Studies," *Journal of Institutional Economics*, forthcoming, 2019; idem., "How Mythical Markets Mislead Analysis." Definitions of a market are suggested elsewhere: cf. Eckehard F. Rosenbaum, "What is a Market? On the Methodology of a Contested Concept," *Review of Social Economy* 58, no. 4 (December 2000): 455–82; Hodgson, "Markets"; idem., *Conceptualizing Capitalism*.

26 Note that a contract does not have to be written down. Some verbal agreements qualify as contracts and may be enforceable in law.

27 See Thomas C. Schelling, "Economics and Criminal Enterprise," in *Choice and Consequence: Perspectives of an Errant Economist* (Cambridge MA: Harvard University Press, 1984), 179–94; Mark Thornton, *The Economics of Prohibition* (Salt Lake City: University of Utah Press, 1991); Boettke, Coyne, and Leeson, "The Many Faces of the Market"; Avinash K. Dixit, *Lawlessness and Economics: Alternative Modes of Governance* (Princeton, NJ: Princeton University Press, 2004); Gary S. Becker, Kevin M. Murphy, and Michael Grossman, "The Market for Illegal Goods: The Case of Drugs," *Journal of Political Economy* 114, no. 1 (Feb-

The difference is important, but it need not delay further our attempt to pin down some minimal and necessary features of a market. These are proposed *minimal requirements* for a market:

1. A market entails a system of accepted rules, enabling multiple traders to enter into voluntary agreements involving mutual obligations.
2. These agreements are made through or between agents that can identify one another and communicate.[28]
3. Their agreed obligations are mutually understood to lead to the agreed delivery of goods, assets or services, in return for some agreed payment.
4. This agreement involves allocations of mutually-endorsed rights to goods or services, according to mutually-accepted rules.[29]

There is some wiggle-room for varied interpretations here, particularly over terms such as *accepted*, *rights*, *obligations*, and *payment*. Most definitions of this kind involve some degree of vagueness.[30] These issues are best addressed using concrete examples, as in the following section.

Note that agreements may be written or unwritten. They may have to be fulfilled over a shorter or longer period. There is no claim here that agreements have always to be enforced by external parties such as the state. Enforcement can be by reputation or by other means.

Markets involve other features such as *competition* and (Weberian) *rational calculation* (on the basis of exchange values). But competition takes place outside markets as well. Weberian rational calculation is a central

28 Note that this allows for the possibility that sellers or buyers are anonymous. It is sufficient that agents acting on their behalf can be identified.

29 Note that institutions are widely defined as systems of rules. See Douglass C. North, *Institutions, Institutional Change and Economic Performance* (Cambridge and New York: Cambridge University Press, 1990); Elinor Ostrom, *Governing the Commons: The Evolution of Institutions for Collective Action* (Cambridge: Cambridge University Press, 1990); Jack Knight, *Institutions and Social Conflict* (Cambridge: Cambridge University Press, 1992); Chris Mantzavinos, *Individuals, Institutions, and Markets* (Cambridge and New York: Cambridge University Press, 2001); Hodgson, *Conceptualizing Capitalism*; and idem., "On Defining Institutions: Rules *versus* Equilibria," *Journal of Institutional Economics* 11, no. 3 (September 2015): 499–505.

30 Bertrand Russell, "Vagueness," *Australasian Journal of Psychology and Philosophy* 1, no. 1 (1923): 84–92.

feature of market economy, but to insert the word *rational* here would be to open up a hornets' nest of contested meanings. Generally, economists do not use *rational* in the Weberian sense. Anyway, to serve our purposes here, the aim is to establish some *minimal* necessary conditions, *not* to list all necessary and sufficient conditions.

Using the above minimal criteria, we can now examine cases where the minimal requirements are *not* satisfied, yet the phenomena are misleadingly described as markets. As we examine these cases it is clear that some market-related elements are present, such as competition (of a kind) and *decentralized coordination systems*. But these elements are insufficient, on their own, to warrant the description of a market. Decentralized coordination systems are a more general form of arrangement of which the market is a special case.

Seeing markets where they do not exist

We are concerned with phenomena that are non-metaphorically described as markets, but are not markets, at least by the minimal requirements laid out in previous section. As noted above, Coase and North have been foremost critics of the failure to address the meaning and nature of markets. Yet ironically, they have also promoted two prominent devaluations of the meaning of the term *market,* by applying it to contexts that clearly fail to meet the minimal requirements above.

Consider the "market for ideas." Early users of the term include Michael Polanyi.[31] For him it was a useful metaphor among others: he also drew analogies from politics and religion. Like his brother Karl,[32] Michael was clear that true markets use explicit prices.[33]

---

[31] See Michael Polanyi, "Patent Reform," *Review of Economic Studies* 11, no. 2 (Summer 1944): 61–76; idem., "The Republic of Science: Its Political and Economic Theory," *Minerva* 1 (1962): 54–73.

[32] Polanyi, *The Great Transformation*, 41–43; 56; 68–72.

[33] Michael Polanyi was a Keynesian liberal who also advocated substantial and redistributive inheritance taxes. Although he attended the founding meeting of the Mont Pèlerin Society in 1947, he parted company in the 1950s because of disagreements over principles and policy. Angus Burgin, *The Great Persuasion: Reinventing Free Markets since the Depression* (Cambridge MA: Harvard University Press, 2012), 116.

Aaron Director played a central role in the development of the Chicago School of Economics. Director seemed to take the "market for ideas" more literally.[34] This could have been valid if he referred to trade in intellectual property. But his usage was much wider: he referred to free speech as a "market for ideas." Similarly, in 1969, the US Supreme Court ruled: "It is the purpose of the First Amendment to preserve an uninhibited marketplace of ideas in which truth will ultimately prevail."[35] This usage too was not confined to intellectual property—as with Director, it referred more broadly to free speech.

In a study from 1974,[36] and later with co-author Ning Wang,[37] Coase repeatedly described and advocated a "market for ideas." They gave no indication that the usage was intended to be metaphorical. Like Director, they used the term not primarily to refer to genuine markets in intellectual property, but to the need for "freedom of speech and expression" and for "the creation and transmission of knowledge" through educational institutions. For them, the "market for ideas" was literal.[38]

Addressing "the market for goods and the market for ideas," Coase went even further: "There is no fundamental difference between these two markets."[39] Given the nature of open conversation and free speech, this implies that contracts, agreements, prices, or allocations of rights are not "fundamental" to markets.[40]

---

34 See Aaron Director, "The Parity of the Economic Market Place," *Journal of Law and Economics* 7 (October 1964): 1–10.

35 Red Lion Broadcasting Co., Inc. v. FCC, 395 U.S. 367 (1969), 395.

36 Ronald H. Coase, "The Market for Goods and the Market for Ideas," *American Economic Review* 64, no. 2 (May 1974): 384–91.

37 Ronald H. Coase and Ning Wang, *How China Became Capitalist* (London and New York: Palgrave Macmillan, 2012), 190–207.

38 Coase and Wang repeated the phrase "market for ideas" about thirty times in their above-cited book, and the "market for goods and the market for ideas … together in full swing" was their main policy recommendation for contemporary China, neglecting other possible institutional reforms in land tenure, corporate law, finance, or the political system. See Geoffrey M. Hodgson and Kainan Huang, "Brakes on Chinese Economic Development: Institutional Causes of a Growth Slowdown," *Journal of Economic Issues* 47, no. 3 (September 2013): 599–622.

39 Coase, "The Market for Goods and the Market for Ideas," 389.

40 See Uskali Mäki, "Science as a Free Market: A Reflexivity Test in an Economics of Economics," *Perspectives on Science* 7, no. 4 (1999): 486–509, for further criticisms of Coase on this issue.

Some ideas—as with patents and copyrights—may be traded, but most are not. We *have* ideas, but mostly they are not deemed objects of property under any accepted system of legal or other rules. The ordinary communication or debating of ideas does not involve agreements with the shared intention of creating obligations according to those rules. Much day-to-day conversation is not a transfer of specific rights. Much broadcasting of information does not identify the individual recipients of the broadcast—so agreements in this case are problematic.

Certainly, there is competition between ideas and there is competition on markets. But this does not mean that all transmission of ideas is via a market. Competition takes place outside markets, as on the sports arena, the TV game show, or the battlefield. Competition as such does not necessarily imply the existence of contracts or markets.

Consider the term "political market." While some political services can be traded on genuine markets, and votes can be traded (illegally) in some countries, it is contestable that all voting and all politics can be regarded as markets. A relatively early use of the term was by W. Mark Crain in a leading economics journal. Crain did not confine his usage to contracted political services. Crain wrote twice that "votes are exchanged for public-policy outcomes."[41] He referred to voters as "buyers" and politicians as "sellers," albeit in scare quotes. But scare quotes are absent in his discussions of political *property rights* and of the *vote market*. He gave no indication that his use of *exchange* or *market* was intended to be metaphorical.[42]

A literature emerged in the 1970s and 1980s that applied the term "political market" both to voting in elections and to measures by lobbyists and pressure groups to gain the support and votes of politicians. North joined this throng,[43] making the important Coasean point that analysis of these "transactions" should take into account the *transaction costs* involved. But North admitted: "It is extraordinarily difficult to measure what is being exchanged

41 W. Mark Crain, "On the Structure and Stability of Political Markets," *Journal of Political Economy* 85, no. 4 (August 1977): 829–30.

42 Much earlier, the Italian economist Maffeo Pantaleoni considered the political system as a market with its own "political prices" alongside the economic market. See Maffeo Pantaleoni, "Considerazioni sulle proprieta di un sistema di prezzi politici," *Giornale degli Economisti* 42 (1911): 9–29, 114–33.

43 See Douglass C. North, "A Transactions Cost Theory of Politics," *Journal of Theoretical Politics* 2, no. 4 (October 1990): 355–67; idem., *Institutions, Institutional Change and Economic Performance.*

in political markets and in consequence to enforce agreements. What is being exchanged are promises for votes."[44] Again, there was no indication by North that the usage of terms like *market* or *exchange* in such contexts was intended to be metaphorical.

Alongside the increasingly fashionable use of market-derived language since the 1970s, there has been a big increase in institutionalized lobbying in major democracies.[45] Insofar as they genuinely compete and trade their services, these "political markets" are real. But this does not necessarily mean that there are "markets for votes."

In many countries (including the US) it is illegal for a lobbyist to pay or to give gifts to a member of the legislature in return for his or her vote. Legal lobbying is an information service, rather than a contract for votes. But of course, there are many ways in which lobbyists use gifts or campaign contributions to sway the votes of legislators. Nevertheless, incautious rhetoric involving "political markets" blurs the distinction between information services and bribery. If lobbying really creates a market for votes, then it is an illegal one. But if there is compliance with the law, then North is wrong: votes are not literally the objects of market-like exchange.[46]

In democracies under the rule of law, a vote by a member of the public for a politician or a party does not typically amount to an agreement that satisfies the minimal requirements of a market. The elected politician or party cannot normally identify all the individual voters who voted for them, so at least one of the minimal conditions for a market is violated. One violation is enough to prove the negative.

The manifesto of a political party is an indication of intent, not an enforceable contract. Typically, politicians cannot be sued for broken promises: the voter has no right of legal redress. A politician's promise is not an "offer" which is "accepted" by casting a ballot: no legally binding agreement is created, involving prices or anything else. The law normally prohibits pay-

44 North, "A Transactions Cost Theory of Politics," 362.

45 Robert G. Kaiser. *So Damn Much Money: The Triumph of Lobbying and the Corrosion of American Government* (New York: Knopf, 2009).

46 The question of de facto legal compliance (or non-compliance) is important for other reasons. There is evidence that compliance with the law has ethical and motivational force for many (but not all) people. See Tom R. Tyler, *Why People Obey the Law* (New Haven: Yale University Press, 1990). Some consequences of this observation are explored in Hodgson, "Much of the 'Economics of Property Rights' Devalues Property and Legal Rights."

ments in return for votes. If there were such a contract, then it would be tantamount to political corruption. Of course, in many countries the rule of law is imperfect. But the point here is not to deny that votes *can* be traded. Instead it is denied that voting *always* involves some market-like deal.

The notion of "political market" is strangely indifferent between less corrupt democracies and others (such as India) where the (illegal) buying of popular votes and the votes of elected politicians is frequent.[47] The latter may legitimately be described as "political markets" because (illegal) contracts for political services are involved. But this does not mean that the entire polity in every democracy is a political market.

Another example concerns the legal system. Bruce Benson and Eric Engen envisioned "the legislative process as a market for laws" where interest groups "pay" legislators for laws as "products."[48] They put quotes around "pay" but that did not inhibit their unequivocal treatment of the legislature as a market (without quotes). But there are rarely any enforceable agreements, involving transfers of rights, between interest groups and legislators in this context. Furthermore, if an interest group successfully lobbies for a new law, then that "product" applies to everyone who is subject to that legal system, not just the lobbyist. It is a strange market where one purchase leads to its delivery to all.

There is another problem here. What is the system of rules under which these supposed "contracts" between legislators and interest groups are formed and enforced? Markets themselves are institutions involving rules. Hence a "market for laws" would require supra-legal institutions with their own (legal or other) rules. Supposedly then, we would need markets for markets-for-laws, or markets for meta-rules. This would go on without end—a problem of infinite regress.[49]

---

47 Anirban Mitra, Shabana Mitra, and Arnab Mukherji. "Cash for Votes: Evidence from India." KDPE 1711, School of Economics Discussion Papers, University of Kent, Kent, UK, 2017.

48 Bruce L. Benson and Eric M. Engen, "The Market for Laws: An Economic Analysis of Legislation," *Southern Economic Journal* 54, no. 3 (January 1988): 732–745.

49 Svetozar Pejovich proposed a "market for institutions." But he avoided the problem of infinite regress by suggesting a given institutional framework within which competition for second-level institutions should take place. The remaining problem in his account is the contentious description of this arrangement as a market. See Svetozar Pejovich, "The Market for Institutions vs. Capitalism by Fiat: The Case of Eastern Europe," *Kyklos* 47, no. 4 (1994): 519–29.

In his work on the family, Gary Becker saw no essential distinction between the commercial world of trade and the emotion-driven intimacy of family life.[50] Apart from the duration of the contract, his analysis acknowledged little difference between sex with a prostitute and sexual relations between married partners. For Becker, they can be analysed with the same theoretical instruments, to the neglect of some distinctive features. Rather than focusing on specific institutions and social structures, his analysis was concerned with abstract allocative choices of a de-institutionalised kind. His work is thus peppered with loose phrases such as "a market for marriages."[51] While marriages themselves are contracts, these particular contracts are not sold. There may be a market for *marriage rights*, as in the auction reported in Babylonia circa 500 BC.[52] But here the primary contract was not between the marriage partners but between the grooms and the fathers of the brides-to-be. Marriages are not bought or sold.[53]

Consider a final example. Henry Manne was one of the founders of the "law and economics" approach. Manne promoted the term "market for corporate control."[54] This referred to struggles by persons or groups to increase control of corporations by means of mergers, takeovers, proxy fights, or the direct purchases of shares. But these methods are not markets for control: instead they are means to gain influence or control. A "market for X" is a market where good or service X is traded by contract. There is no market for corporate control because corporate control is not literally an item for purchase or sale: it may be an *outcome* but it is not an *object* of market transactions.

[50] Gary S. Becker, *The Economic Approach to Human Behavior* (Chicago: University of Chicago Press, 1976); idem., *A Treatise on the Family*, 2nd ed. (Cambridge, MA: Harvard University Press, 1991).

[51] Becker, *The Economic Approach to Human Behavior*, 206.

[52] Ralph Cassady, *Auctions and Auctioneering* (Berkeley and Los Angeles: University of California Press, 1967).

[53] Gary S. Becker and Richard A. Posner claimed that the term "marriage market" means little more than that the matching of partners is "systematic and structured rather than the result of random shots from Cupid's bow." But being "systematic and structured" is not a quality confined to markets. The rhetorical value of this "metaphor" is dubious, particular as it erodes the distinction between marriage and prostitution, which does involve a real market. Gary S. and Richard A. Posner, "Cross-Cultural Differences in Family and Sexual Life: An Economic Analysis," *Rationality and Society* 5, no. 4 (October 1993): 423.

[54] Henry G. Manne, "Mergers and the Market for Corporate Control," *Journal of Political Economy* 73, no. 2 (April 1965): 110–120.

Of course, there are markets for shares—they are known as stock markets. But describing this in particular as a market "for control" is confusing items of purchase with aims or outcomes. There are several reasons to buy shares, including pecuniary gain. Increasing influence or control over a company is but one possible motive. Deploying the term "market for corporate control" is like describing the (actually existing) wine market as the "market for drunkenness." Getting drunk is one of several possible reasons for buying wine. Nevertheless, the term "market for corporate control" is now widely used and it has spread beyond economics, especially into the broader management literature.

These examples show that the use of the term *market* has spread to all sorts of phenomena that, by the requirements laid out above, should not reasonably be described as markets. One possible defence is that the usage is intended to be metaphorical, rather than an accurate acknowledgement of market phenomena.

These examples show that the non-metaphorical use of the term *market* has spread to all sorts of phenomena that, by the minimal requirements laid out above, should not reasonably be described as markets.[55]

Analytical problems with market universalism

The first and most obvious analytical danger is the impoverishment of the concept of a market. The market may be defined in different ways,[56] but no one definition is being promoted here. However, it is reasonable to suggest that markets always involve rights and agreements, according to mutually accepted rules. Hence the appeal to the minimal requirements above.[57]

---

55 For further examples of the questionable use of the term market see Hodgson, *Conceptualizing Capitalism*.

56 Rosenbaum, "What is a Market? On the Methodology of a Contested Concept"; Hodgson, "Markets"; idem., *Conceptualizing Capitalism*.

57 There is also a widespread tendency in both economics and sociology to use the commercial language of money and trade to describe phenomena that are neither traded nor have discernible monetary value. The boldest of these is "social capital." This was abetted by the shift of meaning of "capital" from a monetary phenomenon to any durable and useful entity or arrangement. See Pierre Bourdieu, "The Forms of Capital," in *Handbook of Theory and Research for the Sociology of Education*, ed. John G. Richardson (New York: Greenwood, 1986), 241–258; Edwin

This section does not consider the moral limits to market arrangements or processes. These have been energetically debated elsewhere.[58] The primary focus is analytic.

By the minimal stipulations above, markets involve rules. If "markets for laws"[59] were universal, then there would be markets for all those rules that are required for functioning markets (for laws). This would then require a meta-market for market rules, and a meta-meta-market for those rules, and so on—an infinite regress. By this logic, markets would become more than universal—they would be infinite. It is difficult to imagine how a system of infinite markets could exist, especially as regular trade in infinite markets would require an infinite number of contracts. There must at some point be market rules that are not traded on markets. Consequently, there cannot be markets for all laws.

Émile Durkheim also famously pointed to the necessary existence of rules beyond markets themselves. He argued in 1893 that contracts require preconditions that cannot themselves be fully contracted: "in a contract not everything is contractual."[60] All markets entail rules, and not all rules can be traded.

There are also good practical reasons to prevent key services of the legislature and the judiciary from being traded, including those relating to property and markets. For example, if judicial rulings were for sale to the highest bidder, then the security of property rights and their exchanges would

Cannan, "Early History of the Term Capital," *Quarterly Journal of Economics* 35, no. 3 (May 1921): 469–481; Frank A. Fetter, "Capital," in *Encyclopaedia of the Social Sciences*, vol. 3, ed. Edwin R. A. Seligman and Alvin Johnson (New York: Macmillan, 1930), 187–90; Geoffrey M. Hodgson, "What is Capital? Economists and Sociologists have changed its Meaning—Should it be Changed Back?" *Cambridge Journal of Economics* 38, no. 5 September (2014): 1063–86; idem., *Conceptualizing Capitalism*.

58 See Radin, *Contested Commodities*; John O'Neill, *The Market: Ethics, Knowledge and Politics* (London and New York: Routledge, 1998); Debra Satz, *Why Some Things Should not be for Sale: The Moral Limits of Markets* (Oxford and New York: Oxford University Press, 2010); and Michael Sandel, *What Money Can't Buy: The Moral Limits of Markets* (London: Allen Lane, 2012). Despite its title, *Markets without Limits* by Jason Brennan and Peter M. Jaworski (London and New York: Routledge, 2016) does not claim that markets are ubiquitous. Instead, they argue that any action that is moral, may morally be done for money. We need not evaluate this argument here.

59 See Benson and Engen, "The Market for Laws: An Economic Analysis of Legislation."

60 Émile Durkheim, *The Division of Labor in Society*, trans. W. D. Halls (London: Macmillan, 1984), 158.

be undermined. Hence Michael Walzer established the need for "blocked exchanges" in some spheres,[61] excluding markets from politics, the legislature and the judiciary.

Through the use of patents, licenses, copyright, and so on, some information can become intellectual property and traded on markets. But there would be problems if all information became tradeable property. The extension and subdivision of ownership in a densely interconnected knowledge economy can create an "anti-commons" where extensively divided and interconnected rights—in a real world with positive transaction costs—obstruct investment and trade. The problem applies particularly to patents and other intellectual property and has become more severe in an increasingly knowledge-intensive economy.[62]

While much information and knowledge cannot readily be shared (because of tacitness, interpretative difficulty, or inaccessibility) much else can, and this can be of huge productive value. Over-restriction of the cheaply-acquired benefits of shared possession of non-rivalrous informational assets can generate remarkable inefficiencies. Consequently, the benefits of private and contractual provision of some information may be much less than the overall opportunity costs of charging a price for its use. A healthy market system itself depends on missing or incomplete markets for information.

Other markets are missing or incomplete. In today's developed market economies, most people work under an employment contract. But crucially, employment contracts are for a limited period of time into the future. We cannot legally trade our lives away in lifetime contracts. This would be tantamount to voluntary servitude.

There is some future contracting for labor power, such as when a student receives financial support from a company, in return for a commitment to work for some years in the firm. But the time period is typically a few years, amounting to a small fraction of the student's future working life. There are sometimes "non-compete" agreements with skilled employees, that prevent them leaving a firm and working for a rival for a while. But these are still far short of lifetime contracts.

---

61 Michael Walzer, *Spheres of Justice: A Defence of Pluralism and Equality* (New York: Basic Books, 1983).

62 Michael A. Heller, *The Gridlock Economy: How Too Much Ownership Wrecks Markets, Stops Innovation, and Costs Lives* (New York: Basic Books, 2008); Ugo Pagano, "The Crisis of Intellectual Monopoly Capitalism," *Cambridge Journal of Economics* 38, no. 6 (November 2014): 1409–29.

For this reason, under a market system with employment contracts, there can never be a complete set of markets for labor power. Although capitalism has meant a huge extension of property and markets, and it has made labor power a widespread commodity (as Marx emphasized), it has also, by freeing labor from servitude, sustained *missing* markets for labor futures. For there to be full futures markets for labor, all workers must be able to enter into contracts for every future instant in their expected working life. Such a complete curtailment of future discretion would be voluntary bondage. The uncertainties involved in modern, complex, dynamic economies make such extensive future contracting impractical.

There is in principle no satisfactory contractual solution—within a market economy with wage labor—to missing markets for labor power. Enforcing detailed and extended property and contracting rights would limit the freedom of workers to quit their employment. Typically, workers are employed under a contract that allows exit, subject to notice of a few months. The short-term restriction of extended futures markets for labor is an important safeguard for the freedom of the employee.

Also, the future supply of labor power is not something that can be contracted at source, because babies cannot legally be farmed and sold as commodities within a system without slavery. Because they are not objects of ownership, human infants and their future labor power are not themselves produced under market arrangements. In an economy with markets and free labor, there are unavoidable missing markets for the original production of human resources. These markets are missing because they could exist in other states of the world where slave markets existed, but they are ruled out in states of the world where wage labor is ubiquitous.[63]

The absence of futures markets for labor power creates a problem for the employer with the existing workforce. If the employer spends money on employee training and skill development, then this investment is lost when the worker leaves. As a result, without compensatory arrangements,

[63] Sometimes babies are adopted in return for payment. Becker wrote of babies being sold, e.g., Becker, *A Treatise on Family*, 362 ff. Posner rightly responded: "The term baby selling ... is misleading. A mother who surrenders her parental rights for a fee is not selling her baby; babies are not chattels, and cannot be bought and sold. She is selling her parental rights." Richard A. Posner, *Sex and Reason* (Cambridge, MA: Harvard University Press, 1994), 410.

employers might under-invest in human learning and education. As Alfred Marshall pointed out, "we meet the difficulty that whoever may incur the expense of investing capital in developing the abilities of the workman, these abilities will be the property of the workman himself: and thus the virtue of those who have aided him must remain for the greater part its own reward."[64] The implications of this have been addressed in different ways.[65]

The problem of missing markets has been addressed within general equilibrium theory in the tradition of Kenneth J. Arrow and Gerard Debreu.[66] They investigated a heuristic model where "markets" exist for all possible commodities, in all possible states of the world, for all points of time in the future.

Later authors considered the possibility of missing markets in these models. A missing market is a market that could exist in some possible state of the world, but does not in fact exist. The term "missing market" does not apply to markets that cannot ever exist. If one or more of the commodity-, state-, and time-dependent markets is missing, then the absence of key information concerning prices on that missing market can cascade through the system and affect the overall outcome. The efficiency of other markets can be diminished.

Accordingly, Oliver Hart showed that in "an economy with incomplete markets … the usual continuity and convexity assumptions are not sufficient to ensure the existence of equilibrium." In such circumstances, a market equilibrium may be Pareto suboptimal. Furthermore, "if we start off in a situation where markets are incomplete, opening new markets may make things worse rather than better. In this respect, an economy with incomplete markets is like a typical second-best situation."[67] Likewise, Michael Magill and Martine

---

64 Alfred Marshall, *Principles of Economics: An Introductory Volume*, 8th ed. (London: Macmillan, 1920), 565.

65 Consider the literatures on "non-firm specific human capital" and on training policies: Andres Almazan, Adolfo De Motta, and Sheridan Titman, "Firm Location and the Creation and Utilization of Human Capital," *Review of Economic Studies* 74, no. 4 (October 2007): 1305–27; Kathleen Thelen, *How Institutions Evolve: The Political Economy of Skills in Germany, Britain, the United States and Japan* (Cambridge and New York: Cambridge University Press, 2004).

66 Kenneth J. Arrow and Gerard Debreu, "Existence of an Equilibrium for a Competitive Economy," *Econometrica* 22, no. 3 (1954): 265–90.

67 Oliver D. Hart, "On the Optimality of Equilibrium when the Market Structure is Incomplete," *Journal of Economic Theory* 11, no. 3 (December 1975): 442.

Quinzii showed that missing markets can lead to absent or indeterminate equilibria in existing markets.[68]

Consequently, missing markets mean we are in the world of "second best" solutions. As Richard Lipsey and Kelvin Lancaster famously demonstrated, when one or more optimality conditions cannot be satisfied, it is possible that the next-best solution involves changing other variables away from the values that would otherwise be optimal.[69] If it is infeasible to introduce a well-functioning market in any part of the system, then it is possible that the introduction of further market distortions or restrictions may partially counteract that omission, and lead to a more efficient outcome. There is no "one-size-fits-all" policy solution where the removal of market impediments always brings efficiency or welfare. On the contrary, welfare outcomes of such interventions could be positive or negative—they would be dependent on context.[70]

Markets can be missing for different reasons. Some limits are universal: there cannot be markets for all information or all rules. Other markets are missing because of customary or legislative constraints. These constraints may be removable or irremovable, desirable or undesirable. The relevant problem with market universalism is that missing markets are often overlooked or denied.

Policy temptations of market universalism

Generally, it is difficult or hazardous to derive an *ought* from an *is*—a normative claim from an analytic claim.[71] But statements concerning what things are, or how they work, can aid normative stances without logically entailing

[68] Magill and Quinzii saw missing markets as primarily a result of the limitations of the human psyche. They overlooked the important missing markets for labor power and future skills. See Michael Magill and Martine Quinzii, *Theory of Incomplete Markets* (Cambridge, MA: MIT Press, 1996).

[69] Richard G. Lipsey and Kelvin Lancaster, "The General Theory of Second Best," *Review of Economic Studies* 24, no. 1 (December 1956): 11–32.

[70] Richard G. Lipsey, "Reflections on the General Theory of Second Best at its Golden Jubilee," *International Tax and Public Finance* 14, no. 4 (2007): 349–64.

[71] But pushed to the extreme, the is/ought and fact/value distinctions become challengeable. Hilary Putnam, *The Collapse of the Fact/Value Dichotomy and Other Essays* (Cambridge, MA: Harvard University Press, 2002).

them. Market universalism is an analytic claim that is logically compatible with very different policy viewpoints.

However, the non-metaphorical misuse of the term *market*—to cover arrangements that are not best described in such terms—opens up pro-market normative possibilities. It removes conceptual barriers to pushing actual non-market arrangements towards genuine market mode. If most things are already seen as markets, or they are deemed to have an immanent tendency to become markets, then it would be less consequential to create more markets. Objections to the extension of markets are removed by the claim that existing arrangements are already markets. The temptation then is to ally market universalism with normative policies such as privatization and deregulation.

There is another temptation, with serious consequences. Through notions such as "political markets" and "markets for laws", market universalism conceptually dissolves the state and its legal system into a generally-marketized vision of society. They all become one and the same. The state and law become additional markets alongside others. This temptation within market universalism is the marketization of society and the state, and the denial of the autonomy of politics. The consequent enticement is to downgrade all non-commercial justifications for democracy, law, or social life. Everything is forced into the conceptual straitjacket of property and contract, and evaluated in terms of profit and loss.

One of the achievements of Enlightenment thought—from John Locke and Adam Smith—was the notion of civil society, which was distinguished both from the state and meant more than mere trade or business. Although it is a contested concept, in most accounts civil society includes private business and markets, but it is not reducible to them. As well as trade unions and employer associations, it embraces many forms of social association (including recreation, religion, and philanthropy) that are not necessarily driven by business interests. Civil society is important to develop local knowledge, sustain democracy, and to organize powers to lobby or protest against governments. It is a vital sphere of action and organization between the individual and the state.[72]

---

[72] Jean L. Cohen and Andrew Arato, *Civil Society and Political Theory* (Cambridge, MA: MIT Press, 1992); John Keane, ed., *Civil Society and the State* (London: Verso, 1988); idem., *Civil Society: Old Images, New Visions* (Cambridge: Polity, 1998); Krishan Kumar, "Civil Society: An Inquiry into the Usefulness of an Historical Term," *British Journal of Sociology* 44, no. 3 (September 1993): 375–395; Ernest Gellner, *Conditions of Liberty: Civil Society and its Rivals* (London and New York: Hamish Hamilton, 1994).

Notwithstanding their interdependence, civil society is different from the state. Civil society is also irreducible to market relations, notwithstanding the inclusion of trade and business within its sphere. Market universalism doubly undermines these distinctions. First, civil society is reduced to matters of property and contract. Second, politics is seen as a market as well.

Making everything a market denies the autonomy of law and politics: everything is subsumed within the market zone. All forms of association are regarded as markets. Legal and political relations are reduced to the bland "economic" facts of possession and exchange. Control over property becomes everything. Property moves from being a necessary condition of liberty, as in Enlightenment thought, to being necessary and *sufficient* for the same.

Also transformed is the prominent Enlightenment argument that the government must be legitimated by representative democracy, rather than by tradition or divine rule. Instead, the "political market" helps to promote market criteria as the overriding means to legitimize democracy. Furthermore, democracy itself may be seen as secondary or expedient, especially when property or markets are under threat. By treating democracy as another market, a temptation is to regard markets and property as sovereign, rather than democracy.

Clearly there is a prominent strain of modern thought that tries to justify everything in market-like terms. This suggests that there are no longer any worthwhile moral values or principles—including norms of justice or democratic behaviour—that cannot be given a market price.

We may briefly note a similarity with Marxism in this area, despite other major differences in theory and policy. Marxism does not entail market universalism: on the contrary, it emphasises the historical specificity of the market. But Marx and Engels did reduce civil society to economic matters of money and trade. As Marx wrote in 1843: "Practical need, egoism, is the principle of civil society [...] The god of practical need and self-interest is money."[73] Civil society, for Marx, was the individualistic realm of money and greed. Hence Marx concluded that "the anatomy of civil society is to be sought in political economy."[74] The analysis of the political, legal, and social

---

[73] Karl Marx and Friedrich Engels, *Collected Works*, vol. 3, *Marx and Engels, 1843–1844* (London: Lawrence and Wishart, 1975), 172.

[74] Idem., *Selected Works in Two Volumes*, vol. 1 (London: Lawrence and Wishart, 1962), 362.

spheres was to be achieved with an economics based on the assumption of individual self-interest.

Furthermore, the state, law, and politics under capitalism were made analytically subservient to this dismembered, economistic vision of civil society. Accordingly, Friedrich Engels wrote in 1886 that under capitalism "the State—the political order—is the subordinate, and civil society—the realm of economic relations—the decisive element."[75] Everything was deemed a matter of greed and commerce, to be understood through economic analysis.

Certainly, there are more sophisticated and less reductionist treatments by Marxists of civil society and the state, not least by Antonio Gramsci.[76] But Marx and Engels, alongside recent market universalists, embraced economic reductionism. Everything turns into the economics of trade, eclipsing the autonomy of politics and law, and neglecting the vital importance of non-commercial interaction and association within civil society.[77]

Conclusion

While absolute precision is unattainable, ongoing vigilance in the use of terms and metaphors is vital. It is suggested here that there is much more involved than casual analogy to the persistent use of the term *market* to describe a huge range of economic, political, social, and legal phenomena.

This paper shows that, by reasonable criteria, with minimal attention to the institutions and rules involved in a world of contracts a trade, the term *market* has been misused in instances such as "markets for ideas," "political markets," or "markets for laws." Often, these things are not true markets.

It is necessary to be clear what arrangements are *not* markets. Furthermore, it also must be understood that not everything can be traded on a market. In part this a matter of logic. To avoid an infinite regress, the rules

75 Idem., *Selected Works in Two Volumes*, vol. 2 (London: Lawrence and Wishart, 1962), 394–95.

76 Kumar, "Civil Society: An Inquiry into the Usefulness of an Historical Term."

77 Putnam's (2000) classic study of the erosion of American community life is highly relevant here. But the eager promotion of the language of social capital similarly and ironically nudges the realities of non-commercial interaction and association into the same economistic box; Hodgson, "What is Capital?"; idem, *Conceptualizing Capitalism*.

and institutions used to constitute contracts and enable trade cannot themselves be the objects of market exchange.

Also, a market system with "free" wage labor (in contrast to slavery) always entails some missing futures markets for future labor power. Otherwise the worker would be bonded by contracts for life. Without remedial measures, this lacuna has multiple consequences, including, as Marshall recognized,[78] under-investment in on-the-job training in necessary skills. According to an important theoretical literature, the existence of missing markets means that attempted market solutions to inefficiencies cannot be guaranteed to work.[79]

Although market universalism is not primarily a normative doctrine, it gives rise to major policy temptations. The most serious of these is the conceptual dissolution of the polity and the legal system into the "economic" sphere of the "market." The boundaries between the polity, the economy, and civil society become invisible. In particular, by treating democracy as a market, the temptation is to regard markets as more important than democracy.

Market universalism assails the argument of Enlightenment thinkers that the major role of democracy is to legitimate government. Instead, everything is legitimated by free contract, and by the operation of unfettered markets in all spheres of human interaction, including within the state itself. In this way, by dissolving the distinction between civil society and the state, market universalism enables a radical break from other forms of liberalism, and from all other doctrines that recognize the relative autonomy of the political and legal spheres from the economy and from civil society.

Modern politico-economic systems entail numerous, varied, and decentralized systems of coordination. Kornai's work on socialist economies also shows the role of decentralized coordination systems, even when there are attempts at central planning.[80] As Michael Polanyi argued, "the coordinating functions of the market are but a special case of coordination by mutual adjustment."[81] The polity is one such coordination system. The legal system is another. Organized science is yet another. Civil society involves others. True markets are still others.

---

78 Marshall, *Principles of Economics*, 565.

79 See Lipsey and Lancaster, "The General Theory of Second Best"; Hart, "On the Optimality of Equilibrium when the Market Structure is Incomplete"; Magill and Quinzii, *Theory of Incomplete Markets*; and Lipsey, "Reflections on the General Theory of Second Best at its Golden Jubilee."

80 Kornai, *The Socialist System*.

81 Polanyi, "The Republic of Science," 57.

While these may have common features at some abstract level, the detailed institutional structures and mechanisms are often very different. It is vital that these differences are not ignored, and that they are not all treated as markets.

If the theory of decentralized coordination systems is to be further developed, then it should distinguish between the most general level of analysis and the specific, additional mechanisms that pertain to true markets, including prices and contracts. Because of its diligent attention to institutional detail, Kornai's work is a major inspiration for this research programme.

In Soviet-type systems, the state permeated the entire society and negated the autonomy of both civil society and the legal system. The ideology of market universalism poses a different but related threat: everything is reduced to market relations. Politics and law are mistakenly treated as markets, subject to buyers and sellers rather than ethical principles, thus diminishing justice and morality. Similarly, the plural nature of civil society is eroded by reducing it to a market as well.

The overall danger is that the false market descriptions are corrected by becoming more real. Votes and laws are then literally, and even legally, bought and sold. Market universalism then betokens another dystopia, ruled by a dismal science where everything is judged in terms of profit and loss. Both the public and private spheres of this brave new world, to use Kornai's words, would be ruled by "optimization models and the arsenal of conventional micro- and macroeconomics." Everything, including law and politics, would be run by neoclassical economists.

References

Alchian, Armen A. "Some Economics of Property Rights." *Il Politico* 30, no. 4 (1965): 816–829.

Allen, Douglas W. "The Coase Theorem: Coherent, Logical, and not Disproved." *Journal of Institutional Economics* 11, no. 2 (June 2015): 379–90.

Almazan, Andres, Adolfo De Motta, and Sheridan Titman. "Firm Location and the Creation and Utilization of Human Capital." *Review of Economic Studies* 74, no. 4 (October 2007): 1305–27.

Arrow, Kenneth J., and Gerard Debreu. "Existence of an Equilibrium for a Competitive Economy." *Econometrica* 22, no. 3 (1954): 265–90.

Barzel, Yoram. *Economic Analysis of Property Rights*. Cambridge: Cambridge University Press, 1989.

Becker, Gary S. *The Economic Approach to Human Behavior*. Chicago: University of Chicago Press, 1976.

———. *A Treatise on the Family*, 2nd ed. Cambridge, MA: Harvard University Press, 1991.
———, Kevin M. Murphy, and Michael Grossman. "The Market for Illegal Goods: The Case of Drugs." *Journal of Political Economy* 114, no. 1 (February 2006): 38–60.
———, and Richard A. Posner. "Cross-Cultural Differences in Family and Sexual Life: An Economic Analysis." *Rationality and Society* 5, no. 4 (October 1993): 421–31.
Beckert, Jens, and Matias Dewey. *The Architecture of Illegal Markets: Towards an Economic Sociology of Illegality in the Economy*. Oxford and New York: Oxford University Press, 2017.
———, and Frank Wehinger. "In the Shadow: Illegal Markets and Economic Sociology." *Socio-Economic Review* 11, no. 1 (January 2013): 5–30.
Benson, Bruce L., and Eric M. Engen. "The Market for Laws: An Economic Analysis of Legislation." *Southern Economic Journal* 54, no. 3 (January 1988): 732–745.
Blau, Peter J. *Exchange and Power in Social Life*. New York: Wiley, 1964.
Block, Fred, and Margaret Somers. *The Power of Market Fundamentalism: Karl Polanyi's Critique*. Cambridge MA: Harvard University Press, 2014.
Boettke, Peter J., Christopher J. Coyne, and Peter T. Leeson. "The Many Faces of the Market." *Journal des Economistes et des Etudes Humaines* 14, no. 2 (2004): 71–86.
Bourdieu, Pierre. "The Forms of Capital." In *Handbook of Theory and Research for the Sociology of Education*, edited by John G. Richardson, 241–258. New York: Greenwood, 1986.
Brennan, Jason, and Peter M. Jaworski. *Markets without Limits: Moral Virtues and Commercial Interests*. London and New York: Routledge, 2016.
Burgin, Angus. *The Great Persuasion: Reinventing Free Markets since the Depression*. Cambridge MA: Harvard University Press, 2012.
Cannan, Edwin. "Early History of the Term Capital." *Quarterly Journal of Economics* 35, no. 3 (May 1921): 469–481.
Coase, Ronald H. "The Market for Goods and the Market for Ideas." *American Economic Review* 64, no. 2 (May 1974): 384–91.
———. *The Firm, the Market, and the Law*. Chicago: University of Chicago Press, 1988.
———, and Ning Wang. *How China Became Capitalist*. London and New York: Palgrave Macmillan, 2012.
Cohen, Jean L., and Andrew Arato. *Civil Society and Political Theory*. Cambridge, MA: MIT Press, 1992.
Cole, Daniel H., and Peter Z. Grossman. "The Meaning of Property Rights: Law versus Economics?" *Land Economics* 78, no. 3 (August 2002): 317–330.
Commons, John R. *Legal Foundations of Capitalism*. New York: Macmillan, 1924.
Crain, W. Mark. "On the Structure and Stability of Political Markets." *Journal of Political Economy* 85, no. 4 (August 1977): 829–842.
Deakin, Simon, David Gindis, Geoffrey M. Hodgson, Kainan Huang, and Katharina Pistor. "Legal Institutionalism: Capitalism and the Constitutive Role of Law." *Journal of Comparative Economics* 45, no. 1 (February 2017):188–200.
Director, Aaron. "The Parity of the Economic Market Place." *Journal of Law and Economics* 7 (October 1964): 1–10.
Dixit, Avinash K. *Lawlessness and Economics: Alternative Modes of Governance*. Princeton, NJ: Princeton University Press, 2004.

Durkheim, Émile. *The Division of Labor in Society*, translated by W. D. Halls. London: Macmillan, 1984.

Fetter, Frank A. "Capital." In *Encyclopaedia of the Social Sciences*, vol. 3, edited by Edwin R. A. Seligman and Alvin Johnson, 187–90. New York: Macmillan, 1930. Reprinted as "Frank A. Fetter (1863–1949): Capital (1930)" with editorial introduction by Geoffrey M. Hodgson. *Journal of Institutional Economics* 4, no. 1 April (2008): 127–37.

Gellner, Ernest. *Conditions of Liberty: Civil Society and its Rivals*. London and New York: Hamish Hamilton, 1994.

Goldberg, Victor P. "Relational Exchange: Economics and Complex Contracts." *American Behavioral Scientist* 23, no. 3 (1980): 337–52.

Gravelle, Hugh, and Ray Rees. *Microeconomics*. 2nd ed. Harlow: Longman, 1992.

Hart, Oliver D. "On the Optimality of Equilibrium when the Market Structure is Incomplete." *Journal of Economic Theory* 11, no. 3 (December 1975): 418–43.

Heinsohn, Gunnar, and Otto Steiger. *Ownership Economics: On the Foundations of Interest, Money, Markets, Business Cycles and Economic Development*, translated and edited by Frank Decker. London and New York: Routledge, 2013.

Heller, Michael A. *The Gridlock Economy: How Too Much Ownership Wrecks Markets, Stops Innovation, and Costs Lives*. New York: Basic Books, 2008.

Hodgson, Geoffrey M. *Conceptualizing Capitalism: Institutions, Evolution, Future*. Chicago: University of Chicago Press, 2015a.

———. *How Economics Forgot History: The Problem of Historical Specificity in Social Science*. London and New York: Routledge, 2001.

———. "How Mythical Markets Mislead Analysis: An Institutionalist Critique of Market Universalism." *Socio-Economic Review*. Forthcoming, 2019b.

———. "Karl Polanyi on Economy and Society: A Critical Analysis of Core Concepts." *Review of Social Economy* 75, no. 1 (March 2017): 1–25.

———. "Markets." In *New Palgrave Dictionary of Economics*. 2nd ed. Basingstoke: Macmillan, 2008.

———. "Much of the 'Economics of Property Rights' Devalues Property and Legal Rights." *Journal of Institutional Economics* 11, no. 4 (December 2015c): 683–709.

———. "On Defining Institutions: Rules *versus* Equilibria." *Journal of Institutional Economics* 11, no. 3 (September 2015b): 499–505.

———. "Taxonomic Definitions in Social Science, with Firms, Markets and Institutions as Case Studies." *Journal of Institutional Economics*. Forthcoming, 2019a.

———. "What is Capital? Economists and Sociologists have changed its Meaning—Should it be Changed Back?" *Cambridge Journal of Economics* 38, no. 5 September (2014): 1063–86.

———, and Kainan Huang. "Brakes on Chinese Economic Development: Institutional Causes of a Growth Slowdown." *Journal of Economic Issues* 47, no. 3 (September 2013): 599–622.

Homans, George C. *Social Behaviour: Its Elementary Form*. London: Routledge and Kegan Paul, 1961.

Jevons, William Stanley. *The Theory of Political Economy*. 3rd ed. London: Macmillan, 1888.

Kaiser, Robert G. *So Damn Much Money: The Triumph of Lobbying and the Corrosion of American Government*. New York: Knopf, 2009.

Keane, John, ed. *Civil Society and the State*. London: Verso, 1988.

———. *Civil Society: Old Images, New Visions*. Cambridge: Polity, 1998.

Klaus, Václav, and Dušán Tříska. Review of János Kornai, *The Socialist System: The Political Economy of Communism*. In Václav Klaus, *Renaissance: The Rebirth of Liberty in the Heart of Europe*, 163–9. Washington DC: Cato Institute, 1997.

Knight, Jack. *Institutions and Social Conflict*. Cambridge: Cambridge University Press, 1992.

Kornai, János. "Mathematical Programming as a Tool of Socialist Economic Planning (1965)." In *Socialist Economics*, edited by Alec Nove and D. M. Nuti, 475–88. Harmondsworth: Penguin, 1972.

———. *Anti-Equilibrium: On Economic Systems Theory and the Tasks of Research*. Amsterdam: North Holland, 1971.

———. *The Socialist System: The Political Economy of Communism*. Oxford: Clarendon Press, 1992.

———. *By Force of Thought: Irregular Memoirs of an Intellectual Journey*. Cambridge, MA: MIT Press, 2006.

Kumar, Krishan. "Civil Society: An Inquiry into the Usefulness of an Historical Term." *British Journal of Sociology* 44, no. 3 (September 1993): 375–395.

Lipsey, Richard G. "Reflections on the General Theory of Second Best at its Golden Jubilee." *International Tax and Public Finance* 14, no. 4 (2007): 349–64.

Lipsey, Richard G., and Kelvin Lancaster. "The General Theory of Second Best." *Review of Economic Studies* 24, no. 1 (December 1956): 11–32.

Magill, Michael, and Martine Quinzii. *Theory of Incomplete Markets*. Cambridge, MA: MIT Press, 1996.

Mäki, Uskali. "Science as a Free Market: A Reflexivity Test in an Economics of Economics." *Perspectives on Science* 7, no. 4 (1999): 486–509.

Manne, Henry G. "Mergers and the Market for Corporate Control." *Journal of Political Economy* 73, no. 2 (April 1965): 110–120.

Mantzavinos, Chris. *Individuals, Institutions, and Markets*. Cambridge and New York: Cambridge University Press, 2001.

Marshall, Alfred. *Principles of Economics: An Introductory Volume*. 8th ed. London: Macmillan, 1920.

Marx, Karl, and Friedrich Engels. *Selected Works in Two Volumes*. London: Lawrence and Wishart, 1962.

Marx, Karl, and Friedrich Engels. *Collected Works*. Vol. 3, *Marx and Engels, 1843–1844*. London: Lawrence and Wishart, 1975.

von Mises, Ludwig. *Human Action: A Treatise on Economics*. 1st ed. London and New Haven: William Hodge and Yale University Press, 1949.

Mitra, Anirban, Shabana Mitra, and Arnab Mukherji. "Cash for Votes: Evidence from India." KDPE 1711, School of Economics Discussion Papers, University of Kent, Kent, UK, 2017.

North, Douglass C. "Markets and Other Allocation Systems in History: The Challenge of Karl Polanyi." *Journal of European Economic History* 6, no. 3 (Winter 1977): 703–16.

North, Douglass C. *Institutions, Institutional Change and Economic Performance*. Cambridge and New York: Cambridge University Press, 1990a.

———. "A Transactions Cost Theory of Politics." *Journal of Theoretical Politics* 2, no. 4 (October 1990b): 355–67.

O'Neill, John. *The Market: Ethics, Knowledge and Politics*. London and New York: Routledge, 1998.

Ostrom, Elinor. *Governing the Commons: The Evolution of Institutions for Collective Action*. Cambridge: Cambridge University Press, 1990.

Pagano, Ugo. "The Crisis of Intellectual Monopoly Capitalism." *Cambridge Journal of Economics* 38, no. 6 (November 2014): 1409–29.

Pantaleoni, Maffeo. "Considerazioni sulle proprieta di un sistema di prezzi politici." *Giornale degli Economisti* 42 (1911): 9–29, 114–33.

Pejovich, Svetozar. "The Market for Institutions vs. Capitalism by Fiat: The Case of Eastern Europe." *Kyklos* 47, no. 4 (1994): 519–29.

Pettman, Ralph. *World Politics: Rationalism and Beyond*. London: Palgrave Macmillan, 2001.

Polanyi, Karl. *The Great Transformation: The Political and Economic Origins of Our Time*. New York: Rinehart, 1944.

———. *The Livelihood of Man*, edited by Harry W. Pearson. New York: Academic Press, 1977.

Polanyi, Michael. "Patent Reform." *Review of Economic Studies* 11, no. 2 (Summer 1944): 61–76.

———. "The Republic of Science: Its Political and Economic Theory." *Minerva* 1 (1962): 54–73.

Posner, Richard A. *Sex and Reason*. Cambridge, MA: Harvard University Press, 1994.

Putnam, Hilary. *The Collapse of the Fact/Value Dichotomy and Other Essays*. Cambridge, MA: Harvard University Press, 2002.

Putnam, Robert D. *Bowling Alone: The Collapse and Revival of American Community*. New York: Simon and Schuster, 2000.

Radin, Margaret Jane. *Contested Commodities: Trouble with Trade in Sex, Children, Body Parts and Other Things*. Cambridge, MA: Harvard University Press, 1996.

Red Lion Broadcasting Co., Inc. v. FCC, 395 U.S. 367 (1969).

Rosenbaum, Eckehard F. "What is a Market? On the Methodology of a Contested Concept." *Review of Social Economy* 58, no. 4 (December 2000): 455–82.

Russell, Bertrand. "Vagueness." *Australasian Journal of Psychology and Philosophy* 1, no. 1 (1923): 84–92.

Sandel, Michael. *What Money Can't Buy: The Moral Limits of Markets*. London: Allen Lane, 2012.

Satz, Debra. *Why Some Things Should not be for Sale: The Moral Limits of Markets*. Oxford and New York: Oxford University Press, 2010.

Schelling, Thomas C. "Economics and Criminal Enterprise." In *Choice and Consequence: Perspectives of an Errant Economist*, 179–94. Cambridge, MA: Harvard University Press, 1984.

Simmel, Georg. *The Philosophy of Money*, translated by Tom Bottomore and David Frisby. London and New York: Routledge, 2004.

Soros, George. *The Crisis of Global Capitalism: Open Society Endangered*. New York: Public Affairs, 1998.

———. *The New Paradigm for Financial Markets: The Credit Crisis of 2008 and What It Means*. New York: Public Affairs, 2008.

Stiglitz, Joseph E. "Stiglitz: The Fall of Wall Street Is to Market Fundamentalism What the Fall of the Berlin Wall Was to Communism." By Nathan Gardels. *The Huffington Post*, September 16, 2008. http://www.huffingtonpost.com/nathan-gardels/stiglitz-the-fall-of-wall_b_126911.html. Accessed July 10, 2017.

Thelen, Kathleen. *How Institutions Evolve: The Political Economy of Skills in Germany, Britain, the United States and Japan*. Cambridge and New York: Cambridge University Press, 2004.

Thornton, Mark. *The Economics of Prohibition*. Salt Lake City: University of Utah Press, 1991.

Tyler, Tom R. *Why People Obey the Law*. New Haven: Yale University Press, 1990.

Walzer, Michael. *Spheres of Justice: A Defence of Pluralism and Equality*. New York: Basic Books, 1983.

The System Paradigm and the European Monetary Union

What János Kornai's Contribution to Comparative Economics Can Suggest to the Eurozone

Bruno Dallago

Introduction

The years following the crisis have highlighted the institutional fragility of the Eurozone. While events in the Eurozone during the last decade include important cases of debt and balance-of-payments crises, its essence—which explains why the crisis was much longer and deeper than in other countries—has to do with the institutional construction and governance of the Eurozone system and economy and the resultant policy constraints. This chapter aims at highlighting the deep and complex reasons for the Eurozone conundrum in light of János Kornai's contributions to systemic analysis.

Kornai's systemic perspective looks important because the fundamental question is to explain why the Eurozone crisis was not a simple negative interlude in the progress of European integration, after which European integration would go back to its happy days. The crisis changed the overall process of economic and monetary integration and indeed also political and policy cooperation and coordination among member countries. While proper policy management would be important, even more fundamental is to understand why the institutional construction of the Eurozone is unsustainable in an unfriendly and unstable external context and why this construction prevents the Eurozone and its constituent national governments to adopt policies apt to effectively manage the crisis and promote growth.

The debate following the crisis has been primarily focused on the irrationality of convergence parameters and the incompleteness of the institutional construction, which deprives member countries of fundamental policy instruments. While some progress is under way in softening the former (convergence parameters) and completing the latter (economic institutions and policy instruments), much less if anything has been done on a much deeper and fundamental issue: the coherence and sustainability of the Eurozone system, its relation to diverse national systems, and the institutional difficulty of a broad and deep systemic convergence.

So far, with the partial exception of the first steps of the economic and monetary union, efforts were concentrated on disciplining member countries, which voluntarily transferred their monetary sovereignty to the Eurosystem.[1] The danger of moral hazard and the ways to keep it under control in fiscal governance was, openly after the crisis and more implicitly before the crisis, the fundamental thread of the Eurozone activity. This approach left the fundamental problem of the monetary union unsolved: how can institutionally different countries share the same currency and manage their economies by means of policies? As member of the Eurozone, a country uses a currency that it cannot control, has no sovereignty over monetary policy and has severe constraints over its fiscal policies. This situation creates asymmetries and divergent outcomes among member countries that the monetary union cannot manage for lack of instruments, be their common or national instruments.[2]

Critics of the monetary integration see in this the impossibility and inevitable failure of the Eurozone. Others maintain that this is not necessarily so and that it is the rigidity of the Eurozone construction and its convergence parameters that causes unnecessary costs and damages to its member economies and the integration process, while the lack of policies supporting aggregate demand causes unnecessary stagnation. What is still

---

1 The Eurosystem is the supreme monetary authority of the Eurozone. Its governance is in the Governing Council, which includes the members of the Executive Board of the European Central Bank (ECB) and the governors of the national central banks (NCB) of the Eurozone, with one vote each. The Eurosystem takes decisions on the Eurozone monetary policy through a majority voting system. Such a system requires that NCB governors pursue the common interest, even at the (short-term) disadvantage of the economic and financial interest of their national economy, a situation that may not be guaranteed under the pressure of negative events and difficulties.

2 Bruno Dallago, *One Currency, Two Europes* (Singapore: World Scientific Publishing Co., 2016).

missing in the debate is a comprehensive analysis of how institutionally different countries can share such a fundamental institution as the currency, together with the same monetary policy and fiscal policies constrained by convergence parameters. The present uncertain tittering of the EU amidst growing conflicts and weakening governance ability and capability asks for a deeper analysis: why is the EU incapable of going forward with integration, and why are national idiosyncrasies gaining momentum and leading to policy and political conflict? Kornai's approach and analysis can be of help to highlight this issue.

János Kornai's life-long scientific contributions are important to highlight the deep problems that haunt the Eurozone and which must be resolved in order to assure its long-term sustainability. While the systemic issue was and is considered by a vast array of authors, also in reference to the Eurozone (e.g., the Varieties of Capitalism literature), Kornai's contribution stands out for its ability to conjugate the intimate institutional nature and coherence of an economic system and its relation to the other components of the life of a country (such as politics). Kornai's system paradigm, based on his deep and far-reaching approach, offers the possibility to go to the core of the Eurozone conundrum.

The next section is devoted to Kornai's contribution to systemic analysis and looks at the Eurozone through his concepts and approach. The conclusion is that the Eurozone paradigm is unbalanced and incomplete, while the Eurozone system itself is incomplete and needs a national level. In section 3, the paper looks at the fundamental documents of the European integration as the founding elements that can outline a Eurozone paradigm. Section 4 considers the consequences of the particular features of the Eurozone paradigm and system for the performance of Eurozone economies and shows how these cause the performance of different groups of countries in the Eurozone to diverge above and beyond their merit and demerit. Section 5 looks at the Eurozone system starting from Kornai's view, to stress how its incompleteness causes serious problems to those countries whose national system is at odds with the Eurozone paradigm. As shown in section 6, this incompleteness and systemic oddity causes divergence within the Eurozone and makes policies and reforms problematic and often ineffective. Section 7 concludes by assessing the ongoing Eurozone attempts to overcome its main problems in light of Kornai's teaching.

Kornai's contribution: paradigms, systems and the Eurozone

Kornai defines a paradigm as a "long-lasting common way of thinking by a scientific community."[3] The paradigm is the outcome of a long intellectual and scientific development which, once defined and accepted, "... provides a certain circle of researchers with the intellectual guidance that paradigms should provide."[4]

The system paradigm is a particular kind of paradigm, one which has a composite origin. A system paradigm refers to a paradigm with the following six attributes.[5] First, researchers are concerned with the system as a whole and with the relations between the whole and its parts. Second, the attention of researchers is focused on more permanent institutions and on system-specific attributes of the operation of a society. Third, researchers must search for an explanatory theory in historical terms. Fourth, individual preferences are considered largely as the product of the system itself. Fifth, researchers recognize that all systems have shortcomings or dysfunctions specific to them. Sixth, the characteristic research and analysis method is comparison.

While the term paradigm usually refers to a scientific community, the use of the term for analyzing European integration is justified by the ideal and scientific origin of the process and the many analyses and reports which were conducted alongside the construction of the European Union and the Eurozone. All these led to commonly accepted and shared treaties that address and constrain policies and action. These highlight the existence of a sufficiently coherent and shared vision of the process and its expected outcome that should generate compatible behavior by member countries. In this perspective, the "Eurozone paradigm" can be considered equivalent to a system paradigm. This is not to say that there are no different and conflicting visions of the economic and monetary integration. They exist, are spread, and shared

---

3 János Kornai, "The System Paradigm," in *Paradigms of Social Change: Modernization, Development, Transformation, Evolution*, ed. Waltraud Schekle, Wolf-Hagen Krauth, Martin Kohli, and Georg Elwert (Frankfurt and New York: Campus Verlag; New York: St. Martin's, 2000), 113.

4 Ibid.

5 Kornai, "The System Paradigm," 118–121.

by many Europeans, including respected scholars,[6] let alone political leaders. Yet these visions represent critical voices and play little role in the construction and governance of the Eurozone. The latter forms a coherent and shared process based on treaties that all national governments have freely and voluntarily subscribed to and with which they are compelled to comply.

The Eurozone paradigm is not the outcome of pure scientific analysis, but rather involves political interaction and compromise, so the use of the term paradigm may look unjustified in this case. Yet, in Kornai's words, "…the methodology of the system paradigm lacks models based on exact assumptions and theorems…"[7] Yet, "it requires of its exponents the consistency of logic, with statements supported by argumentation and comparison with similar or contrasting cases. The stringency of the argumentation is increased by quantitative analysis, which has to be done wherever possible." Equally important is that in dealing with the paradigm, history and politics should be given proper consideration.

It is also important to clarify in which sense the Eurozone can be considered as a system. The term system "… conveys the meaning that several lesser parts form a coherent whole. These parts interact … there are comprehensible relations among them organizing them into a structure."[8] The economic system of a country includes the coordinated set of all relevant formal and informal institutions and organs necessary for an economy to work: coordinate the activity of economic and social actors, provide incentives, generate information flows and lead to proper decision making, organize production, and be able to manage uncertainty and conflicts and solve them.[9]

In economics, and particularly in comparative economics, the term system is used to identify "a distinct combination of forms of political power, dominant ideology, ownership relations, and coordination of social activities" that distinguish a country or a group of countries from others and that have evolved through time. Typical examples are the capitalist and socialist

---

[6] Joseph E. Stiglitz, *The Euro: How a Common Currency Threatens the Future of Europe* (New York: W.W. Norton, 2016); Paolo Savona, *Come un incubo e come un sogno*. (Soveria Mannelli: Rubbettino, 2018).

[7] Kornai, "The System Paradigm," 123

[8] Idem., "The System Paradigm Revisited: Clarifications and Additions in the Light of Experiences in the Post-socialist Region," *Acta Oeconomica* 66, no. 4 (2016): 549.

[9] Idem., *The Socialist System: The Political Economy of Communism* (Princeton: Princeton University Press, 1992).

systems. Here, the term "points to the mutual effects of various elements in the public state of affairs, operation of the country, and structure of the machinery of power."[10]

The primary characteristics mentioned above (political power, dominant forms of property, and coordination mechanism) define the system as a whole and distinguish different systems. Along with these, there are six secondary characteristics that are determined stochastically by primary characteristics. They include the working of the goods and labor markets, technical progress, income distribution, microeconomic budget constraint, and corruption.[11] This definition highlights the important conclusion that these are systemic differences among Eurozone member countries and that these differences have implications.

The official vision of the European monetary union as a system foresees that, under the effect of common institutions, the pressure of consistent European action and procedures, based on convergence parameters and the active effort of member countries through policy compliance and structural reforms, national economic systems would converge to what is foreseen by the Eurozone paradigm. While the goal of political unification remained alive, it was not considered essential for a smooth and strong working of the European economy, even in the case of the Eurozone. This created a discontinuity between the Eurozone paradigm and the set of national systems, which did not converge sufficiently to form a consistent Eurozone system.

Referring to the socialist system, Kornai wrote: "… despite all the individual attributes that distinguish each of these socialist countries from all the others, they resemble one another and exhibit important attributes in common. Even though their actual systems differ in many details, they are all members of a broader, clearly identifiable class of socio-political-economic systems…"[12] This statement also applies to the group of countries forming the Eurozone.

Although it is evident that the Eurozone member countries belong in the capitalist system, each one also presents distinct systemic features. Along with systemic variability, the Eurozone includes countries with limited sovereignty, which transferred important parts of their sovereignty to the European Union, in particular to the common monetary authorities. At the same time,

---

10 Idem., "The System Paradigm Revisited," 549.
11 Idem., "The System Paradigm Revisited," 553.
12 Idem., *The Socialist System*, 5.

the Eurozone as a supranational construction remains incomplete as a system, because it includes countries that keep their sovereign idiosyncratic institutions in many fields, particularly in political matters, plus all informal institutions. This opens the possibility of multiple equilibria, which lead to coordination failure and moral hazard among member countries. Member countries could achieve a more desirable equilibrium, but fail to do so since they do not coordinate their decision making due to their diverse interests and goals following from their different institutions and situations. A typical case is the lack of institutionalized policy complementarity, in particular when a member country in a fiscally balanced situation is afraid of destabilizing its finances or current account and fails to expand its demand, so to support other member countries in a deficit or distress situation. Coordination failure can thus lead to an underemployment equilibrium. This opens the questions of the relation between national and Eurozone institutions and policies and the intercountry interaction. Given national idiosyncrasies, difficulties and problems in the Eurozone differ among member countries, which would require different policy instruments and adjustment processes.

A common paradigm imposed on national systemic variety causes a problem. A common paradigm foresees similar behavior of countries adopting it. In centrally planned economies, in which markets had negligible roles and competition on the supply market was inexistent, differences among national systems could be smoothed away through political and administrative decisions and action. Market economies are different. If the paradigm would concern only the broad primary characteristics, the Eurozone system could work smoothly. This is indeed the case of the common market based on the four fundamental freedoms, albeit the ongoing negotiations on Brexit show how complex this less demanding example of integration can be.

Kornai's primary aim is to distinguish the different outcomes of the process of transformation of former socialist countries in capitalist countries, yet his approach is useful to highlight the varieties existing within the Eurozone. Kornai's main organizing criterion is the politico-governmental form of different countries. He stresses "what a huge effect political structures and political ideas have, and how vital it is to examine in detail the course of history for an understanding of the transformations of society."[13] While

[13] Idem., "The System Paradigm Revisited."

Kornai refers to the shift from socialism to capitalism, these words can be applied to the "great" change that monetary unification represents in the Eurozone. Yet the devil is often in the particulars and the two cases are not identical and have important differences.

Kornai distinguishes between four primary characteristics of democracy, autocracy, and dictatorship, and six secondary characteristics.[14] Based on these characteristics, all EU member countries are democracies, with the exception of Hungary, which is a non-Eurozone autocracy. So, no member country of the Eurozone is under dictatorships nor is it an autocracy. Yet Kornai's analysis is interesting in a different sense. Eurozone member countries gave up an important part of their sovereignty: money and its management, and accepted to limit their financial sovereignty, submitting it to commonly devised and shared convergence parameters. Moreover, they granted common bodies—the European Council and the European Commission in particular—the power of inspection and enforcement of common rules.

The fundamental problem, then, is to assess whether the governance of the Eurozone lacks democratic legitimacy. Indeed, various authors theorize the existence of a "democratic deficit" in the Eurozone.[15] In short: democratically elected governments agree to submit their country's sovereignty to a set of parameters whose compliance with is checked and enforced by an organ without a formal decision- or law-making role (the European Council) and an organ set up through the interaction among national governments and only then formally approved by the democratically elected European Parliament (the European Commission).

The two most striking examples of the supposed democratic deficit are the apparent mistreatment of Greece and its government in summer 2015 and the imposition of selected austerity policies against the will of the democratically elected Greek government. A second example is when, in fall 2011, the democratically elected government of Italy resigned following a not-yet-clear ploy at European level, apparently with domestic support. Yet, in other

---

[14] Idem., "The System Paradigm Revisited," 565.

[15] Simona Piattoni, "The European Crisis: Testing the Trust Foundations of an Economic and Monetary Union," in *A Global Perspective on the European Economic Crisis*, ed. Bruno Dallago, Gert Guri and John McGowan (Abingdon, Oxfordshire: Routledge, 2016), 79–95; Paolo Savona, *Come un incubo e come un sogno*; but see Andrew Moravcsik, "The Myth of Europe's Democratic Deficit," *Intereconomics: Journal of European Public Policy* (November–December 2008): 331–340.

cases, the mechanism worked the other way around: Germany and France in 2003 and 2004 did not comply with the excessive deficit rules and forced a softening of the original version of the Stability and Growth Pact.[16] In recent years, Germany and the Netherlands did not comply with excessive current account surplus, so far without being obliged to do so.[17]

These cases highlight the danger that a possible democratic deficit is strengthened by asymmetric and unequal treatment of different countries, depending on their political power, contingent situations, or their alignment with the Eurozone paradigm. This may jeopardize the neutrality of Eurozone rules. If so, some member countries of the Eurozone may appear to have limited domestic democracy and others to extend the power of their *domestically* elected governments over others through the Eurozone organs. In the spirit of Kornai's approach we can conclude that the European Union, and even more so the Eurozone, have too many political and administrative filters between the democratic principal, the citizens, and the common decision-making agents. This is a dysfunctional way to pursue the coordination and cooperation of different and diverse countries, which is apparently firing back, particularly in national political spheres. A further teaching by Kornai is that politics should be an integral component of the construction of a Eurozone system and considered in the Eurozone paradigm.

Monetary integration and the Eurozone paradigm

The management of the common currency is complex. The Euro is a fiat money without a government. Eurozone national finances are in a currency that national governments do not control, except very indirectly and minimally

[16] Horst Feldmann, "From Initiating to Breaching to Diluting the Stability and Growth Pact," in *Germany's Economic Performance: From Unification to Euroization*, ed. Jens Hölscher (Houndmills–Basingstoke: Palgrave Macmillan, 2007), 134–136; Victor Ngai, "Stability and Growth Pact and Fiscal Discipline in the Eurozone," Working Papers no. 12-10, University of Pennsylvania, Wharton School, Weiss Center, 2012. https://ideas.repec.org/p/ecl/upafin/12-10.html.

[17] Alice Zoppè. *Implementation of the Macroeconomic Imbalance Procedure: State-of-play* (Brussels: European Parliament, Economic Governance Support Unit, September 2019), http://www.europarl.europa.eu/RegData/etudes/IDAN/2016/497739/IPOL_IDA(2016)497739_EN.pdf.

through the Governing Council of the European Central Bank.[18] Any decision by the ECB and action by the European Commission restrict and sometimes determine policy making by democratically elected national governments.

The European paradigm evolved through time.[19] Monetary integration and the formation of the Eurozone through the Economic and Monetary Union (EMU) are the clearest and most demanding core of the paradigm. The requirements and the consequences of a common currency were the concern of the European Community as early as the late 1960s. An important step in this perspective is the "Report to the Council and the Commission on the Realisation by Stages of Economic and Monetary Union in the Community," better known as the Werner Report.[20] This report outlines a first, comprehensive vision of the future monetary union and is therefore the first clear definition of the Eurozone paradigm, a more complete and encompassing vision compared to what was later foreseen by the Delors Report and was actually implemented so far.[21]

In the vision of the Werner Report, what really matters is the overall process of economic, financial, and institutional convergence of the entire community (now Union). This means that only the external equilibrium of the entire community is important. At the same time, internal equilibrium is considered as the outcome of the "mobility of the factors of production and financial transfers by the public and private sectors."[22] The Report is fully aware of the implications and does not rely only on market instruments. Indeed, it considers the necessity of both convergence of and interdependence among member countries in any economic domain, and the development of the powers of the common organs. Along with policies, convergence must also concern institutions at both national and Community level.

---

[18] The Governing Council of the European Central Bank is the main decision-making body of the ECB, responsible for formulating monetary policy for the Eurozone. It comprises the members of the Executive Board of the European Central Bank and the governors of the National Central Banks of the Eurozone's member countries.

[19] Dallago, *One Currency, Two Europes.*

[20] Council—Commission of the European Communities, *Report to the Council and the Commission on the Realisation by Stages of Economic and Monetary Union in the Community—"Werner Report"* (Luxembourg, 1970), http://aei.pitt.edu/1002/1/monetary_werner_final.pdf.

[21] *Report on Economic and Monetary Union in the European Community* (Brussels: Committee for the Study of Economic and Monetary Union, 1989), http://ec.europa.eu/economy_finance/publications/publication6161_en.pdf.

[22] Council—Commission of the European Communities, *"Werner Report,"* 10.

The necessity to have a complete governance of European integration and the severe problems that would descend from the inability to implement the integration agenda were thus clear as early as 1970. The Werner Report can accordingly be considered as the main reference of the ideal Eurozone paradigm and as the basis for its future system, a reference that leaves to the political will of member countries the solution of the problems that a premature monetary union would create.

The disruption of the Bretton Woods system and the oil crisis prompted member countries to adopt idiosyncratic national policies. The 1974 Council Decision on economic convergence moved in the direction of financial convergence, while paying lip service to the necessity of real economic and institutional convergence. The publication of the Delors Report in 1989 followed long bargaining and contrasts among member countries. Accordingly, the Report envisages a greater role for national governments and places confidence in the inter-country mobility of resources, but also in the necessity to place decisions within an agreed macroeconomic framework and bind the financial freedom of member countries through procedures and rules to keep stability of the monetary union.

Unfortunately, the Delors Report's trust in self-adjusting mechanisms—geographical and sectorial mobility of resources, price flexibility, and lack of structural impediments—does not sufficiently match European reality. Here lies much of the problem of the Eurozone compared to the premises of its paradigm: insufficient resource mobility (particularly in the labor market), institutional idiosyncrasies and structural problems, together with unbalanced public finances in some countries and their national management and accountability. To be sure, the Report is aware of the existence of impediments and their asymmetric consequences on the internal cohesion of the EU, but it apparently supposes that they can be effectively removed through market processes and reforms.

The Delors Report, together with various treaties, represents the high moment of a pragmatic technical adjustment of aspirations to European integration. While this adjustment worked reasonably well for decades and produced wellbeing and political stability for Europeans, it nevertheless contributed to create an incomplete and unbalanced Eurozone paradigm and consequently inhibited the development of a full Eurozone system. The Eurozone paradigm evolved thus in an unbalanced way, giving strong priority to fiscal stability and inflation control, while downplaying the needs of the real economy. The Eurozone paradigm is also incomplete, since it does not cover important aspects of the governance of the common currency, including a full banking union and a truly unified capital market. It downplays fundamental economic and social institutions other than the currency, including growth, technical progress and full employment, and overlooks the idiosyncratic working of markets in different member countries. The latter goals were left to *ad hoc* agendas, such as the Lisbon Strategy. The inadequacy of this approach became evident during the crisis.

The basic reference frame for the Eurozone, the paradigm, is thus unbalanced and incomplete, and runs the risk of being ineffective as a guide for analyzing, understanding, calculating, deciding, and acting, in particular in non-standard circumstances such as a crisis. The final word is left to the political will of member countries and the governments' ability to compromise.

The consequences of paradigm incompleteness and systemic duality

The Euro, the legal tender in nineteen EU member countries, is a fiat money without a state and even lacking a complete government. In fact, national governments agreed to establish the euro as their sole and irreversible common currency and delegated the Eurosystem and the European Central Bank (ECB) as the only repository of the monopoly to issue money. All this has important consequences for the economic system, discussed in the next section.

These same governments keep their institutional and policy sovereignty in many important fields, although they agree to behave in ways compatible with monetary stability. First among these is financial stability. European treaties do not foresee the possibility to abandon the Eurozone.[23] The need to provide other member countries with credible commitments requires that each government's activity is based on simple and transparent rules, whose compliance is easy to check and enforce by third parties. In the Eurozone

[23] There is presently some debate on the need to foresee the exit from the Euro for countries willing (or perhaps obliged) to do so. The high moment in this debate was the manifesto published by 154 distinguished German economists in the *Frankfurter Allgemeine Zeitung* on May 21, 2018. See "Der Euro darf nicht in die Haftungsunion führen!" *Frankfurter Allgemeine Zeitung*, May 21, 2018, http://www.faz.net/aktuell/wirtschaft/eurokrise/oekonomen-aufruf-euro-darf-nicht-in-haftungsunion-fuehren-15600325.html.

these are the convergence criteria, checked and enforced by the European Commission, the European Council, and the European Central Bank.

Thus, the Euro is established as an irreversible, incomplete, inter-government, and inter-state contract among politically sovereign countries, which voluntarily accept to submit their financial behavior to commonly devised and enforced parameters. Incompleteness creates uncertainty, and consequently the danger of moral hazard in the behavior of member countries crops up. Moral hazard and uncertainty lead to the predominance of short-term goals and achievements, primarily short-term balanced budgets. A rational adaptation to such a situation, and an effective way to keep moral hazard under check, is to impose hard budget constraints across the board, in particular to national finances and the ECB mandate, and avoid setting up funds for supporting the common currency in case of distress.

The institutional and policy incompleteness of the monetary union is bound to create serious problems, particularly in case of unforeseen events. Moreover, the concept of policy coordination continues to be unclear and the way for pursuing economic convergence remains in need of elaboration. What stays unsolved, in particular, is whether and how it is possible to have effective common policies for member countries in different real and financial conditions and situations and with different economic systems, policies which are compatible with the Eurozone paradigm.

This solution is politically rational in an incomplete monetary union, but is not efficient. One currency with a unique exchange rate plus hard budget constraints on national public finances and no compensating mechanisms causes the economic performance of countries with different systems and in different situations to diverge significantly (Chart 1).[24] This effect is enlarged by the free flow of financial resources which, following the international crisis, went through a sudden stop and escaped risky vulnerable countries.

[24] Vulnerable countries (VULN) in Chart 1 are those member countries of the EU which, due to their difficult economic or financial position (such as having an uncompetitive economy expressed by sizeable current account deficits, or being in an unbalanced macroeconomic or financial situation, or both), need to strengthen and adjust their situation by means of policies. However, they miss policy sovereignty to do so following their membership in an incomplete monetary union. Conversely, resilient countries (RESIL) have balanced finances and competitive economies and do not need policies to adjust their economies. In the chart, vulnerable countries are Cyprus, Greece, Ireland, Italy, Portugal, Spain. Resilient countries are Austria, Belgium, Finland, France, Germany, Luxembourg, the Netherlands.

Chart 1. Quarterly GDP, Percentage change over previous period (Q4 2007=100)

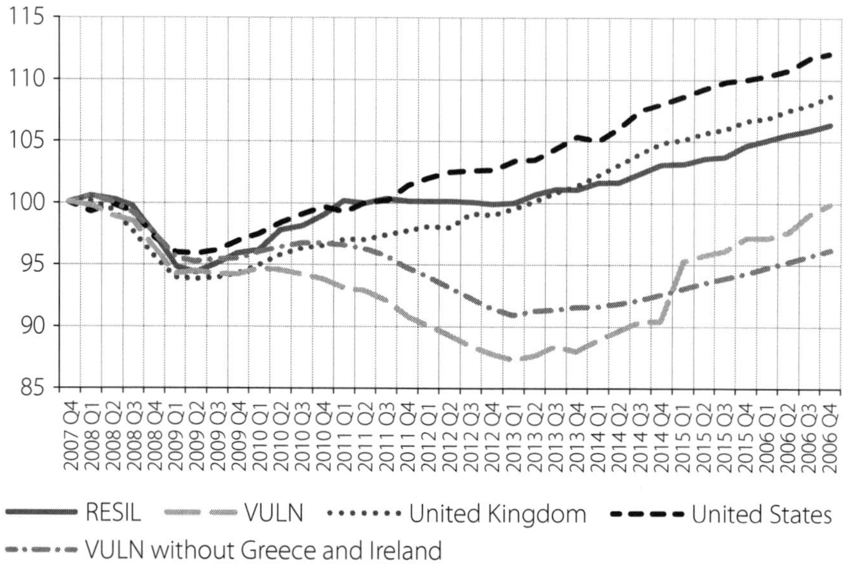

Source: Own calculation based on Eurostat data

Looking at the post-crisis policy proposals which circulate in the Eurozone, it may appear that there may be two different and competing approaches. For simplicity, I'll call one the mainstream policy approach and the other one the neo-Keynesian policy approach. The mainstream policy approach privileges a restrictive reading of the Eurozone paradigm, strongly influenced by the ordoliberal perspective, stressing the need to have balanced finances in each member country.[25] It also succeeded in escaping the establishment of a Eurozone stabilization fund to avoid the threat of political bargaining, thus relying on the IMF for stabilization purposes until the ECB decided to act in 2012, when the ECB's president Draghi pronounced his famous "whatever it takes" speech. While having balanced national finances is fundamental for the ongoing cooperation and trust among the member countries of an incomplete monetary union, such balance can be reached in different ways: by imposing

[25] See Hans-Werner Sinn, *The Euro Trap: On Bursting Bubbles, Budgets, and Beliefs* (Oxford: Oxford University Press, 2014).

a hard budget constraint in the short run or by balancing finances in the long run through growth and competitiveness. So far, the mainstream approach failed to balance finances and promote growth, while the flows of private resources among member countries often promoted the creation of financial and real estate bubbles and, after the crisis, fled distressed vulnerable countries. Thus, this reading of the Eurozone paradigm actually boils down to the short-run interest of financial stability.

Dissimilarly, the neo-Keynesian policy approach, particularly after the start of the crisis, proposes that public budgets are used to revitalize growth.[26] This means easing convergence parameters. It also supposes that countries, particularly resilient ones, agree to extend joint support to vulnerable countries, based on trust and without any threat of moral hazard, thus de facto easing their budget constraint.[27] In this, they overlook the fact that vulnerable countries typically failed to reform and stabilize their economies in due time and delayed reforms afterwards, although alternative explanations for this inability stress important institutional differences.[28]

A more reasonable alternative was requiring that surplus countries, Germany in particular, expand their domestic demand to create domestic expansion and, in this way, create similar chances for vulnerable economies. A particular version of this approach was proposed by the US Department of Treasury, which strongly criticized Germany for failing to do so while continuing to pursue a sizeable current account surplus.[29] Kornai stressed the

---

[26] Hansjörg Herr, Jan Priewe, and Andrew Watt, eds., *Saving the Euro: Redesigning Euro Area economic governance* (SE Publishing, 2017), https://www.socialeurope.eu/book/saving-euro-redesigning-euro-area-economic-governance.

[27] On the consequences of the soft budget constraint, see János Kornai, "The Soft Budget Constraint: An Introductory Study to Volume IV of the Life's Work Series," *Acta Oeconomica* 64, no. 1 (2014): 25–79.

[28] Alison Johnston and Aidan Regan, "European Monetary Integration and the Incompatibility of National Varieties of Capitalism," *Journal of Common Market Studies* 54, no. 2 (2016): 318–336; Andreas Nölke, "Economic Causes of the Eurozone Crisis: the Analytical Contribution of Comparative Capitalism," *Socio-Economic Review* 14, no. 1 (2016): 141–161.

[29] US Department of Treasury, *Report to Congress on International Economic and Exchange Rate Policies* (Washington, DC: US Department of the Treasury, Office of International Affairs, 2013), https://www.treasury.gov/resource-center/international/exchange-rate-policies/Documents/2013-10-30_FULL%20FX%20REPORT_FINAL.pdf.

importance of this approach for countries pursuing a combination of financial discipline, growth, and competition with institutional transformation.[30]

As a matter of facts, given the Eurozone paradigm and system, there really was no free policy choice and mainstream policies dominated easily. Deficit spending at the national level is simply not viable in an incomplete monetary union, because this would have exported problems to all the other countries. Yet more could have been done at the Eurozone level to provide better coordination, give support for reforms in vulnerable countries, and set up common resources for supporting countries with liquidity problems, even on the shaky construction of the Eurozone. However, the real challenge has been to balance and complete the Eurozone paradigm and system and promote transformation of vulnerable countries.

The Eurozone system

The international financial crisis revealed that the Eurozone paradigm was dangerously unbalanced and incomplete; the kind of Eurozone cooperation and instruments it foresaw were insufficient and should have been urgently developed. This was apparently recognized by such an odd couple as Wolfgang Schäuble and Yanis Varoufakis, the German and Greek finance ministers in 2015, respectively.[31] The Eurozone problem has two components. First, when a political or economic formation—be it an empire, an economy, or a transnational company—includes parts which are different or operate in different contexts, unique and uniform central decisions have asymmetric effects. Second, asymmetric effects foster the aspiration of the parts for autonomy. To avoid negative consequences, countries should either converge their institutions and economic situations or countervailing mechanisms should be set up to balance negative outcomes.

Decentralization—federalism or multi-divisional organization—is the typical solution keeping only strategic decisions in the hands of the center (e.g., a central government, CEO). This solution is apt to support the integra-

---

[30] János Kornai, *The Road to a Free Economy: Shifting from a Socialist System: The Example of Hungary* (New York: W. W. Norton; Budapest: HVG Kiadó, 1990).

[31] Dani Rodrik, "Does Europe Really Need Fiscal and Political Union?" *Social Europe*, January 8, 2018, https://www.socialeurope.eu/europe-really-need-fiscal-political-union.

tion of markets or customs unions, which require only few common norms (e.g., avoiding state help to firms or practices of unfair competition). A monetary union is more demanding and the challenge for the Eurozone is to combine the advantages of the common currency with the historical legacy of countries keeping political, economic, and social idiosyncrasies. Money needs one unique central institution for all countries. Yet money cuts across the board in that it influences all economic (and social and political) activities of a country.

Given its nature, a system should be complete. Indeed, the overall system of Eurozone countries is complete, although made of two incomplete systems: the national system and the common Eurozone system. Hence, the allocation of precise competences and the coordination between the two levels are fundamental and the risks of ambiguity, overlapping, and conflicts are pervasive. Unfortunately, the two partial systems are at mutual odds in case of many, mostly vulnerable countries.

The common level includes monetary institutions and organs, identical for all Eurozone member countries. Moreover, the EU has exclusive competence in a number of important fields, while in other fields it coordinates and supports national competences. Finally, various competences are shared with national governments. National governments continue to be sovereign in important fields (e.g., welfare, employment, legal matters, the pension system, police, administration) and also informal institutions are national or local.[32]

An important issue in this construction is the nature of common institutions and the distance of national institutions from the common paradigm.[33] The larger the difference, the greater are problems, difficulties and costs of national adaptation and compliance. Being the mandate of the ECB quite restrictive and the convergence parameters in the spirit of German ordoliberalism, it is easy to infer that countries used to have a national central bank with a broader mandate and less stringent policy making should have more problems, difficulties and costs in complying with the Eurozone paradigm. These are mostly vulnerable countries. Only the political determination to cooperate helped the working of the dual level system.

[32] Dallago, *One Currency, Two Europes*.

[33] The author has recently started a research project together with Sara Casagrande at the Department of Economics and Management at the University of Trento on measuring the distance.

If institutions were irrelevant and markets perfect, having a unified and effective system would be unimportant. If there were no transaction costs to economic activity, if resources were perfectly mobile and substitutable, if the allocation of resources were always to the socially most productive use, if national borders were not mattering, if countries were sharing exactly the same goals and ideals, if decision makers were perfectly rational and forward-looking, then the Eurozone were a perfect optimum currency area (OCA) and systemic incompleteness or differences would be irrelevant. Even an imperfect OCA such as the United States—a country with an effective common government—fares clearly better than the Eurozone (Chart 2).[34]

Chart 2. Optimum currency areas compared

OCA criterion	Eurozone	United States
Labor mobility[35]	Low	Yes
Trade openness[36]	Yes	Yes
Product diversification[37]	Yes	Yes
Fiscal transfers	Low	Yes
Homogeneity of preferences	Partial	Yes
Commonality of destiny	Partial	Yes

Source: Own elaboration

[34] Robert Mundell considers that asymmetric shocks do not undermine the common currency, which acts as a shock absorber. Indeed, the currency union spreads the shocks by allowing the negatively hit region or country to rely on the resources of the rest of the union, thus spreading the effect of the shock over a much larger area. However, this requires at least coordinated and complementary policies.

[35] Robert Mundell, "Uncommon Arguments for Common Currencies," in *The Economics of Common Currencies*, ed. Harry G. Johnson and Alexander K. Swoboda (London: Routledge, 1973), 114–132.

[36] Ronald McKinnon, "Optimum Currency Areas," *American Economic Review*, 53, (September 1963): 717–724.

[37] Peter Kenen, "The Theory of Optimum Currency Areas: An Eclectic View," in *Monetary Problems of the International Economy*, ed. Robert Mundell and Alexander K. Swoboda (Chicago: University of Chicago Press, 1969), 41–60.

In the Eurozone, then, the smooth and effective working of the economic system is all the more important. Institutional and systemic analysis contributed to show that it is different institutions and systems that cause different economic behavior, including fiscal behavior.[38] Under these conditions, the need to place the common currency under the unique formal Eurozone paradigm must disadvantage the countries whose national economic system is further from the Eurozone system paradigm. This raises the question of whether the Eurozone should promote the convergence of national systems to the Eurozone system paradigm, through harder budget constraints or else, or transfer additional national competences to the Eurozone level, so to complete the Eurozone system or find more flexible instruments to support the two levels' cooperation.[39]

The internal divergence of an unbalanced Eurozone

The problem, then, is how to deal with this disadvantage in a construction that lacks political union.[40] This case of implicit discrimination, a discrimina-

---

[38] Joachim Ahrens, Rainer Schweickert, and Juliane Zenker, "Varieties of Capitalism and Government Spending in Developed and Developing Countries," *Journal of Economic Development* 40, no. 1 (2015): 113–136; Peter A. Hall, and David W. Soskice, eds., *Varieties of Capitalism: The Institutional Foundations of Comparative Advantage* (Oxford: Oxford University Press, 2001); Alison Johnston and Aidan Regan, "European Monetary Integration and the Incompatibility of National Varieties of Capitalism"; Andreas Nölke, "Economic Causes of the Eurozone Crisis: the Analytical Contribution of Comparative Capitalism"; David W. Soskice, "Macroeconomics and Varieties of Capitalism," in *Beyond Varieties of Capitalism*, ed. Bob Hancké, Martin Rhodes, and Mark Thatcher (Oxford: Oxford University Press, 2007), 89–121.

[39] Dani Rodrik presents an interesting analysis on the necessity for a sustainable globalization to allow for national institutional differences, although he admits that the EU can provide an exception and can lead to institutional convergence. See Dani Rodrik, *The Globalization Paradox: Democracy and the Future of the World Economy* (New York: W.W. Norton, 2011).

[40] The literature on transplanted institutions offers an interesting hint on this mechanism. It shows that the introduction of alien institutions renders an economic system unbalanced and ineffective, which causes inefficiency of economic activity. While this analysis refers usually to former colonies, the process is similar in many ways to what happens in the Eurozone: without external colonization, but voluntarily submitting countries to alien institutions. See Rafael La Porta, Florencio Lopez-de-Silanes, and Andrei Shleifer, "The Economic Consequences of Legal Origin," *Journal of Economic Literature* 46, no. 2 (2008): 285–332.

tion that is "*unintentional* and outside of the discriminator's awareness,"[41] has real consequences. Economies further from the Eurozone paradigm (i.e., vulnerable economies) meet an internal appreciation of the real exchange rate, among other unfavorable and favorable effects, such as lower interest rates. In order to avoid jeopardizing their competitiveness in the short run, they can only use internal devaluation (i.e., decrease directly wages and other costs). This shrinks the domestic market and weakens incentives, an effect which exports can compensate only in small open economies. Hence the divergence of economic performance compared to resilient countries may become permanent.

Economic systems and economies may change, though. Italy and Germany provide good examples in a way that is opposite to the present situation. In the 1950s and the 1960s, the Italian Lira was a strong and stable currency, able to keep a fixed exchange rate within the Bretton Woods system.[42] Moreover, until mid-1960s, when full employment was reached, wages increased less than productivity and prices were stable. The following years were different, and the drift of the Italian economy became evident particularly in the 1980s. Since then, the Italian economy met clear and growing difficulties in complying with the Eurozone rules. The fair success in stabilizing public finances did not translate into economic growth, while attempted reforms had scant outcomes in improving economic performance.

In 1999, *The Economist* labelled Germany as the "sick man of the euro."[43] However, the German economy improved remarkably in the following years, mainly thanks to the reforms of 2003–2005. This suggests a possible solution of the present dichotomy within the Eurozone between vulnerable and resilient countries: reforms and investment in due consideration of the conditions that determine when such reforms and investments can be successful. Why did they work in Germany and not in Italy?

[41] Marianne Bertrand, Dolly Chugh, and Sendhil Mullainathan, "Implicit Discrimination," *American Economic Review Papers and Proceedings* 95, no. 2 (2005): 94.

[42] An international committee established by the Financial Times declared the lira as the best currency of 1960. Giorgio Mori, "L'economia italiana del dopoguerra," in *Storia della economia mondiale*, vol. 10, ed. Valerio Castronovo (Rome and Milan: Editori Laterza-Il Sole 24 Ore, 2009), 288.

[43] "The Sick Man of the Euro," *The Economist*, June 3, 1999, https://www.economist.com/node/209559.

Reforms are often problematic for different reasons:[44] they may create uncertainty, cause too many losers, or impose sacrifices and costs in the short run in exchange for unknown advantages and gains in the long run. This may create a complex problem of collective action that may be overcome by external pressure and/or support (Greece), the reputation of reformers and a cohesive society (Germany), and the existence or lack of devices and structures, such as a well-developed and financially sound welfare system attenuating social costs (Germany, the Netherlands, Scandinavian countries). The lack or ineffectiveness of any of these factors is likely to slow down reforms or frustrate the effort (Italy).

In the Eurozone, reforms meet additional problems: they should concern both common and national institutions and their costs and benefits may be distributed differently among member countries. Particularly important is that countries having to reform the most, because they are farther away the Eurozone paradigm, are the countries that were more accustomed to make more intensive use of devices excluded from the Eurozone paradigm, in particular the exchange rate adjustment. They are also the ones which suffered the most losses due to the crisis and are under the most severe financial constraints.

Structural reforms are fundamental, since they address impediments to the fundamental drivers of growth by unshackling labor, product, and service markets, foster job creation, investment, and productivity, as the EU and international organizations stress.[45] The problem is that in policy practice

---

44 See János Kornai, "The Hungarian Reform Process: Visions, Hopes and Reality," *Journal of Economic Literature* 24, no. 4 (1986): 1687–1737, and his many publications on transformation in Central-Eastern Europe. For an interesting political economy analysis of reforms, see Frank Bönker, *The Political Economy of Fiscal Reform in Central-Eastern Europe: Hungary, Poland and the Czech Republic from 1989 to EU Accession* (Cheltenham: Edward Elgar, 2006); and Katharina Müller, *The Political Economy of Pension Reform in Central-Eastern Europe* (Cheltenham: Edward Elgar, 1999).

45 European Commission, "Structural Reforms," Brussels: Economic and Financial Affairs, European Commission, 2015, http://ec.europa.eu/economy_finance/structural_reforms/index_en.htm; see also Alberto Alesina, Silvia Ardagna, and Vincenzo Galasso, "The Euro and Structural Reforms," NBER Working Paper no. 14479, National Bureau of Economic Research, Cambridge, MA, November 2008, http://www.nber.org/papers/w14479; Erik Canton et al., "The Role of Structural Reform for Adjustment and Growth," *ECFIN Economic Brief* 34 (June 2014), http://ec.europa.eu/economy_finance/publications/economic_briefs/2014/pdf/eb34_en.pdf.

the accent is placed on changes to the labor market or the pension system in order to decrease costs and public expenditures, and ease dismissals. There is no clear evidence that these changes improve the microeconomic efficiency and effectiveness of European economies, particularly so for late comers in reforms. Moreover, these changes contribute to decreases in the size of the domestic market and worsen incentives and the economic, social, and political mood of most consumers and may fire back in politics.

Other reforms, in particular decreasing transaction costs (e.g., administrative costs and costs of contract enforcement) and decreasing the tax wedge over economic activity (including broadening the tax base through fighting tax evasion) are mentioned, but are rarely the focus of policymaking. Other important reforms are improving productivity by more and better investment and organization, liberalization and competition, research and development, improving the quality of human capital, strengthening innovation, including social innovation, better infrastructure, leaner and more efficient public administration, more effective justice, fighting corruption and tax evasion. These were important components of the Lisbon strategy and play an important role in the Europe 2020 strategy, so far without much actual importance, let alone priority. The problem, then, is not with reforms, but with the mix of reforms that is required and the priority attached to them.

The restrictive meaning attached to structural reforms means giving top priority to financial stability over long run convergence of all member countries to the Eurozone paradigm and economic performance. The pressure on vulnerable countries to implement structural reforms, including their being part of conditionality packages in exchange for financial support, may be important to overcome national stalemate and foot dragging. However, the pressure led to disregard the more fundamental need for institutional reforms, such as the efficiency of markets and the public administration. Indeed, these reforms became even more difficult, since the necessary financial resources are lacking and the citizens are less receptive.

Conclusion: the way forward

It is useful to summarize the conclusions reached so far, taking the perspective of Kornai's systemic analysis. First, the construction of the Eurozone is insecure because it is based on an unbalanced and incomplete paradigm. Second, policy action and coordination among countries is problematic and often ineffective because there is no complete Eurozone economic system. The actual system is a hybrid of common and national components that often do not fit well together and create different mixes in different countries. Third, the ways in which the Eurozone was constructed and works causes implicit discrimination to the disadvantage of vulnerable countries, which have no alternative instruments to compensate for their disadvantage. Fourth, macroeconomic adjustment was left largely, if not exclusively, to vulnerable countries. Eurozone coordination and cooperation in reforms ailed, while, after the crisis, short-term perspectives and priorities linked only to financial stability took hold. Fifth, while vulnerable countries tried to free ride on Eurozone advantages, resilient countries did not provide leadership in the form of policies compatible with the common good, and even provided even less in the form of support—nor did the European Commission act in a sufficiently strong manner in the field of support for growth, with the partial exception of the European investment plan implemented since 2015.[46] The outcome was a prolonged "transitional recession" in vulnerable countries similar to the effect of reforms and structural change with no growth policies in transition countries noticed by Kornai.[47]

These problems did not go unnoticed by Eurozone organs and national governments. In the last two years, many projects were advanced and efforts were implemented, often in an episodic and contradictory way, in good part out of line with Kornai's perspective. For some time, the main approach was muddling through: extend the flexibility existing in the treaties as much as possible, softening the stringency of convergence parameters, taking into consideration exceptional circumstances to postpone the required compliance with fiscal parameters. The institutional architecture was not modified, but the implementation of the budget constraint was somehow postponed and accompanied by moral suasion and peer pressure more than by administrative sanctions. Also, fiscal policies in the Eurozone became mildly expansionary

46 Grégory Claeys, André Sapir, and Guntram B. Wolff, "Juncker's Investment Plan: No Risk—No Return," *Bruegel*, November 28, 2014; Reinhilde Veugelers, "The Achilles' Heel of Juncker's Investment Plan," *Bruegel*, December 8, 2014. See also, European Commission, "Investment Plan for Europe: the Juncker Plan," https://ec.europa.eu/priorities/jobs-growth-and-investment/investment-plan_en.

47 János Kornai, "Transformational Recession: The Main Causes," *Journal of Comparative Economics* 19, no. 1 (1994): 39–63.

since 2014,[48] thus supporting the strongly expansionary monetary policy implemented by the ECB. These contradictory moves were unable to move the Eurozone out of its prolonged instability and dismal performance, as Kornai's approach predicts. However, the mild softening of national budget constraints gained some time to look for more consistent and effective solutions.

Action for institutional completion was most noticeable, although not uncontested, in the monetary sector. Not only did the ECB take on the role of lender of last resort for private banks. The ECB also became a quasi-lender of last resort to governments with liquidity problems, albeit through the secondary market. Long postponed institutions and organs of full monetary unification started to be created. Following the single rulebook prepared by the European Commission, a single supervisory mechanism (SSM) and a single resolution mechanism (SRM) for banks were set up starting from 2014. These are important steps for the banking union, which gave the ECB new roles for pursuing greater transparency, lower risk, and stronger stability for European banks. However, the European deposit insurance scheme is still to come.

Action resumed also in the direction of creating a unified European capital market in order to overcome its persisting national character and help the development of a more complete and consistent Eurozone system. The crisis caused the accumulation of massive amounts of non-performing loans (NPL) at commercial banks, both because of mismanagement of banks and the inability of many borrowers to honor their duties.[49] This phenomenon jeopardizes the solvency of many banks and, consequently, economies and governments, since commercial banks own a significant share of public debt of their country. To deal with this problem, the proposal of establishing a European Asset Management Company for NPLs was advanced and is being discussed.

These moves are largely out of tune with Kornai's perspective, being they weakly coordinated in the direction of a complete Eurozone system. The

48 European Commission, *Towards a Positive Fiscal Stance for the Euro Area* (Brussels: European Commission, 2016), https://ec.europa.eu/info/publications/2017-european-semester-communication-fiscal-stance_en.

49 The amount of NPLs is estimated at 7 percent of EU GDP and 5.4 percent of bank loans, but in 10 countries this latter amount exceeds 10 percent. See European Commission, *First Progress Report on the Reduction of Non-Performing Loans in Europe* (Brussels: European Commission, 2018), http://eur-lex.europa.eu/legal-content/EN/TXT/PDF/?uri=CELEX:52018SC0033R(01)&from=EN.

move that better incorporates Korai's perspective—consistently combining fiscal rigor with support for growth and institutional reform in a long-term perspective—came in late 2017. The Commission presented new documents that suggest a more consistent, better coordinated and ambitious way to move ahead. The European Commission Roadmap presented on December 6, 2017, looks particularly important.[50] The Roadmap foresees progress in three areas: financial union, economic and fiscal union, and democratic accountability and governance. The core of the financial union is the completion of the banking union by mid-2019, including risk reduction, a European deposit insurance scheme, and a single resolution fund. The agenda also foresees a framework for European sovereign bond-backed securities for the Eurozone within 2018 and finalizing all pending legislative initiatives for the capital markets union by mid-2019.

Writing in the final quarter of 2019, it appears that institutional progress lost impetus and new complexities and difficulties appeared. The uncertainty created by growing political concerns and inter-country divergences, the results of the May 2019 elections for the new European Parliament, the appointment of the new von der Leyen Commission and the bumpy negotiations for the implementation of Brexit have slowed down reform processes and partly diverted attention to political issues. Only the process for appointing the new ECB President entering office at the end of Mario Draghi's term on October 31, 2019 did not slow down the ECB action. The appointment of Christine Lagarde as the incoming president apparently had an invigorating effect on the ECB role.

The reform agenda looks more prudent in the institutional economic field than envisaged in the Roadmap and is overlapping with complex and urgent political priorities (such as setting up migration policies), divergent inter-country aims, worsening economic situation, debate over the next EU budget for 2021–2027 and the economic and political consequences of Brexit. However, important reforms in the economic and fiscal union proceed, albeit at a slower pace. These include structural reform support, dedicated convergence facility for non-Euro member countries, the establishment of a European monetary fund and a European minister of economy and finance.

[50] European Commission, *The Commission's Roadmap for Deepening Europe's Economic and Monetary Union* (Brussels: European Commission, 2017), https://ec.europa.eu/commission/news/deepening-europes-economic-and-monetary-union-2017-dec-06_en.

Neither of these fundamental issues reached a no-return stage, yet they continue to be on the agenda and slow steps towards their implementation continue. More important, the political determination seems to be alive.

The Roadmap represents clear progress in the completion of the economic and monetary union. Yet, there are some critical issues: the actual power and role of the European minister, the amount and use of the resources the minister will manage, the conditions attached to their use, the features and management of the European monetary fund, the way in which the fiscal compact will be incorporated into EU law, whether there will be sufficient support for structural reforms in member countries and at which conditions. There are strikingly dissimilar proposals on the floor presently, which would lead each to significantly different Eurozones: a compromise is clearly necessary. This will obviously require more time than envisaged in the Roadmap, but nevertheless the existence of a plan is important in Kornai's consistent approach.

While Kornai does not deal directly with the European Union and the Eurozone, his approach and method are important for understanding the reasons of the Eurozone's difficulties and for finding solutions. The most important teachings that can be taken from Kornai's work in reference to the Eurozone problems can be summarized as follows. First, the comprehensiveness of the system paradigm is fundamental, as much as system completeness and consistency. To do this, a form of political union seems necessary, a request that descends from the relevance that Kornai gives to politics in his analyses. Second, keeping a sufficiently hard budget constraint in the long-run is fundamental, as much as growth policies and innovation. The economic and monetary union has been rather far away from this perspective and this helps to explain its lack of economic dynamism, its financial vulnerability, and political and social problems. The recent initiatives apparently go in a direction that opens up hopes of a better and stronger correspondence with Kornai's perspective and the problems that the Eurozone has to solve. It is yet to be seen whether the political will and courage of member countries and common organs are sufficiently strong to this end. The key of the future of the Eurozone is more in politics than economics.

References

Ahrens, Joachim, Rainer Schweickert, and Juliane Zenker. "Varieties of Capitalism and Government Spending in Developed and Developing Countries." *Journal of Economic Development* 40, no. 1 (2015): 113–136.

Alesina, Alberto, Silvia Ardagna, and Vincenzo Galasso. "The Euro and Structural Reforms." NBER Working Paper no. 14479, National Bureau of Economic Research, Cambridge, MA, November 2008. http://www.nber.org/papers/w14479.

Bertrand, Marianne, Dolly Chugh, and Sendhil Mullainathan. "Implicit Discrimination." *American Economic Review Papers and Proceedings* 95, no. 2 (2005): 94–98.

Bönker, Frank. *The Political Economy of Fiscal Reform in Central-Eastern Europe: Hungary, Poland and the Czech Republic from 1989 to EU Accession*. Cheltenham: Edward Elgar, 2006.

Canton, Erik, Isabel Grilo, Josefina Monteagudo, Fabiana Pierini, and Alessandro Turrini. "The Role of Structural Reform for Adjustment and Growth." *ECFIN Economic Brief* 34 (June 2014). http://ec.europa.eu/economy_finance/publications/economic_briefs/2014/pdf/eb34_en.pdf.

Claeys, Grégory, André Sapir, and Guntram B. Wolff. "Juncker's Investment Plan: No Risk—No Return." *Bruegel*, November 28, 2014.

Council—Commission of the European Communities. *Report to the Council and the Commission on the Realisation by Stages of Economic and Monetary Union in the Community*. Luxembourg, 1970. http://aei.pitt.edu/1002/1/monetary_werner_final.pdf.

Dallago, Bruno. *One Currency, Two Europes*. Singapore: World Scientific Publishing Co., 2016.

European Commission. *First Progress Report on the Reduction of Non-Performing Loans in Europe*. Brussels: European Commission, 2018. http://eur-lex.europa.eu/legal-content/EN/TXT/PDF/?uri=CELEX:52018SC0033R(01)&from=EN.

European Commission. *Rome Declaration of the Leaders of 27 Member States and of the European Council, the European Parliament and the European Commission*. Brussels: European Commission, 2017. http://europa.eu/rapid/press-release_STATEMENT-17-767_en.htm.

European Commission. "Structural Reforms." Economic and Financial Affairs, European Commission, 2015. http://ec.europa.eu/economy_finance/structural_reforms/index_en.htm.

European Commission. *The Commission's Roadmap for Deepening Europe's Economic and Monetary Union*. Brussels: European Commission, 2017. https://ec.europa.eu/commission/news/deepening-europes-economic-and-monetary-union-2017-dec-06_en.

European Commission. *Towards a Positive Fiscal Stance for the Euro Area*. Brussels: European Commission, 2016. https://ec.europa.eu/info/publications/2017-european-semester-communication-fiscal-stance_en.

European Council. *Report on Economic and Monetary Union in the European Community*. Brussels: Committee for the Study of Economic and Monetary Union, 1989. http://ec.europa.eu/economy_finance/publications/publication6161_en.pdf.

Feldmann, Horst. “From Initiating to Breaching to Diluting the Stability and Growth Pact.” In *Germany’s Economic Performance: From Unification to Euroization*, edited by Jens Hölscher, 134–136. Houndmills–Basingstoke: Palgrave Macmillan, 2007.

Hall, Peter A., and David W. Soskice, eds. *Varieties of Capitalism: The Institutional Foundations of Comparative Advantage*. Oxford: Oxford University Press, 2001.

Herr, Hansjörg, Jan Priewe, and Andrew Watt, eds. *Saving the Euro: Redesigning Euro Area Economic Governance*. SE Publishing, 2017. https://www.socialeurope.eu/book/saving-euro-redesigning-euro-area-economic-governance.

Johnston, Alison, and Aidan Regan. “European Monetary Integration and the Incompatibility of National Varieties of Capitalism.” *Journal of Common Market Studies* 54, no. 2 (2016): 318–336.

Kenen, Peter, “The Theory of Optimum Currency Areas: An Eclectic View.” In *Monetary Problems of the International Economy*, edited by Robert Mundell and Alexander K. Swoboda, 41-60. Chicago: University of Chicago Press, 1969.

Kornai, János. “The Hungarian Reform Process: Visions, Hopes and Reality.” *Journal of Economic Literature* 24, no. 4 (1986): 1687–1737.

———. *The Road to a Free Economy: Shifting from a Socialist System. The Example of Hungary*. New York: W. W. Norton; Budapest: HVG Kiadó, 1990.

———. *The Socialist System: The Political Economy of Communism*. Princeton: Princeton University Press, 1992.

———. “The Soft Budget Constraint: An Introductory Study to Volume IV of the Life’s Work Series.” *Acta Oeconomica* 64, no. 1 (2014): 25–79.

———. “The System Paradigm.” In *Paradigms of Social Change: Modernization, Development, Transformation, Evolution*, edited by Waltraud Schekle, Wolf-Hagen Krauth, Martin Kohli and Georg Elwert, 111–33. Frankfurt and New York: Campus Verlag; New York: St. Martin’s, 2000.

———. “The System Paradigm Revisited: Clarifications and Additions in the Light of Experiences in the Post-socialist Region.” *Acta Oeconomica* 66, no. 4 (2016): 547–596. Republished in *Revue d’études comparatives Est-Ouest* 48, no. 1–2 (2017): 239–296.

———. “Transformational Recession: The Main Causes.” *Journal of Comparative Economics* 19, no. 1 (1994): 39–63.

La Porta, Rafael, Florencio Lopez-de-Silanes, and Andrei Shleifer. “The Economic Consequences of Legal Origin.” *Journal of Economic Literature* 46, no. 2 (2008): 285–332.

McKinnon, Ronald (1963), “Optimum Currency Areas,” *American Economic Review*, 53, (September): 717–724.

Moravcsik, Andrew. “The Myth of Europe’s Democratic Deficit.” *Intereconomics: Journal of European Public Policy* (November–December 2008): 331–340.

Mori, Giorgio. “L’economia italiana del dopoguerra.” In *Storia della economia mondiale*, vol. 10, edited by Valerio Castronovo, 265–298. Rome and Milan: Editori Laterza-Il Sole 24 Ore, 2009.

Müller, Katharina. *The Political Economy of Pension Reform in Central-Eastern Europe*. Cheltenham: Edward Elgar, 1999.

Mundell, Robert. “Uncommon Arguments for Common Currencies.” In *The Economics of Common Currencies*, edited by Harry G. Johnson and Alexander K. Swoboda, 114–132. London: Routledge, 1973.

Ngai, Victor. "Stability and Growth Pact and Fiscal Discipline in the Eurozone." *Working Papers,* no. 12–10, University of Pennsylvania, Wharton School, Weiss Center, 2012. https://ideas.repec.org/p/ecl/upafin/12-10.html.

Nölke, Andreas. "Economic Causes of the Eurozone Crisis: the Analytical Contribution of Comparative Capitalism." *Socio-Economic Review* 14, no. 1 (2016): 141–161.

Piattoni, Simona. "The European Crisis: Testing the Trust Foundations of an Economic and Monetary Union." In *A Global Perspective on the European Economic Crisis*, edited by Bruno Dallago, Gert Guri, and John McGowan, 79–95. Abingdon, Oxfordshire: Routledge, 2016.

Rodrik, Dani. "Does Europe Really Need Fiscal and Political Union?" *Social Europe*, January 8, 2018. https://www.socialeurope.eu/europe-really-need-fiscal-political-union.

———. *The Globalization Paradox: Democracy and the Future of the World Economy.* New York: W.W. Norton, 2011.

Savona, Paolo. *Come un incubo e come un sogno*. Soveria Mannelli: Rubbettino, 2018.

Sinn, Hans-Werner. *The Euro Trap: On Bursting Bubbles, Budgets, and Beliefs*. Oxford: Oxford University Press, 2014.

Soskice, David W. "Macroeconomics and Varieties of Capitalism." In *Beyond Varieties of Capitalism*, edited by Bob Hancké, Martin Rhodes, and Mark Thatcher, 89–121. Oxford: Oxford University Press, 2007.

Stiglitz, Joseph E. *The Euro: How a Common Currency Threatens the Future of Europe.* New York: W.W. Norton, 2016.

US Department of Treasury. *Report to Congress on International Economic and Exchange Rate Policies*. Washington, DC: US Department of the Treasury, Office of International Affairs, 2013. https://www.treasury.gov/resource-center/international/exchange-rate-policies/Documents/2013-10-30_FULL%20FX%20REPORT_FINAL.pdf.

Veugelers, Reinhilde. "The Achilles' Heel of Juncker's Investment Plan." *Bruegel*, December 8, 2014.

Zoppè, Alice. *Implementation of the Macroeconomic Imbalance Procedure: State-of Play*. Brussels: European Parliament, Economic Governance Support Unit, September 2019. http://www.europarl.europa.eu/RegData/etudes/IDAN/2016/497739/IPOL_IDA(2016)497739_EN.pdf.

Independent Fiscal Institutions

"New Kids on the Block" in Economic Policy

László Jankovics *

Introduction

Fiscal rules and independent fiscal institutions (IFIs) have recently emerged as complementary institutions to address deficit bias and, more generally, pro-cyclical policy stances. While fiscal rules were typically introduced first, a growing awareness of disappointing outcomes in terms of enforcement put the spotlight on the potential benefits of independent bodies. Also, through their continuous monitoring of numerical rules, IFIs are expected to promote transparency and accountability, thereby reducing information asymmetries and raising the quality of fiscal policy debates. The significance of involving IFIs in the budgetary processes has been increasingly acknowledged both by the economic literature and policy-makers in the recent years, in particular in EU member states.

IFIs differ significantly from one country to another in terms of the set-up, mandate, resources, degree of visibility, etc., reflecting differences in national political, administrative, and budgetary arrangements. In his introductory remarks at the spring 2010 international conference "The Role of Independent Fiscal Institutions," organized by the first Fiscal Council of Hungary, János Kornai elaborated his views on the suitable set-up for IFIs.[1] He emphasized the

* The views expressed in the article are solely those of the author, and do not necessarily reflect the official position of the European Commission.

[1] János Kornai, "Opening Remarks," Conference on Independent Fiscal Institutions, Budapest, March 18, 2010. Subsequently published as idem., "Where is the Line

importance of limiting the mandate of IFIs in the sphere of positive economics, and to refrain from assigning these bodies a normative remit or formal competences (such as veto rights), as the executions of these latter functions would necessarily involve value judgments, which should be reserved for elected politicians.[2] In the area of positive economics, he identified three crucial tasks that should stand at the core of the operation of IFIs (without any order of importance): (1) Analyzing the consistency of planned fiscal measures with the available fiscal space, (2) policy costing, and (3) enhancing the transparency of public finances. As all countries with an IFI have at least one numerical rule in force, the firstly mentioned task is tantamount to checking the *ex ante* compliance with fiscal rules since fiscal elbow room could be defined as the gap between targeted and projected fiscal variables.

This paper will investigate to what extent the existing IFIs in the European Union match the advice of Professor Kornai about the key design features of such institutions.[3] The geographical coverage has been limited to the EU for three main reasons: (1) the knowledge constraints of the author, (2) extensive information in a comparable format are only available on IFIs in

between Independent Economic Analysis and Active Policy Making? The Example of the Independent Fiscal Councils," *Acta Oeconomica* 60, no. 3 (2010): 249–254.

[2] The desirability of a clear and transparent delineation of the potential roles taken up by economists in public life (e.g., decision-makers, advisers, academics focusing on positive research) is a recurrently expressed conviction in the works of János Kornai. See János Kornai, "Ten Years after 'The Road to a Free Economy': The Author's Self-evaluation," in *Annual World Bank Conference on Development Economics 2000*, ed. B. Pleskovic and N. Stern (Washington: World Bank, 2001), 49–66; or János Kornai, "György Surányi, Governor of the MNB—Through the Eyes of a Former Member of the Central Bank Council" [Surányi György, az MNB elnöke—egy egykori jegybanktanács-tag szemével], in *Surányi György hatvanéves*, ed. K. Sebestyén (Budapest: Pénzügykutató Alapítvány, 2014), 110–122, for a more recent example.

[3] Information contained in this paper derives from several sources, in particular the relevant section of the European Commission's Fiscal Governance database, the IMF's Fiscal Council Dataset, the OECD's case studies, IFI's own websites, as well as the Commission's report on the transposition of the Fiscal Compact, which includes subsections on all national monitoring institutions. For a relevant OECD case study, see Lisa von Trapp, Ian Lienert, and Joachim Wehner, "Principles for Independent Fiscal Institutions and Case Studies," *OECD Journal of Budgeting*, no. 2 (Paris: Organisation for Economic Cooperation and Development, 2016). Also see European Commission, *Report from the Commission presented under Article 8 of the Treaty on Stability, Coordination and Governance in the Economic and Monetary Union — C(2017)1201* (Brussels: European Commission, 2017).

the EU, and (3) with the recent mushrooming of IFIs in the region, a clear majority of them by now are located within the EU. However, the following analysis does not discuss the supranational European Fiscal Board, since it has a unique mandate to advise the European Commission on its responsibility in implementing the EU fiscal framework, and therefore does not act as a direct watchdog in the budgetary arena, unlike national IFIs. In the context of their key activities, the paper will also discuss the operational role played by IFIs in national budgetary processes. However, one has to bear in mind an important caveat: assessing the policy impact of IFIs may require the passage of more time, since many of them have only been recently operationalized. Moreover, comprehensive assessments of the fiscal councils are fiendishly difficult to conduct in isolation, not least because the other building blocks of national fiscal frameworks (numerical rules, medium-term budgetary frameworks, and public financial management procedures) are intertwined with each other.

This paper is organized as follows. The next section presents a succinct literature review about the rationale of IFIs. Section 3 discusses the main features and working relations characterising EU IFIs, putting stress on their variety. Section 4 gives some provisional observations and lessons learned in relation to the three core tasks identified by Kornai, also the light of the evolving literature attempting to measure the effectiveness of IFIs. Finally, Section 5 concludes with a number of potential ideas for strengthening the role of IFIs to the benefit of sound fiscal policymaking.

The economic rationale for IFIs

Discretionary fiscal policy was consensually identified in the economic literature as suffering from two interrelated shortcomings: deficit bias and procyclicality. The persistent deviation from an optimal policy path, resulting in sustained debt accumulation, has primarily been explained by political economy considerations,[4] ranging from fiscal illusions by an ill-informed electorate to the time inconsistency phenomenon, and more recently including models on indebtedness as a strategic tool by incumbents to limit the fiscal space of a successor government. Partly linked to this, the pro-cycli-

[4] For a recent survey of the related political economy models, see Alberto Alesina, and Andrea Passalacqua, "The Political Economy of Government Debt," NBER Working Paper, no. 21821, National Bureau of Economic Research, Cambridge, MA, 2015.

cality of fiscal policy, especially as regards good economic times, has also been convincingly documented,[5] which entails two important drawbacks. First, pro-cyclical policies tend to exacerbate the volatility of output and employment, thereby depressing the accumulation of capital via increased uncertainty. Second, they lead to insufficient elbowroom for cyclical downturns, essentially undermining the stabilisation function of fiscal policy.

Fiscal rules and IFIs have recently emerged as complementary institutions to address the deficit bias and, more generally, the pro-cyclical policy stance. While fiscal rules were typically introduced first in order to address the above described fiscal biases, a growing awareness of disappointing outcomes in terms of fiscal rule enforcement put the spotlight on the potential benefits of independent bodies as an additional feature of the fiscal landscape (i.e., not as a substitute for fiscal rules). In fact, IFIs can tangibly increase the level of scrutiny and visibility of numerical rules. Also, through their continuous monitoring, IFIs are expected to promote transparency and accountability, thereby reducing information asymmetries and raising the quality of fiscal policy debates. Indeed, a recent IMF empirical paper showed that only fiscal rules equipped with independent monitoring arrangements were associated with lower sovereign debt financing costs.[6] This result held even for countries with a mixed track record of fiscal responsibility.

IFIs are generally not meant to be granted formal policy-making competences. Xavier Debrun and his co-authors propose differentiating between two distinct models of independent public bodies, depending on the scope of their intervention in fiscal policy: "Independent Fiscal Authorities," which are entrusted to set annual budgetary and debt targets or even to adjust the level of taxation and public expenditure; and "Fiscal Councils," which can shape fiscal policy by independent analyses, projections, and advice.[7] Noting the atypical cases of Hungary and more recently of Greece,[8] the IFIs in the

[5] See Alessandro Turrini, "Fiscal Policy and the Cycle in the Euro Area: The Role of Government Revenue and Expenditure," Economic Papers, no. 323, European Commission, Brussels, 2008, for the euro area evidence.

[6] International Monetary Fund, "A Greater Role for Fiscal Policy," in *Fiscal Monitor—April 2017*. (Washington: International Monetary Fund, 2017).

[7] Xavier Debrun, David Hauner, and Manmohan S. Kumar, "Independent Fiscal Agencies," *Journal of Economic Surveys* 23, no. 1 (2009): 44–81.

[8] Since 2012, the Hungarian Fiscal Council has a constitutionally enshrined veto right over the annual budget bill if it detects *ex ante* non-compliance with the domestic debt reduction requirement. The veto right is exercised via the procedural

EU belong to the latter type. It also means that from this point of view their set-up is in harmony with the above-recalled recommendation of János Kornai, who advised against formally involving IFIs in the political decision-making processes. This being said, the idea to delegate fully or partly the budgetary powers to independent fiscal institutions or non-elected technocrats has recurrently been put forward in the literature.[9]

The policy avenue of delegation could, however, be criticized from both theoretical and democratic legitimacy point of views. First, there is non-negligible uncertainty even in professional circles regarding the optimal level of deficit and debt, and consequently little prospect for political consensus on the appropriate policy course to set. Second, fiscal policy in all aspects has distributional consequences: even if the fiscal council's prerogative were limited to deciding on the size of the annual balance with the legislature remaining the final arbiter for the structure of the budget, there would still be redistributional aspects among generations involved. Hence, deferring responsibility to technocrats in fiscal councils would interfere with a fundamental right of the voter, since accountability in modern economies is established through the ballot box.

A key question surrounding the decision to create a fiscal council is: why would such an entity have a potentially greater disciplining effect than other existing bodies active in fiscal policy analysis? In many countries, a number of official entities (such as national audit offices or central banks) or other, private entities (independent research institutions and academic bodies) had potentially already been influential through vigorous participation in public policy debates. However, the resulting scattering of different watchdog functions across heterogeneous institutions could weaken their potential impact. Indeed, the establishment of a fully-fledged fiscal council enables the pooling of local expertise (creating analytical synergies) and access to financial and

rule that the final parliamentary vote on the draft cannot be organized without the consent of the body. With a spring 2017 amendment, the Hellenic Fiscal Council is charged to assess the compliance of the draft annual budget bill—before its submission to Parliament—with the provisions of the Fiscal Compact. The Minister's Explanatory Report accompanying the draft budget bill must contain the affirmative opinion of the Council on this matter.

9 Famously proposed in Charles Wyplosz, "Fiscal Policy: Institutions versus Rules," CEPR Discussion Papers, no. 3238, Centre for Economic Policy Research, Geneva, 2002; see also a recent example in Martin Larch and Thomas Braendle, "Independent Fiscal Councils: Neglected Siblings of Independent Central Banks? An EU Perspective," *Journal of Common Market Studies* 56, no. 2 (2018): 267–283.

informational resources (including access to confidential data) not otherwise available to unofficial bodies.[10]

Lars Calmfors has pointed out that the impact of a given IFI on fiscal performance depends also on country-specific factors.[11] If the primary source of the deficit bias in an economy has traditionally been various types of informational problems (e.g., fiscal illusions stemming from the insufficient understanding of the government's budget constraint, including common pool issues, or failures to timely detect unsustainable booms), the activities of an independent fiscal institution would be likely to mitigate the underlying causes of fiscal profligacy. However, if other motives resulting in deliberate policy choices dominate the deficit bias (e.g., strategic indebtedness in the context of political polarisation or exploitation of future generations), the ruling authorities could be inclined to ignore or even push back their independent counterparts. In such cases, the effectiveness of IFIs is naturally more limited, although they could still elevate the reputational costs incurred by the budgetary authorities when opting for a less responsible fiscal behavior. In a more radical form of this notion, Jürgen von Hagen posits that the prevailing model of advisory fiscal councils, which is also the model currently reflected in the European legislation, is fundamentally non-viable in the longer term.[12] This is because they are fighting the wrong battle when they are addressing information asymmetries. The implementation of their core tasks (most notably the assessment of macrofiscal plans, the monitoring of rules) is likely to improve the transparency of public finances, but, in his view, the dominant sources of the deficit bias have not been information asymmetries, but common pool problems. He concludes that fiscal councils must possess some form of veto powers over the government's budget (such as the imposition of across-the-board spending cuts) in order to tackle the common pool problems, and thereby to be useful for the general public, and not only for the academic community. This rather revolutionary path, however, also

---

10 See László Jankovics, "Independent Fiscal Institutions" [Független költségvetési intézmények], *Public Economics* 7, no. 1 (2012): 147–164, for a more detailed discussion on these considerations.

11 Lars Calmfors, "The Roles of Fiscal Rules, Fiscal Councils and Fiscal Union in EU Integration," IFN Working Paper, no. 1076, Research Institute of Industrial Economics, Stockholm, SE, 2015.

12 Jürgen von Hagen, "Are Fiscal Councils Here to Stay?" in *Independent Fiscal Councils: Watchdogs or Lapdogs?* ed. Roel Beetsma and Xavier Debrun (Vox.eu eBook, 2018), 187–196.

raises some fundamental economic and institutional accountability questions beyond the contentious issue of political feasibility (as was set out above).

Overview of IFIs in the EU and their structural characteristics

In the context of successive economic governance reform waves, and with a view to the envisaged benefits outlined in the literature (as detailed above in the previous section), a number of legislative initiatives at the EU level provided a significant impetus for IFI development. First, the EU Directive 2011/85 on requirements for national budgetary frameworks (a component of the Six-Pack adopted in 2011) introduced, for the first time, a reference to the need for involving independent institutions or "bodies endowed with functional autonomy" in the budgetary processes.[13] It is imperative to clarify that compliance with the Directive does not necessitate the establishment of a fully-fledged fiscal council. The related provisions could be fulfilled by other arrangements as well, e.g., in case of Poland, the monitoring of numerical rules is carried out by the Supreme Audit Office. Subsequently, the Fiscal Compact came in 2012, with its compulsory structural balanced-budget rule equipped with monitoring by designated IFIs in the signatory member states.[14] Finally, in 2013, the "Two-Pack" Regulation, which only concerns euro area member states, introduced the requirement for national medium-term fiscal plans and draft budgets to be based on independently produced or endorsed macroeconomic forecasts as well as conferred on IFIs a formal monitoring role in all numerical fiscal rules in force. These reform steps have also been resulted from a wide-spread view that the strengthening of the EU architecture should go hand in hand with improving national budgetary frameworks.

It should be stressed that, in spite of all these European level requirements concerning IFIs, member states have retained a significant degree of freedom in term of designing their own IFIs. Given that existence of IFIs in

[13] Council of the European Union, Council Directive 2011/85 on requirements for budgetary frameworks of the Member States," *Official Journal of the European Union* 54 (2011): 43.

[14] The inter-governmental Treaty on Stability, Cooperation and Governance (TSCG) in the Economic and Monetary Union entered into force on January 1, 2013 and its Title III, i.e., the Fiscal Compact, binds twenty-two member states (nineteen euro area countries and, on a voluntary basis, Bulgaria, Denmark, and Romania).

some countries predated legislative momentum at European level, and also as a recognition of the diversity of national fiscal and administrative settings, there was no attempt to impose a one-size-fits-all model in the EU legislation, which therefore only set general minimum criteria for Eurozone countries.

Mainly driven by the aforementioned legislative requirements, the number of IFIs has more than tripled in the recent past: out of the 35 IFIs that were present in EU member states at the end of 2017, only 10 were active in 2010. The latest arrivals on the scene are the Slovenian Fiscal Council, which has become operational in late spring 2017, and the Czech Fiscal Council, whose members were appointed in January 2018. It is also worthwhile to add that in 8 member states (Austria, Belgium, Greece, Finland, Luxembourg, the Netherlands, Slovenia, and Slovakia), there are two institutions mandated to carry out core IFI functions. In these cases, the division of tasks is typically arranged in a way that there is a forecasting institution (which is in charge of providing the official macroeconomic forecasts used for budgetary planning), and a council with a wider remit.

Graph 1. The rise of IFIs since the eruption of the euro area crisis[15]

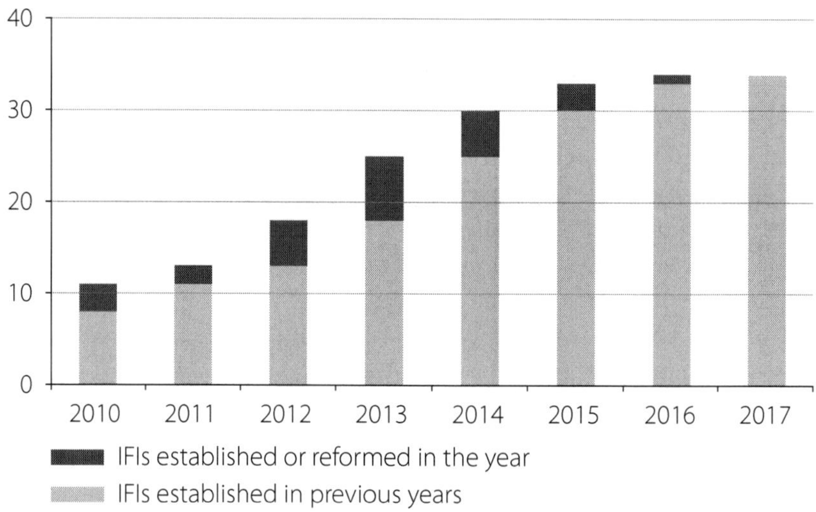

Note: Years denote date of legal establishment, it may differ from the date of effective start of operations.

[15] Source data reproduced from László Jankovics and Monika Sherwood, "Independent Fiscal Institutions in the EU Member States: The Early Years," European Economy Discussion Papers, no. 67, European Commission, Brussels, 2017, 11–12.

In terms of independence safeguards, a very large majority of EU IFIs rely on a statutory base grounded in ordinary legislative provisions or those of higher legal standing (in Estonia, France, Hungary, Ireland, Italy, Lithuania, and Spain, the IFIs are established through provisions in their constitutions, or laws with qualified majority quorums). Requirements for IFI decision-making members typically include qualification criteria as well as provisions aimed at avoiding conflicts of interest with other public or private capacities. Across the EU, 21 out of 35 IFIs (ca. 60%) function as a detached body (i.e., operating on a standalone basis), while the remaining ones are either attached to or embedded[16] in other existing domestic institutions (typically national parliaments, central banks or courts of auditors). The main rationale for attachment is that it facilitates access to resources (offices, IT equipment, etc.) and enables a smooth start-up.

IFIs exhibit a large variance in allocated budgets and human resources, partly reflecting the differences in their mandate. There are a number traditionally sizeable "forecasting institutions" (most notably, the Austrian Institute for Economic Research, the Belgian Federal Planning Bureau, and the Dutch Bureau for Economic Policy Analysis [CPB]), which employ a couple dozen staff who undertake technical and administrative work (mostly economists and statisticians, but also legal experts, accounting and budgeting staff, and IT personnel). Among the recently established ones, there are a number of bodies with solid analytical capacities (most notably, the Spanish Independent Authority for Fiscal Responsibility, the Italian Parliamentary Budget Office [PBO], and the United Kingdom Office for Budget Responsibility [OBR]), with staffs of 20 or more people. This being said, most institutions employ fewer than ten support staff[17] and, on average, four economists and/or statis-

[16] "Attached" means that the IFI has financial and organizational links with the host institution (e.g., the Italian Parliamentary Budget Office is attached to the legislature), whereas "embedded" signifies that the IFI is a section of the host institution (e.g., Lithuanian Budget Policy Monitoring Department is embedded in the National Audit Office). It should be noted that some of the standalone institutions (e.g., the Bulgarian and the Hungarian Fiscal Councils) also receive administrative support from existing public bodies.

[17] It is worth pointing out that the resources of the EU IFIs are in general rather modest in comparison to their equivalents outside Europe. The endowment of IFIs with budgetary resources and the corresponding staff numbers in the USA, Korea, Mexico, and Australia surpass by far those of most EU IFIs.

ticians are working in non-forecasting EU IFIs.[18] Funding for standalone IFIs is typically included in the central budget; other examples involve the central bank's budget (e.g., Slovak Council for Budget Responsibility) or the parliament's budget (e.g., Bulgarian Fiscal Council). In the case of attached/embedded IFIs, funding is generally provided via an earmarked appropriation within the budget of the host institution.

EU IFIs' mandates differ significantly in scope and, in addition, many of them perform tasks based on their own initiative, e.g., beyond those explicitly laid down in their statutory provisions (legislation or statutes). The remits typically consist of a subgroup of the following activities: (1) Macroeconomic and/or budgetary forecasting (autonomous production of such forecasts or the endorsement/assessment of the government's forecasts), (2) Assessment of compliance with fiscal rules, (3) Quantitative policy costing, (4) Analysis of the long-run sustainability of public finances, (5) Promotion of fiscal transparency, (6) Recommendations on fiscal policy (e.g., on the fiscal stance, on the composition of fiscal measures, or the consequences of alternative policies). It is worth recalling that European legal requirements concern only the first two items, and naturally these are laid down as compulsory tasks for virtually all IFIs. The remaining elements are typically carried out on the own initiative of the councils (legally sometimes underpinned by a broad optional reference in the mandate, such as the body "may" prepare a report on any issues deemed to be relevant for public finances).

Based on its Fiscal Governance Database, the Commission has recently started calculating a Scope Index of Fiscal Institutions (SIFI) that aims to measure the breadth of tasks discharged by IFIs. The index covers the above mentioned six dimensions of IFIs' mandates. The relevant scores in each category are adjusted with a "legal force coefficient" in order to capture the elements of the official mandates. The scores are then weighted so that tasks stemming from the EU legislation carry greater importance. The computed

[18] The International Monetary Fund outlines some broad principles for determining the size of the support staff: it argues that a mandate consisting of macrofiscal assessments could properly be carried out with a staff of less than ten analysts, the production of a fully-fledged independent forecasts would necessitate a staff of at least twenty, while the preparation of regular policy costings would demand the work of another twenty professionals. See International Monetary Fund, *The Functions and Impact of Fiscal Councils* (Washington: International Monetary Fund, 2013), 35–36.

SIFI values for years 2015 and 2016 range from 20 to close to 80, with an average value of some 48 (see graph below). The distribution of institutions across the scale does not seem to reveal any meaningful grouping according to the most used criteria (e.g., "large" vs. "small," or "old" vs. "new" member states; North vs. South). An important disclaimer is that the results simply reflect the extent of the mandate, hence they should not be read as a proxy for the effectiveness of the respective IFIs.

Graph 2. The Scope Index of Fiscal Institutions (SIFI)

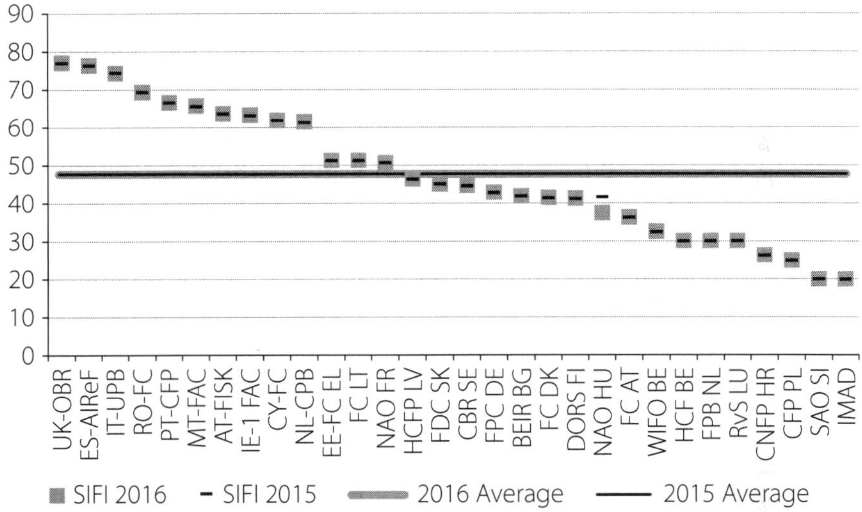

Source: Commission's Fiscal Governance Database

Zooming in on the IFI tasks defined by Kornai

As recalled in the introduction, János Kornai saw three core functions for IFIs: (1) Analyzing the consistency of planned fiscal measures with the available fiscal space, (2) policy costing, and (3) enhancing the transparency of public finances. As already argued, the first activity could be equalled with the task of *ex ante* compliance assessment with numerical fiscal rules. It is instructive to cross-check these "Kornai functions" with the findings of some recent empirical papers attempting to gauge the effectiveness of IFIs. Even though the relevant studies underline the difficulty of a proper assessment against the backdrop of the IFIs' relative novelty and their considerable heterogeneity, some tentative conclusions can be drawn.

Based on a stylized model showing how a fiscal council can effectively promote fiscal discipline, Beetsma and Debrun examine to what extent the key characteristics of IFIs, as contained in the IMF dataset,[19] are in line with the model-inspired ideal type. The dimensions, which are considered key to the effectiveness of IFIs, are the following: (1) breadth of the mandate, (2) ability to communicate freely, (3) the channels of direct influence on the budgetary process, and (4) statutory as well as functional independence. Overall, the paper finds that three-quarters of the IFIs analysed broadly possess features that are indispensable for effective operation. In the remaining cases, typically the independence dimension is most in need of reinforcement. Based on the previous version of the above-mentioned IMF dataset, Debrun and Kinda empirically investigate whether the observed design of independent bodies possesses a discipline-enhancing power.[20] Overall, they conclude that only well-designed IFIs are associated with better fiscal outcomes and less biased forecasts, so the mere existence of IFIs is not by itself conducive to sound public finances.[21] Specifically, the identified key characteristics for an effective operation are the following ones: (1) the independent functioning, (2) a visible presence in the public debate, (3) the mandate to monitor numerical rules, and (4) to assess/produce the official macro-fiscal forecasts.

It can broadly be concluded that the key areas of IFI tasks identified in the papers rhyme with the "Kornai functions." In fact, a profound impact on the budget formation process and a notable orientating role in the public debate cannot be really established without the preparation of regular moni-

[19] The analysis covered thirty fiscal councils, out of which twenty-one were from the EU (for the excluded ones, too much information was missing). According to this ranking, the two most effective IFIs are the UK Office for Budgetary Responsibility and the Portuguese Public Finance Council. See Roel Beetsma and Xavier Debrun, "Fiscal Councils: Rationale and Effectiveness," IMF Working Paper, no. 16/86, International Monetary Fund, Washington, DC, 2016.

[20] Xavier Debrun and Tidiane Kinda, "Strengthening Post-Crisis Fiscal Credibility: Fiscal Councils on the Rise—A New Dataset," IMF Working Paper, no. 14/58, International Monetary Fund, Washington, DC, 2014.

[21] The authors stress that even significantly positive correlations should not be interpreted as a causal relation as these may simply reflect deeper, often unobservable factors. Moreover, the limited time span for many of the IFIs in the database may also affect the empirical results.

toring reports and dedicated policy costing studies. In parallel, improving on the transparency of public finances can help both tame some eminent sources of the deficit bias as well as solidify the independence of the IFI. Overall, carrying out these functions is assumed to increase the persuasive powers of fiscal watchdogs. In the following subsections, this paper will therefore present an overview how and to what extent these tasks are undertaken by EU fiscal councils.

ASSESSMENT OF COMPLIANCE WITH FISCAL RULES

As was documented in the literature survey, there are clear synergies between IFIs and fiscal rules. Specifically, only well-designed fiscal rules, i.e., those accompanied by independent monitoring mechanisms, were found to have positive impacts on fiscal policy (e.g., improved budgetary outcomes, lowered borrowing costs). Also inspired by this empirical evidence, the notion that an independent assessor is an essential ingredient in the design of an effective numerical rule has become part in many national fiscal governance frameworks.

In the EU, disregarding the "pure forecasters," all IFIs are charged with verifying compliance with general or central government rules. However, extending the monitoring to other specific sectors of the general government (such as social security) or to the subnational level is much less common. Indeed, around a quarter of EU IFIs are compelled by legislation to assess compliance at the subnational level, typically in federal state structures (Austrian Fiscal Advisory Council, the Belgian High Council of Finance, or the Spanish Independent Authority for Fiscal Responsibility). A peculiar case in point is Bulgaria, where the Fiscal Council is charged with assessing both *ex ante* and *ex post* compliance with the numerical rules laid down for the national social insurance funds. Regarding the frequency of monitoring reports, the most typical solution is that IFIs release two main reports annually, where typically the spring edition analyzes the country's medium-term budgetary plans (linked to the submission date of Stability/Convergence Programmes), and the autumn one deals with the planned (or adopted) budget (e.g., Cyprus, Ireland, and Italy belong to this category). These reports encompass many aspects of fiscal policy, with the monitoring part usually being a dedicated subchapter of the document.

Most of the IFIs are undertaking both forward-looking and backward-looking compliance assessments. In fact, there are only a few countries where the monitoring mandate calls solely for an *ex ante* perspective. This is the case for Denmark, Finland, and the United Kingdom. In the latter case, the OBR is specifically required to judge in its semi-annual reports whether the government's fiscal policy as announced to that date remains consistent with a greater than 50 percent chance of achieving the so-called fiscal mandate constituting the main UK numerical rule. The nature of this task is also influenced by the design of UK rules, which are defined over a multi-annual horizon without containing specific targets for the intervening years.

A genuine dialogue between the fiscal authorities and IFIs on the findings and recommendations contained in the monitoring reports benefits greatly the transparency of public finances. For the 22 member states, which are bound by the Fiscal Compact, such a dialogue is facilitated by the so-called comply-or-explain provisions (the governments "shall be obliged to comply with, or alternatively explain publicly why they are not following the assessment of these bodies [IFIs]"), which principle is typically enshrined in law in the concerned countries.[22] However, this Fiscal Compact requirement covers only a number of targeted cases linked to the structural balanced-budget rule (activation of the correction mechanism; monitoring the correction process and triggering, extending and exiting escape clauses). Moreover, as documented by Michal Horvath, in the majority of cases the official responses to IFI opinions are neither systematic nor always pertinent to the issues raised.[23] This also calls for more broadly defined and formally stipulated comply-or-explain arrangements. Irrespective of the regulation, the visibility of fiscal policy debates could be greatly enhanced by a publication schedule, which allows for intensive reporting by the media on government reactions. For instance, in Ireland, based on its own initiative, the government responds in a detailed open letter of up to 10–12 pages within 6–8 weeks following the publication of the semi-annual Fiscal Assessment Reports by the Council. The letter covers not only the recommendations issued by the Irish IFI, but also its analytical findings and technical issues.[24]

---

22 See a systematic overview in the report of European Commission (2017) taking stock of compliance of national legal provisions with the Fiscal Compact.

23 Michal Horvath, "EU Independent Fiscal Institutions: An Assessment of Potential Effectiveness," *Journal of Common Market Studies* 56, no. 3 (2018): 504–519.

24 There are also some more contentious examples as well. In Italy, exchanges between the IFI and the government take place at parliamentary debates/hearings (available *ex post* as part of the proceedings on the parliament's webpage) and

POLICY COSTING

Policy costing consists in providing—at various stages of the budgetary cycle—estimates of the budgetary impact of new measures envisaged by fiscal authorities. Independent estimates could be essential to ensure an informed public debate and parliamentary deliberation, in particular if the government does not release its budgetary impact assessments in a consistent and timely manner. On the revenue side, accurate costing requires first-hand knowledge of the often complex tax legislation and access to non-public databases. On the expenditure side, it often relies on detailed data, which only relevant line ministries responsible for spending programmes can provide. These challenges coupled with the inevitable human resource need for undertaking rigorous computations result in that around half of the EU IFIs ("pure forecasters" are taken out of the sample) are active in this field in any way. A further important qualification is that this group is roughly evenly split between those institutions who prepare quantitative stand-alone cost estimates and others who provide only plausibility assessment of official budgetary estimates for new measures as part of their opinion on the feasibility of fiscal plans. Overall, only a quarter of EU IFIs are engaged in dedicated costing activity, the most notable examples are the IT PBO, OBR, and CPB.

At this point, a brief look beyond Europe to North American experiences seems to be warranted, since the IFIs in the United States and Canada have an extensive track-record in costing. Probably the most well-known IFI in the world is the US Congressional Budget Office (CBO). It is practically a "factory" of impact assessment with its mammoth 250-strong staff. Its comprehensive obligation to supply the US Congress with cost estimates does result in around 600–650 published budgetary impacts assessments per calendar year (beyond fiscal, these cover effects on intergovernmental budgetary relations or on the private sector, where relevant). Moreover, in its advisory function, CBO is reported to informally prepare more than 1000 additional impact assessments for senators and Congress members per year (which are, in turn, not published). The Canadian Parliamentary Budget Officer (PBO)

---

not in the form of a publicly traceable written response. A further case in point is Hungary. Over the recent years the Hungarian authorities regularly included in the explanatory annexes of the budget bill a written response to the Fiscal Council's remarks based on the preliminary draft. However, this commendable own-initiative practice could not gain any meaningful traction in the media, as the response was part of a bulky set of legal documents of possibly more than 1000 pages.

and its Office could provide even more useful insights for many EU IFIs, given its comparable endowment with resources (a staff of around 15 experts). On top of regular forecasts and monitoring publications, around 12–15 costing studies and one-off thematic reports are published per year. A deliberate selectivity of topics is applied, based on the budgetary stakes involved and the potential value added of a PBO report. Resource constraints could occasionally be further eased through the leveraging of external specialists, who are incentivised through access to data and joint academic publications.

There are a number of dimensions to be considered when setting the analytical framework for policy costing. First, in terms of coverage of budgetary items, costing could usefully focus on non-discretionary revenues and expenditures, i.e., those which are primarily determined by economic developments and demographic trends (prime examples are tax revenues and social allowances). Second, regarding methodological options, it is increasingly acknowledged that in many cases, it is not adequate to capture only static impacts, and it is necessary to extend the analysis to macroeconomic feedbacks (or second-round effects). In the event of a wide-ranging tax-benefit reform package, it is justified to try to incorporate the full spectrum of dynamic effects, which would imply a further extension to behavioural changes as well. Third, estimates should, if possible, be compared to a well-defined macro-fiscal baseline (i.e., technical projections prepared under the assumption of unchanged legislation or unchanged policies). Fourth, the standard time horizon of the projections should, as a rule, be extended to the medium-term, which is relevant for capturing dynamic effects and also to fully understand impacts on fiscal sustainability. Setting a multi-year timespan is not only essential for prudently quantifying the impact of welfare reforms, like parametric pension reform steps, but it is also of key importance for many other budgetary measures as well (for instance, bank transaction taxes are notorious for their declining revenue yields some time after their introduction, since economic agents adjust their financial dealings to avoid or minimize their tax obligations).

PROMOTION OF FISCAL TRANSPARENCY

There are only a few countries where there is an explicit mention about transparency as a self-standing objective or activity for IFIs. This may be explained by the fact that fostering transparency may be indirectly fulfilled by discharging other tasks (e.g., assessment of official macro-fiscal plans and review of the government's budgetary impact studies). It is therefore rather exceptional that the Swedish Fiscal Policy Council is explicitly charged in its founding ordinance to "examine the clarity of the budget bills." It shall also "...contribute to more transparency and clarity about the aims and effectiveness of economic policy" and "work to stimulate more public debate on economic policy."[25] The Slovak Council for Budget Responsibility is tasked by the Fiscal Responsibility Act to prepare annually an evaluation report on budget transparency rules, including an assessment on the quality and availability of important information and data on public finances.

Furthermore, some other IFIs pursue transparency operations in practice. Indeed, as users of budgetary accounts, statistics, and documentation, IFIs are well placed to assess the quality and timeliness of information on budgetary matters. Some IFIs have been advising governments on how to improve the availability of fiscal statistics for sub-sectors and functional classifications, or to provide more detailed breakdowns for the annual and medium-term fiscal plans. Specific examples of active IFIs in the field include the Spanish Independent Authority for Fiscal Responsibility (with its interactive web-based Data Lab, which provides easy access to and visualisation of many relevant data series), and the Romanian Fiscal Council (with a regular dedicated chapter on fiscal transparency issues in its Annual Report). The OBR contributed to transparency and public awareness by producing an easy-to-read guide on public finance for the public.[26]

Conclusions

Independent fiscal institutions have recently spread across the EU, largely thanks to the general enhancements made to European fiscal policy framework since the crisis. Indeed, today, virtually all EU member states have at least one IFI that provides independent advice and input for fiscal policy-making. Given the relatively short period of time since most IFIs took up

[25] See the translation of the relevant legal provisions at the Swedish Fiscal Policy Council's webpage: http://www.finanspolitiskaradet.se/english/swedishfiscalpolicycouncil/abouttheswedishfpc/ordinance.4.4c1b31c91325af4dad3800020198.html .

[26] See Office for Budget Responsibility, *A Brief Guide to the UK Public Finances* (London: Office for Budget Responsibility, 2017) for the most recent edition.

their duty, it is difficult to assess (both quantitatively and qualitatively) the impact of IFIs on budgetary outcomes and the quality of fiscal policy. Nonetheless, early (primarily anecdotal) evidence suggests that these institutions do play a useful role in budgetary processes. They exert a positive influence mainly through positive analysis, embodied in the flagship IFI tasks advocated by Kornai: monitoring of compliance with fiscal rules, preparing policy costings, and improving the transparency of public finances.

Assessment of compliance with fiscal rules is well-recognized as the core mission of an IFI in both the economic literature and the EU legislation. In the context of monitoring the respect of fiscal rules, some EU IFIs have already been successful in engaging national governments in a debate on fiscal execution and planning. They have thereby contributed to enhancing the public's awareness of fiscal issues, in particular regarding the estimated size the available fiscal space, which could potentially be used to finance additional spending plans or tax cuts. This being said, further efforts should be made (by legislation or in practice) so that all IFIs charged to publish both forward-looking as well as backward-looking assessments in a timely manner, and covering most, if not all, of the domestic fiscal rules in force.

Currently, only subgroups of EU IFIs are active in the preparation of independent budgetary impact assessments (or alternatively the certification of official costing estimates) and the promotion of fiscal transparency. Based on European and non-European experiences, it seems to be beneficial to extend the mandate of IFIs to include these responsibilities as well. Since such activities are quite labor-intensive, such considerations should be accompanied by a reflection on appropriate additional resources for IFIs.

The above overview of the current practices in the EU member states suggests that IFIs would benefit from a further strengthening of their legal standing vis-à-vis governments. To this end, it would make sense to recommend that Member States create a proper legal basis for the comply-or-explain principle according to which budgetary authorities should react publicly to IFIs' opinions, and thus oblige governments to respond to the assessment of IFIs within deadlines defined by law. Given that in most cases the role of IFIs is broader than checking compliance with numerical rules, this reinforced comply-or-explain mechanism should ideally cover most (if not all) reports issued by independent fiscal councils.

References

Alesina, Alberto, and Andrea Passalacqua. "The Political Economy of Government Debt." NBER Working Paper, no. 21821, National Bureau of Economic Research, Cambridge, MA, 2015.

Beetsma, Roel, and Xavier Debrun. "Fiscal Councils: Rationale and Effectiveness." IMF Working Paper, no. 16/86, International Monetary Fund, Washington, DC, 2016.

Calmfors, Lars. "The Roles of Fiscal Rules, Fiscal Councils and Fiscal Union in EU Integration." IFN Working Paper, no. 1076, Research Institute of Industrial Economics, Stockholm, SE, 2015.

Debrun, Xavier, David Hauner, and Manmohan S. Kumar. "Independent Fiscal Agencies." *Journal of Economic Surveys* 23, no. 1 (2009): 44–81.

Debrun, Xavier, and Tidiane Kinda. "Strengthening Post-Crisis Fiscal Credibility: Fiscal Councils on the Rise—A New Dataset." IMF Working Paper, no. 14/58, International Monetary Fund, Washington, DC, 2014.

European Commission. *Report from the Commission presented under Article 8 of the Treaty on Stability, Coordination and Governance in the Economic and Monetary Union — C(2017)1201.* Brussels: European Commission, 2017.

International Monetary Fund. *The Functions and Impact of Fiscal Councils.* Washington: International Monetary Fund, 2013.

———. 2017. "A Greater Role for Fiscal Policy." In *Fiscal Monitor—April 2017.* Washington: International Monetary Fund, 2017.

Horvath, Michal. "EU Independent Fiscal Institutions: An Assessment of Potential Effectiveness." *Journal of Common Market Studies* 56, no. 3 (2018): 504–519.

Jankovics, László. "Independent Fiscal Institutions." *Public Economics* 7, no. 1 (2012): 147–164.

———, and Monika Sherwood. "Independent Fiscal Institutions in the EU Member States: The Early Years." European Economy Discussion Papers, no. 67, European Commission, Brussels, 2017.

Kornai, János. "Ten Years after 'The Road to a Free Economy': The Author's Self-evaluation." In *Annual World Bank Conference on Development Economics 2000*, edited by B. Pleskovic and N. Stern, 49–66. Washington: World Bank, 2001.

———. "Opening Remarks." Conference on Independent Fiscal Institutions. Budapest, March 18, 2010. Subsequently published as "Where is the Line between Independent Economic Analysis and Active Policy Making? The Example of the Independent Fiscal Councils." *Acta Oeconomica* 60, no. 3 (2010): 249–254.

———. "György Surányi, Governor of the MNB—Through the Eyes of a Former Member of the Central Bank Council." In *Surányi György hatvanéves*, edited by K. Sebestyén, 110–122. Budapest: Pénzügykutató Alapítvány, 2014.

Larch, Martin, and Thomas Braendle. "Independent Fiscal Councils: Neglected Siblings of Independent Central Banks? An EU Perspective." *Journal of Common Market Studies* 56, no. 2 (2018): 267–283.

Office for Budget Responsibility. *A Brief Guide to the UK Public Finances.* London: Office for Budget Responsibility, 2017.

Turrini, Alessandro. "Fiscal Policy and the Cycle in the Euro Area: The Role of Government Revenue and Expenditure." Economic Papers, no. 323, European Commission, Brussels, 2008.

von Hagen, Jürgen. "Are Fiscal Councils Here to Stay?" In *Independent Fiscal Councils: Watchdogs or Lapdogs?* edited by Roel Beetsma and Xavier Debrun, 187–196. Vox.eu eBook, 2018.

von Trapp, Lisa, Ian Lienert, and Joachim Wehner. "Principles for Independent Fiscal Institutions and Case Studies." *OECD Journal of Budgeting*, no. 2. Paris: Organisation for Economic Cooperation and Development, 2016.

Wyplosz, Charles. "Fiscal Policy: Institutions versus Rules." CEPR Discussion Papers, no. 3238, Centre for Economic Policy Research, Geneva, 2002.

Modified Management Thinking in Health Care

The Impacts of Centralization and the Soft Budget Constraint

Éva Krenyácz

The renaissance of centralization

Nowadays, all over the world, health care faces intense challenges in the form of growing health care needs, aging populations, or exponentially developing medical technology. Governments try to use stronger cost control mechanisms and transform the structure of the health care sector through re-centralization, consolidation, mergers of institutions, or privatization. By contrast, some decades ago, the dominant trend was decentralization, because it "[brought] government closer to the people and so the political process [became] more tangible and transparent and more people [could] become involved."[1] Concerning health care and the improvement of health performances and quality, the process of democratization, as well as the minimization of inequalities and ethnic disparities (or tensions), were the main reasons for "redistributing central authorities and responsibilities to local governments."[2]

In their 2008 study, Haldor Byrkjeflot and Simon Neby divided periods of hospital centralization/decentralization according to further divisions among different respective state models. These periods were structured around: (1) the making of the decentralized model (before 1970), (2) the

---

1 Axel Hadenius, *Decentralisation and Democratic Governance* (Stockholm: Elanders Gotab, 2003), 1.

2 Krishna Regmi, *Decentralizing Health Services: A Global Perspective* (New York: Springer, 2014), 3.

heyday of the decentralized model (1970–early 2000s), and (3) challenging the decentralized model (after 2000), when even Scandinavian countries are arguably becoming more centralized.[3]

Table 1. The process of decentralization and re-centalization in Europe[4]

	Decentralized model	Challenging the decentralized model
Tax-funded health systems in Nordic countries	Most administrative and managerial responsibility, as well as substantial political (policy) and fiscal decision-making control, decentralized inside the public sector	*Norway*: Government takes over political and administrative/managerial responsibility from all hospitals and transfers the administrative roles to five newly-created regional bodies *Denmark*: Fiscal—and most political—responsibilities are re-centralized back to the national government; regional governments reduced *Finland, Sweden*: Number of regional-level governments or municipalities reduced
Tax-funded health systems in Southern Europe	Most administrative and managerial, as well as many political (but not key fiscal), responsibilities devolved from national to regional governments	Continued regional decentralization of health sector decisions; and the design of new national programs to monitor performance or set standards for quality and outcomes
Social health insurance-funded countries in continental Europe	Most administrative and managerial, as well as many fiscal (but not key political), decisions delegated to private not-for-profit bodies	Move toward centralizing fiscal responsibilities away from private not-for-profit funds and into the hands of a national government body
State-based social insurance systems	Decentralized ownership of hospitals from national to regional and local governments, or municipal governments, as "privatization"	National governmental ministries regain operational control over their social health insurance systems from regional funds

[3] Haldor Byrkjeflot and Simon Neby, "The End of the Decentralised Model of Healthcare Governance?" *Journal of Health Organization and Management* 22, no. 4 (2008): 331–349.

[4] Own table, derived from Richard B. Saltman, "Decentralization, Re-centralization and Future European Health Policy," *European Journal of Public Health* 18, no. 2 (2008): 104–106.

Richard B. Saltman observed that it appears that only administrative and managerial authority will remain decentralized at a lower level, or with non-governmental organizations, because of worries about the aging of the population, the rapid growth of expensive new clinical technologies, and the economic constraints on the health sector in general.[5] Beyond centralization—or as an expectation related to centralization—the rationalization (or, in other terms, the decrease) of hospital bed capacity also arises: "The broader re-organization of hospital care provision involving ways of centralizing hospital care provision and of reducing hospital infrastructure has also been a reform target."[6]

Tim Xu and his co-authors, in their 2015 report, highlight that hospital consolidation (understood as a merger of institutions) has increased substantially, and that it has some benefits: increased quality control, lower patient mortality, and improved outcomes achieved by concentrating patients in high-volume centers.[7] However, increases in hospital market concentration lead to increases in the price of hospital care.[8] In tax-funded countries, the expenditures of health insurance funds are rising, and deficits have become constant. Furthermore, budget deficits were seen as a means of getting more resources from the owner and were, in reality, considered as flexible budgets.[9]

The overall approach of the soft budget constraint originates in the work of János Kornai, with a focus on the behavior of socialist companies (at present, this phenomenon has been noticed in every country in both public and private sectors).[10] Kornai states that decision-makers wait to be saved in

[5] Saltman, "Decentralization, Re-centralization and Future European Health Policy."

[6] Timo Clemens et al., "European Hospital Reforms in Times of Crisis: Aligning Cost Containment Needs with Plans for Structural Redesign?" *Health Policy* 117, no. 1 (2014): 6–14.

[7] Tim Xu, Albert W. Wu, Martin A. Makary, "The Potential Hazards of Hospital Consolidation: Implications for Quality, Access, and Price," *JAMA* 314, no. 1 (2015): 1337–1338.

[8] Martin Gaynor and Robert Town, "The Impact of Hospital Consolidation—Update," Policy Brief no. 9, The Synthesis Project, Robert Wood Johnson Foundation, June 2012.

[9] Kari Nyland and Inger Johanne Pettersen, "The Control Gap: the Role of Budgets, Accounting Information and (non-) Decisions in Hospital Settings," *Financial Accountability & Management* 20, no. 1 (2004): 77–102.

[10] János Kornai, "A hiány újratermelése" [The reproduction of deficit] *Közgazdasági Szemle* 25, no. 9 (September 1978): 1034–1050; and idem., "The Soft Budget Constraint Syndrome in the Hospital Sector," *International Journal of Health Care Finance and Economics* 31, no. 1 (2009): 5–31.

the event of a low *ex ante* budget; then, excesses in expenditure will be paid by some other institution, typically by the state.[11] As he writes, "the stronger the hospital manager's position is in relation to the hospital's superior organizations, the insurer providing the funds and the institutional owner providing the subsidy, the greater the hope of rescue."[12] Csaba Dózsa demonstrates similarly that hospital indebtedness depends on the macro-level financing situation as well as on management decisions.[13] He showed that indebted and financially stable institutions could be found among hospitals with the same characteristics.

The context of the Hungarian health care system

Trends of debt settlement and consolidation, as a certainty paired with soft budget-constrained health care deficits, is a worldwide problem due to expenditures rising above revenues. Health care providers do not pay their suppliers, and as such providers lobby governments for support, even though optimal distribution decisions are not supported by debt settlement.[14] Since the mid-90s, the Hungarian health care sector has been stuck in a "vicious circle," with continuously decreasing resources becoming insufficient to resolve the sector's structural problems.[15] As in other countries, the fund of Hungarian health care is constantly shrinking—in numbers, health care spending in Hungary as a percentage of total GDP is currently 7.6% (the average among OECD member states is 9%).[16] The average drop in GDP—resulting from economic crisis—was almost twice as much in Central and

[11] Kornai, "The Soft Budget Constraint Syndrome in the Hospital Sector." *International Journal of Health Care Finance and Economics* 9, no. 2 (2009): 117–135.

[12] Ibid., 125.

[13] Csaba Dózsa, "Strategic Responses of Hospitals in Hungary to the Changing Environment in the Early 21st Century," PhD diss., Corvinus University of Budapest, 2011.

[14] Jack Langenbrunner et al., "Purchasing and Paying Providers," in *Purchasing to Improve Health System Performance*, ed. Joseph Figueras, Ray Robinson and Elke Jakubowski (Berkshire: Open University Press, 2005), 236–264.

[15] József Bodrogi, *A magyar egészségÜGY* [Hungarian health care system] (Budapest: Semmelweis Kiadó, 2010).

[16] OECD/Eurostat/WHO (2017), A System of Health Accounts 2011: Revised edition, (OECD Publishing, Paris, 2017, 134-135) http://dx.doi.org/10.1787/9789264270985-en.

Eastern European countries as the drop in the Eurozone, which caused already insufficient health care resources to shrink further.[17]

Figure 1. Financing after accounting for performance,[18] 2009–2015[19]

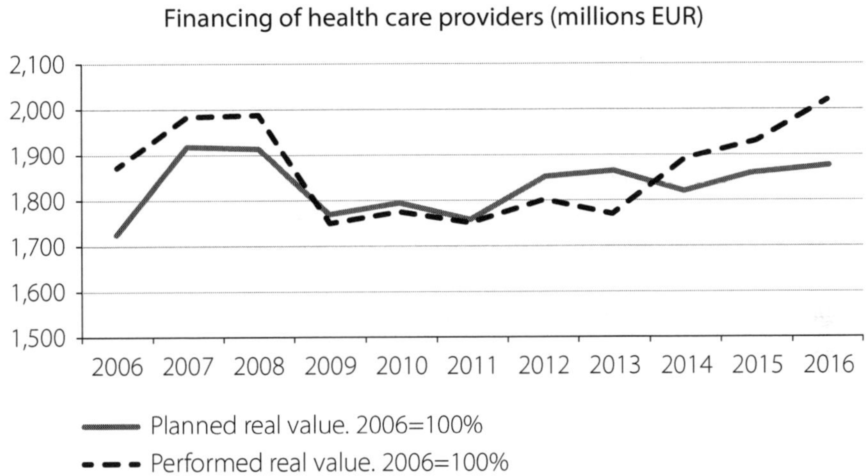

As an effect of the economic crisis, between 2009 and 2013, actual health insurance payments to hospitals were lower than budgeted payments. From 2014, insurance payments exceeded budgeted amounts by 3–8%, but that increase was paid only at the end of the year. Moreover, the deficit has been continuously generated, and the financing amount has not been corrected by increases in employee wages, inflation, and rises in VAT rate over the previous period.

According to regular practice in recent years, resources are provided by the financier (owner) for the settlement of hospital debts and for the reduction of supplier debt services and waiting lists. As Kornai said:

---

17 Petra Baji et al., "The Impact of the Recession on Health Care Expenditure—How Does the Czech Republic, Hungary, Poland and Slovakia Compare to Other OECD Countries?" *Society and Economy* 37, no. 1 (2015): 73–88.

18 Definition of performance (interpretation of the author): value of health cases provided by in-patient and out-patient institutions and financed by social insurance.

19 Own figure, based on data of National Health Insurance Fund of Hungary (Hungarian acronym NEAK), published online, http://www.neak.gov.hu/felso_menu/szakmai_oldalak/publikus_forgalmi_adatok/gyogyito_megelozo_forgalmi_adat?pagenum=2.

> The process is self-reinforcing. If many organizations expect and receive bailouts, so that they become frequent, even more will come to expect them. And with many organizations, the sequence of events starts again as before, after the bailout, in the knowledge that another rescue will be accomplished if need be.[20]

Lenient budgets are a state of mind: the decision-maker waits to be saved and acts accordingly. In 1996, and again in 2002, there was a massive consolidation of the entire Hungarian health care sector, after which the reduction in the number of hospitals with debts had only been temporary—overspending restarted soon after.[21] By now, covering hospital debts is taken for granted in this system, where hospital leaders expect to be bailed out at the end of year.

Figure 2. Consolidation amount compared to the total amount of hospital funding[22]

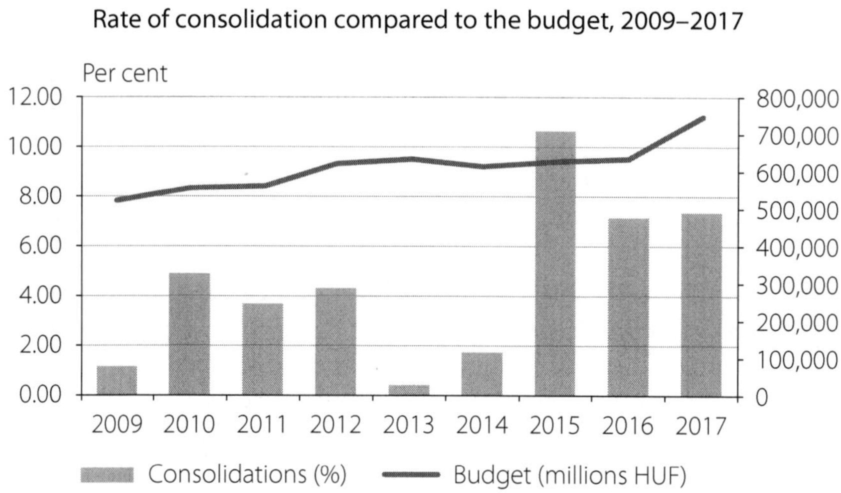

In the last decade, the monthly funding amount was less than one twelfth of the annual amount, so there was the possibility of, and expectation for, year-end payments. Thus, the government created "end-of-year consolidations",

[20] Kornai, "The Soft Budget Constraint Syndrome in the Hospital Sector," 119–120.
[21] Ibid., 122.
[22] Own figure, data asked directly from NEAK.

which hospitals called "the sweep out of health insurance cash."[23] From time to time, suppliers of hospitals raise their voices about the magnitude of debt that hospitals owe them, and they reinforce the need for consolidation. Later, debt settlement financing has appeared beside "the sweep out" in amounts of 189 million EUR in 2015, 145 million EUR in 2016 and 177 million EUR in the year of 2017.[24]

The cash-sweeping, and then a significant amount of debt settlement, was divided between the hospitals by an unknown or non-existing algorithm until last year. According to a recent law, the ratio of debt financing depends on the expiration (thirty, sixty, or ninety days) of the debts. Although, it has also been added that hospitals may ask for individual aid for institutional renewal, investment, or development.

Ownership: nationalization, as a process of centralization

Due to the system change after 1989, central governmental control in the health care sector was replaced by decentralization. The control of local governments remained, with only minor changes, until 2012. Health care reform in Hungary started with a huge change in politics—the Ministry of Health was merged into one "giga-ministry" with education, social care, culture, and sport, headed by the state Secretary of Health. Then, a health policy program described the main goals of a proposed new health care governance system, envisioning coordination bodies at national, regional, and local levels. Regarding the ownership of hospitals, the policy document was clearly against private, for-profit hospitals, and also proposed to provide even higher autonomy for hospital managers. In several steps, the ownership of previously county-owned hospitals was transferred to the central government (both local and county-level governments were affected). The health care institutions (after carrying out several hospital mergers as well) have moved under a centralized professional managing institution (Állami Egészségügyi Ellátó Központ, Hungarian National Healthcare Services), the largest supplier and supporter of health care services. It has numerous authorities, such as budget,

23 Cited from personal interview of health care experts.

24 State Audit Office of Hungary. *Elemzés az egészségügy finanszírozásáról* [Analysis of health financing], 2019, 22. https://asz.hu/storage/files/files/elemzesek/2019/egeszsegugy_finanszirozasa20190628.pdf.

control, and asset management, consolidated public procurement, and care management. A few, but significant, hospitals have continued to be supervised by other bodies of the central government (e.g., university hospitals directly supervised by the Ministry, or one of the biggest community hospitals by the Ministry of Defense). In the new structure, numerous tenders were announced for top manager positions and most hospital managers were changed.

The structural change resulted in a national decrease in the number of active beds. Instead of eliminating active beds, institutions could apply for a conversion to one-day and outpatient hospital services. According to the latest statistics of National Health Insurance Fund of Hungary, Hungarian acronym NEAK (Nemzeti Egészségbiztosítási Alapkezelő) —released December 31, 2016—167 health institutions provide services financed by social security.[25] The supervisory institutions that maintain these health institutions, and their size, are demonstrated in Table 2.

Table 2. Number of institutions and beds, presented by maintenance[25]

Institutions by maintenance	2003		2011		2016	
	Number of institutions	Number of beds	Number of institutions	Number of beds	Number of institutions	Number of beds
Health care institutions maintained by local government	117	60,747	112	55,404	15	93
Health care institutions maintained by central government	26	9,846	15	6,492	96	58,187
University	4	7,446	4	7,359	4	7,328
Enterprises	1	68	12	187	27	1,906
Religious institutions	9	1,609	7	1,463	6	1,432

[25] Own table, based on data of NEAK, http://www.neak.gov.hu/felso_menu/szakmai_oldalak/publikus_forgalmi_adatok/gyogyito_megelozo_forgalmi_adat/fekvobeteg_szakellatas/korhazi_agyszam.html.

Institutions by maintenance	2003		2011		2016	
	Number of institutions	Number of beds	Number of institutions	Number of beds	Number of institutions	Number of beds
Others (foundations, etc.)	19	526	21	592	18	561
Hungarian Prison Service	2	608	2	608	1	311
Total	178	80,850	173	72,105	167	69,818

Table 2 shows the process of centralization in Hungarian health care services financed by social security. Private-funded care currently holds only a marginal portion of the total number of beds, and these are mostly found in state-based social insured institutions.[26]

In the public health care system, the state secretary[27] has wanted to introduce a chancellor system since the year 2016, but it generated a widespread refusal by hospital managers, health workers, and experts, so the introduction of the system was postponed for April 2018. Finally, the chancellor system has not yet been introduced. According to the state secretary, the chancellor model can improve control and transparency as well as contribute to the reduction of human resources crises. According to the hospital managers, interviewed in this research, the chancellor is a position of power that will be appropriate to implementation of management decisions and hospital should not serve themselves, but the patients.

Research method

The research presented in this paper focuses on the characteristics of hospital management. I examine the interpretations, tools, and daily practices of management, as well as the incorporation of these into the decision-making

[26] Péter Gyenes et al., *A magyar egészségügyi rendszer teljesítményértékelése 2013–15* [The performance evaluation of Hungarian health care system 2013–15] (Budapest: Állami Egészségügyi Ellátó Központ, 2016).

[27] In 2010, the Ministry of Health had been merged into one "giga-ministry" together with education, social care, culture, and sport and each sector has a state secretary.

process. The central research question of this paper is: What kind of tools do top managers use for decisions in a centralized and continuously consolidated health care system?

For presenting how the Hungarian health care system modifies management tools in hospitals, a qualitative research method was used. The research question was examined from the managers' point of view. For deeper recognition and detailed presentation, individual and focus group interviews were made—top managers, health care experts, and decision supporters (including a chief financial officer and controller) were interviewed from different hospitals. The sample includes different types and sizes of institutions and private hospitals, paying particular attention to the responses of medical universities. Community health centers, regional hospitals, national institutions, medical universities, and rehabilitation centers are contained in the sample. For the selection of the institutions, the statistical analysis of health care management control systems was taken into consideration.[28] Table 3 shows information about the different hospital owners and the role of the institutions that employ the interviewees, including three profit-based and two state-owned enterprises, financed by social insurance.

Table 3. Ratio of surveyed institutions according to the role and the owner of the hospitals

Owner of the institution	Ratio of interviewed institution
State health institution	11.0%
University hospital	25.0%
For-profit institutions	12.5%

Role of institution	Ratio of interviewed institution
Community health center	5.9%
Community hospital	6.3%
National hospital	33.3%
Specialized hospital	12.5%
Regional center and co-center	33.3%
Multi-profile hospital	17.4%

[28] Éva Krenyácz, "A hazai egészségügyi intézmények kontrolling-rendszere" [The management control system of Hungarian health care institutions], *Statisztikai Szemle* 93, no. 8–9 (2015): 823–857.

A total of eight personal interviews were made with top managers of hospitals (citation with MI notation) and one homogeneous focus group interview (FGI) with decision supporters. To better understand information about the procedure and process of hospital management, Hungarian health care sector experts (EI) were also consulted.

An advantage of focus group interviews is that the more efficient the data collection, with the careful preparation,[29] the more information that can be gained by using synergies between group members.[30] The internal dynamic of the focus groups have a strong social influence on the members and so the collective responses of the focus group,[31] which is more dominant in the homogenous group of decision supporters (mainly controllers). The implementation of the focus group research unit was an enormous challenge because of the overladen hospital managers; speaking to some colleagues through Skype solved the problem for the second interview. The focus group was small (five persons), as the interviewees have experience from several institutions. Moreover, they are—according to their self-declaration—highly motivated and committed to managerial decision support. The following list gives some characteristics of the focus group:

1. A homogenous group with two represented areas (finance and controlling), which are closely linked;
2. Participants have experience working in various hospitals (different locations, size, structures, management);
3. Dedication, and the formation of strong, definite opinions, have all been assumed based on the questionnaire;
4. Open and inquisitive team, and with participants typically being women (this may be representative of the profession as well).

During individual and group interviews, a semi-structured interview situation was generated and the "funnel technique"[31] was applied—the structure of the interview was increased, thus taking advantage of both strong and weakly structured questions. The interviews were built on each other: expert inter-

[29] György Becker, "Hogyan nézzünk fókuszcsoportot?" [How do we look at focus groups?], *Marketing & Management* 40, no. 2–3 (2006): 4–8.

[30] Gábor Héra and György Ligeti, *Módszertan* [Methodology] (Budapest: Osiris Kiadó, 2006).

[31] Lilla Vicsek, *Fókuszcsoport* [Focus group] (Budapest: Osiris Kiadó, 2006).

views came first (1.5 hours) followed by the focus group (1.5 hours). With the expansion of this knowledge, the interview questions of hospital managers were specified. The length of interview decreased from 1.5 hours to 1 hour, due to recurring information. The interviews were typed—after having read them several times, a quick report was prepared to keep as a guideline during the final analysis.

Based on the text from the experts' interviews, major categories were marked with open source coding in Verbi MAXQDA 12 software, and then these were divided into subcategories during the encoding.

Results: management devices used and attitudes

Hungarian law names the top hospital managers: the general director (hereafter, the manager or top manager), the finance director, the medical director (who supervises and coordinates the medical and pharmaceutical activity; controls the operation of departments), and the nursing director (who monitors and coordinates care activities). The manager is responsible for the optimal (professional and financial) operation of the hospital. My research highlights that the managements of the examined hospitals use different systems for managing their institutions, which can be classified in three categories. (1) Almost every interviewee mentioned that there are leaders who manage from the "heart," as interviewed experts said, they do not use decision support systems, or they manage intuitively. (2) Other managers use special financial tools for liquidity control and debt balance, and, (3) finally, less typical is the management control system.

Before alternations were made to the practice of health care financing in 2004, the use of management control was popular among top managers. A management control system is basically an approach, or method, to analyze the organization of the hospital. In the thinking of public hospitals, it is a tool for retrospective analysis, not for providing rapid response; practically, its tasks are the registering and processing of past data rather than planning, forecasting, and feedback. Because of this misinterpretation of the management control system, two other devices (i.e., management without tools and special financial tools) are more deeply examined. The presentation of the relationship between the system of public health care and the thinking of management will include the experiences of using management control systems.

Managing intuitively

Hospital management is formed in many institutions along particular lines. Some managers do not apply decision support systems—information is rather in the head of the top manager. According to the interviewees, managers use less data for decision-making due to the lack of IT systems, the lack of knowledge among management, questioning the validity of data (most importantly in terms of cost), or other problems. Experts added that:

> At many hospitals, I can see the leader managing from their "heart-pocket-booklet" and it would be difficult to say how many—obviously top managers do not readily admit that of course ... in certain areas there are calculations and data … but with a lot of improvisation. (EI)

According to several interviewees, top management manages from the "heart-pocket-booklet" (intuitively without calculable information) because of underdeveloped IT systems and the lack of data validity; however, solving and eliminating these tasks is the responsibility of the manager. Therefore, we can conclude that this management style is generated by the managers' lack of knowledge or the importance of "leadership as a status symbol" (MI):

> "The manager is elected politically and this is the symbol of power and status honor … he/she is engaged on the base of power and not value." (MI)

> "For the general director, the main motivation is status." (MI)

> "The manager manages from booklet because they do not have management science knowledge, managers vein or not aware of what he/she can do." (MI)

"By applying a management control system, the fault of organizational operation can be discovered, and it shows the managers' mistakes as well." This can only be corrected by exploring conflicts and tensions, and it is difficult to estimate the consequences of undertaking conflict (e.g., a decision could paralyze the operation of a hospital), and can even affect the status of the top manager.

> "After defining the expectations for performance, 40% of physicians left the hospital, causing a three-month loss." (MI)

> "The medical staff itself actually operates incorrectly when it is not working as an organization ... for example, it took me three years to make it so that the *consilium* really could work according to the intended purpose." (MI)

Another reason for the legitimacy of this management type is the continuous decrease in managerial room for maneuver, e.g., with the implementation of the chancellery system in health care (as in other parts of the public sector). It is a vicious circle, which further devalues the devices available to hospital management. The introduction of the chancellery system into the health care sector reinforces this process by "arguing against the responsibility and competence of the general manager" (MI). It could also carry the demands of management and control activities into the sectoral level, which is progressively outlined by the process of centralization.

The use of special financial management tools

The majority of the surveyed institutions use specific instruments to manage the economic balance:

1. The limitation of performance in each medical department and its continuous control;
2. Special row budgets divided to departments; and
3. Liquidity and debt monitoring and managing.

The two main reasons behind these financial management tools is (1) underfinancing and (2) the existence of performance-volume limits, which is a specific phenomenon in Hungarian health care.[32]

[32] David Dankó et al., "A teljesítményvolumen-korlát hatásai a kórházak magatartására a HBCs alapú finanszírozás kontextusában. I. rész" [The effect of performance volume limit on the behaviour of hospitals in the context of DRG financing system, part I], *Interdiszciplináris Magyar Egészségügy* 5, no. 8 (2006a): 20–28; and idem., "A teljesítményvolumen-korlát hatásai a kórházak magatartására a HBCs

In Hungary, there is not an accepted definition of performance, but the actors (sectoral management, funding agent, providers, consultants, doctors, etc.) of health care use it as a value of health cases (given generally in diagnosis-related groups, i.e. DRGs[33] and in German points) provided by in-patient and out-patient institutions and financed by social insurance. The social insurance finances the value of DRGs and German points in a fixed rate.

Hospitals can account for their performance up to a fixed amount in the budget: social security financing revenues are maximized at the beginning of the year. Therefore, the available performance of hospitals is divided into professions/medical departments as a performance-volume limits ((hereinafter PVL) "quota." This restriction of funding requires the limitation of hospital performances in active and outpatient care (with the exception of some major illnesses and chronic care). Managers can reach the maximum financed revenue by continuing to control and reallocate institutional PVL. This mechanism is largely explained by the strong revenue focus of hospitals: in this context, the main managing role is to achieve the maximum possible revenue. And so, the reported performance to health insurance fund is always monitored:

> "Rule of thumb: Perform as is needed to achieve the correct PVL ... of course it is a bit more refined ..." (MI)

> "They are able to define the gap above the level of PVL where it can perform without much deficit. Obviously, they can find interventions in the narrow digression gap, which is to cover the fixed costs, and it is worth performing. But, above the gap, zero-percent financing guarantees the deficit. The question is: How much is the deficit? Because of the interest in patient care ... we provide care to patients, free for some, and, if we balance well, the hospital won't be bankrupt." (EI)

This financial management tool contains the achieving of maximum performance (maximization of health care revenue) on minimum cost level. The cost of human resources is about 70% of the budget, but managers think that

alapú finanszírozás kontextusában. II. rész" [The effect of performance volume limit on the behaviour of hospitals in context of DRG financing system, part II], *Interdiszciplináris Magyar Egészségügy* 5, no. 9 (2006b): 5–12.

33 Diagnosis-related group (DRG) is a system to classify hospital cases for categorizing and then financing health care services (or rarely products) in an integrated way.

the only limitable cost is the special medical row of the budget: professional material, medicines, blood utilization, and laboratory and CT budget. But ultimately those budgets which are associated with the use of direct patient care cost is more flexible than the others (e.g., bloodwork and medicines).

> "To tell the truth, even the budget is not a budget; because it may be exceeded, with perhaps an awfully confusing administration belonging to it." (EI)

> "In principle, the department cannot exceed the budget; but, in health care, it is very difficult to keep to it. If a department runs out of medicine, I can only ask them to tell me why. It is so infantile." (MI)

The third element among the available financial management tools is liquidity monitoring and debt managing; financial processes are reflected in the handling of bank accounts and the settlement of debts. Hospitals must report stock of cash and suppliers on a monthly basis to the maintainer. The financial director monitors the cash balance on a daily basis and decides to pay the bills. This is a key for lobbying because the timetable and the balance of the debt settlement define the amount of future consolidation.

Relation of public health care and management thinking

After the introduction of performance-based financing in 1993, hospital management was regulated by managers enhancing performances.

> "Since 1995—from the first cases of controlling, to the appearance of PVL—the easiest and most popular tools enhancing management were all offensive; all based on revenue growth, and not on restrictions on expenses or cutbacks. As a stoppage to that, they introduced PVL, a revenue stopper, and by that and thus cutting back expenses, in-house results, coverage, and institution-wide results could be enhanced." (EI)

The performance limit turned financing into base-financing and generated new ways of thinking and managing, pushing controlling tools into the background. Handling PVL and distributing them between professions became the main focus.

"With the appearance of PVL financing immobilized in the system, compromising the otherwise so strong controlling." (EI)

"Due to patient care being the main interest of hospitals, if need be, they can go above; and they do. This means patients are cared for, some of them for free actually. If they kept the balance in the meantime, bankruptcy would not occur." (EI)

In a hospital, knowing the costs—fixed or varied—is essential. This, however, was only recognized by some of the state-owned institutions with enhanced controlling systems. So, these institutions:

"Tend to do fewer expensive activities because the more they go above the PVL, the more deficits these activities cause." (FGI)

"More expensive professions based on cases, i.e., optometry, surgery or orthopedics, induce higher costs over PVL, while fixed-rate medicinal or psychiatric professions are otherwise expensive due to HR expenses; it does not actually matter if 100 or 110 patients are treated, since those few extra cases make no significant difference in expenses." (MI)

The amount remaining in the National Insurance budget at the end of the year is distributed in order to settle outstanding debts at year-end or to reduce waiting lists, etc. This amount had been distributed between institutions based on performance in previous years. However, recent years' experience indicates that the bailout amount depends on the debt service of individual hospitals and their ability to lobby.

"Are there any outstanding debts of the hospital older than 60 days? … They all had it … they started to compensate suppliers in a different manner." (EI)

"This is bad practice, since they are kept in a state where they are not interested in keeping liquidity. Thus, there is no retaliation if supplier debt service is overrun … the government rather injects a single amount, not believing at all in the possibility of reproduction in the case of a 100 billion [HUF] raise in financing." (MI)

Debts concern heads of institutions, but they do not incite them to take on more effective management, because their message is essentially this: "Due to debts, my losses will be compensated, so why should I make an effort to stand against the clinic," and so on. Operational budgets, economics, and other features were much more transparent in the decentralized municipal system.

> "As the head of an institution, I was completely aware of the fact that if I became indebted and bankrupt then someone would have to stand up … but I was completely aware of its relations with the hospital and also with its financial situation. I could actually influence this too. But only as far as that: if I become bankrupt, then no more care. No care means scandal. In case of a scandal, I become headlines. Headlines mean replacement, and so on… There was once some kind of a red line, up until which the owner could have helped, but only to a certain limit." (EI)

> "In the past decade, if financing changes happened only three times a year, it was a quiet year." (FGI)

Uncertainty, legislative changes, under-financing, and year-end extra financing —all of them justify the need for and use of financial management devices.

Conclusion

Even though the theory of decentralization in the health care sector unfolded in Europe two or three decades ago, governments started using recentralization with the aim of improving health care performance and quality, respectively minimizing inequalities and ethnic disparities. In Hungary, decentralization started after the regime change, and remained until 2012. Through centralization, institutions came under state supervision and ownership; several hospitals were merged, and there was a corresponding rationalization of (read: decrease in) hospital bed capacity. The current government has continuously extracted resources from health care, reduced funding—actual health insurance payments to hospitals have been consistently lower than budgeted financing. Thus, year-end funds became regular and expected. In the last three years, debt settlement financing has appeared to a significant extent. This soft budget constraint, noted by Kornai, and the continued process of centralization, has had a strong influence on the managers' way of thinking.

The managers interpret these changes as a serious issue, as a sensitive area driven by politics and personal relationships, with common problems yet unsolved, as well as untold or hidden expectations. The debts of hospitals do not drive the hospital leaders toward more effective management practices, since their message is "my losses will be compensated due to debts; so why should I make any effort to oppose the clinic," and so on.

Operational budgets, management control, and other features, were more transparent in the decentralized municipal system; confirming the idea that "decentralization brings the government closer to people, thus the political process becomes more tangible and transparent."[34] In this period, the tools of management control (reporting by controller, coverage calculation, analyses of capacity, etc.) are preferred. Because of centralization and the phenomenon of debt consolidation, financial perspectives are present in the thoughts of hospital top manager—they strive to achieve economic stability while simultaneously monitoring liquidity and lobbying for bailout, these being the most common management tools for top managers. At the same time, some of the managers do not apply any decision support systems: information is united in their person because of underdeveloped IT systems, the lack of data validity, and because of the managers' lack of knowledge or the importance of leadership being a "status symbol."

Due to end-of-year consolidations, the phenomenon of the soft budget constraint modified the attitudes of top hospital managers toward a particular financial perspective: the managers prefer to lobby for extra-funds instead of avoiding deficit and improving efficiency. Even though changes in financing or the introduction of performance limitations has a powerful effect on the health care system, interviewed managers and experts perceive that the centralized restructuring and the bailout phenomenon has modified their way of thinking. Since debt settlement is regular, it has become expected, and thus has been incorporated into the managers' regular toolbox.

[34] Hadenius, *Decentralisation and Democratic Governance*, 1.

References

Baji, Petra, Márta Péntek, Imre Boncz, Valentin Brodszky, Olga Loblova, Nóra Brodszky, and László Gulácsi. "The Impact of the Recession on Health Care Expenditure—How Does the Czech Republic, Hungary, Poland and Slovakia Compare to Other OECD Countries?" *Society and Economy* 37, no. 1 (2015): 73–88.

Becker, György. "Hogyan nézzünk fókuszcsoportot [How do we look at focus groups?]." *Marketing & Management* 40, no. 2–3 (2006): 4–8.

Bodrogi, József. *A magyar egészségÜGY* [Hungarian health care system]. Budapest: Semmelweis Kiadó, 2010.

Byrkjeflot, Haldor, and Simon Neby. "The End of the Decentralised Model of Healthcare Governance?" *Journal of Health Organization and Management* 22, no. 4 (2008): 331–349.

Clemens, Timo, Kai Michelsen, Matt Commers, Pascal Garel, Barrie Dowdeswell, and Helmut Brand. "European Hospital Reforms in Times of Crisis: Aligning Cost Containment Needs with Plans for Structural Redesign?" *Health Policy* 117, no. 1 (2014): 6–14.

Dankó, David, Norbert Kiss, Márk Molnár, and Éva Révész. "A teljesítményvolumen-korlát hatásai a kórházak magatartására a HBCs alapú finanszírozás kontextusában. I. rész" [The effect of performance volume limit on the behaviour of hospitals in the context of DRG financing system, part I]. *Interdiszciplináris Magyar Egészségügy* 5, no. 8 (2006a): 20–28.

——, "A teljesítményvolumen-korlát hatásai a kórházak magatartására a HBCs alapú finanszírozás kontextusában. II. rész" [The effect of performance volume limit on the behaviour of hospitals in context of DRG financing system, part II]. *Interdiszciplináris Magyar Egészségügy* 5, no. 9 (2006b): 5–12.

Dózsa, Csaba. "Strategic Responses of Hospitals in Hungary to the Changing Environment in the Early 21st Century." PhD diss., Corvinus University of Budapest, 2011. http://phd.lib.uni-corvinus.hu/550/.

Gaynor, Martin, and Robert Town. "The Impact of Hospital Consolidation—Update." Policy Brief, no. 9, The Synthesis Project, Robert Wood Johnson Foundation, June 2012.

Hadenius, Axel. *Decentralisation and Democratic Governance*. Elanders Gotab, Stockholm, 2003.

Héra, Gábor, and György Ligeti. *Módszertan* [Methodology]. Budapest: Osiris Kiadó, 2006.

Kornai, János. "A hiány újratermelése" [The reproduction of deficit]. *Közgazdasági Szemle* 25, no. 9 (September 1978): 1034–1050.

——. "The Soft Budget Constraint Syndrome in the Hospital Sector." *International Journal of Health Care Finance and Economics* 9, no. 2 (2009): 117–135.

Krenyácz, Éva. "A hazai egészségügyi intézmények kontrolling-rendszere" [The management control system of Hungarian health care institutions]. *Statisztikai Szemle* 93, no. 8–9 (2015): 823–857.

Langenbrunner, Jack, Joe Kutzin, Eva Orosz, and Miriam Wiley. "Purchasing and Paying Providers." In *Purchasing to Improve Health System Performance*, edited by Joseph Figueras, Ray Robinson and Elke Jakubowski, 236–264. Berkshire: Open University Press, 2005.

Gyenes, Péter, Balázs Babarczy, Fanni Farkas Borbás, Péter Kiefer, and Péter Mihalicza. *A magyar egészségügyi rendszer teljesítményértékelése 2013–15* [The performance evaluation of Hungarian health care system 2013–15]. Budapest: Állami Egészségügyi Ellátó Központ, 2016.

Nyland, Kari, and Inger Johanne Pettersen. "The Control Gap: the Role of Budgets, Accounting Information and (non-) Decisions in Hospital Settings." *Financial Accountability & Management* 20, no. 1 (2004): 77–102.

OECD/Eurostat/WHO. *A System of Health Accounts 2011: Revised Edition*, Paris: OECD Publishing, http://dx.doi.org/10.1787/9789264270985-en.

Regmi, Krishna. *Decentralizing Health Services: A Global Perspective*. New York: Springer, 2014.

Saltman, Richard B. "Decentralization, Re-centralization and Future European Health Policy." *European Journal of Public Health* 18, no. 2 (2008): 104–106.

State Audit Office of Hungary [Állami Számvevőszék, ÁSZ]. *Elemzés az egészségügy finanszírozásáról* [Analysis of health financing]. 2019. https://asz.hu/storage/files/files/elemzesek/2019/egeszsegugy_finanszirozasa20190628.pdf.

Vicsek, Lilla. *Fókuszcsoport* [Focus group]. Budapest: Osiris Kiadó, 2006.

Xu, Tim, Albert W. Wu, and Martin A. Makary. "The Potential Hazards of Hospital Consolidation: Implications for Quality, Access, and Price." *JAMA* 314, no. 1 (2015): 1337–1338.

Resource Reallocation and Ambiguous Economic Performance in a Captured State

The Case of Hungary

József Péter Martin

Introduction

By now, it has become an academic cliché that institutions "matter," or might even be decisive when it comes to economic development.[1] After "new economic institutionalism" became mainstream, the genesis and nature of institutions fostering or impeding development, the interactions between institutions and elites, the role of the society in forming the institutions, and the interactions between institutions and policies became subjects of widely held academic discussions that complemented—or, at some points, challenged—this paradigm.[2]

---

[1] See, Douglass North, *Institutions, Institutional Change and Economic Performance* (Cambridge: Cambridge University Press, 1990); World Bank, *Building Institutions for Markets. World Development Reports* (Washington, DC: World Bank, 2002); Dani Rodrik, Arvind Subramanian, and Francesco Trebbi, "Institutions Rule: The Primacy of Institutions Over Geography and Integration in Economic Development," NBER Working Paper, no. 9305, National Bureau of Economic Research, Washington, DC, October 2002; Daron Acemoglu, Simon Johnson, and James A. Robinson, "Institutions as the Fundamental Cause of Long-Run Growth," NBER Working Paper Series, no. 10481, National Bureau of Economic Research, Washington, DC, May 2004.

[2] Dani Rodrik, "The Past, Present, and Future of Economic Growth," Global Citizen Foundation Working Paper, no. 1, Global Citizen Foundation, Isle of Man, UK, 2013; Gabriella Ilonszki, and György Lengyel, "An Elite Divide: Irresponsible Elites in Opposition and in Government," Conference paper, presented at the conference "Farewell to the Elites?" Jena, Germany, September 25–26, 2014; Alina Mungiu-

Economic stability, a precondition for sustainable, long-term growth, stems from an optimal mix of economic policy and institutional factors, although the difference between the two is murky.[3] On one hand, policies could be defined as a set of formal institutions; on the other, economic policy should serve as a means to establish an institutional set-up inducing sustainable growth for the long term. Economic policy can enhance long-term development via the optimal allocation of resources, if the institutions, in Acemoglu's terms, are inclusive by warranting a level playing field, i.e., serving the public good and not only the endeavors of the ruling elite. Inclusive institutions emerge among groups where access to resources and positions is open, thus it is more difficult to form political and economic monopolies.[4]

János Kornai's initial system paradigm made clear distinctions between the characteristics of socialist and capitalist systems.[5] Then, his revisited paradigm made further distinctions among three—in the Weberian sense—ideal types of governance, namely democracy, autocracy, and dictatorship.[6] Among these three types of polities, institutions function in inherently different ways. In democracies, institutions guarantee the conditions of removing the government (a "primary characteristic") and thus operate as controls on the central government ("secondary characteristic"). In autocracies, these control institutions are either just formalistic or weak. In dictatorships, institutions of checks

Pippidi, *The Quest for Good Governance: How Societies Develop Control of Corruption* (Cambridge: Cambridge University Press, 2015); József Péter Martin, "Continuity or Disruption? Changing Elites and the Emergence of Cronyism after the Great Recession—The Case of Hungary," *Corvinus Journal of Sociology and Social Policy* 8 (2017): 255–281; Antoaneta L. Dimitrova, "The Uncertain Road to Sustainable Democracy: Elite Coalitions, Citizen Protests and the Prospects of Democracy in Central and Eastern Europe," *East European Politics* 34, no. 3 (2018): 257–275.

3 Dani Rodrik, "The Past, Present, and Future of Economic Growth."

4 Max Weber, *Economy and Society*, vols. 1–2, ed. Günther Roth and Claus Wittich (Berkeley: University of California Press, 1978 [1921]); Douglass C. North, J. J. Wallis, and B. J. Weingast, *Violence and Social Orders*. (Cambridge: Cambridge University Press, 2009); Daron Acemoglu and James A. Robinson, *Why Nations Fail: The Origins of Power, Prosperity, and Poverty* (Cambridge, MA: Harvard University Press, 2012), 529.

5 János Kornai, "The System Paradigm," in *Paradigms of Social Change*, ed. Waltraud Schelkle, Wolf-Hagen Krauth, Martin Kohli, and Georg Elwert (Frankfurt: Campus Verlag; New York: St. Martin's, 2000), 111–134.

6 Idem., "The System Paradigm Revisited: Clarification and Additions in the Light of Experiences in the Post-Socialist Region," *Acta Oeconomica* 66, no. 4 (2016): 547–596.

and balances do not exist, thus the possibility of removing the government does not exist.

In both new institutionalism and Kornai's revised system paradigm, institutions have a crucial role in how capitalism delivers economic performance. In Acemoglu et al.'s growth model, economic performance is determined by economic institutions (e.g., property rights) and eventually by political institutions (e.g., the rule of law).[7] Growth can only be sustainable if impartial governance and the rule of law persist. However, as North pointed out thirty years ago, not only formal but also informal institutions matter when it comes to economic development.[8] (Other studies have also highlighted the primacy of informal institutions over formal ones.[9])

Elites are not a central subject of new economic institutionalism (or if they are, only in an indirect or controversial way). Rather, this paradigm is prone to attribute occasional roles to actors and personalities. For a number of institutionalists, elites remain an abstract category. However, at certain points the new elite paradigm opposes institutionalism by claiming that actors will eventually become game changers, constantly overwriting existing rules.[10] In this paradigm, trust or distrust among elites would be logically and factually prior to institutional arrangements. According to a typology of political regimes,[11] the characteristics of political institutions are interlinked with elite configurations. Democratic polities, by virtue of their existence, imply certain elite consensus.

In this paper, I discuss the Hungarian case in the context of Central and Eastern Europe (CEE), focusing on why and how some resources have been reallocated in this captured state. After describing the specificities of backsliding and the interplay of policies and institutions, varied manifestations of emerging cronyism will be revealed beyond the frequently discussed public procurement system. The economic situation shows a conspicuously ambiguous character. We discuss how varied and polarized perceptions feed-

7 Acemoglu et al., "Institutions as the Fundamental Cause of Long-Run Growth."

8 North, *Institutions, Institutional Change and Economic Performance.*

9 World Bank, *Building Institutions for Markets: World Development Reports*; Claudia Williamson, "Informal Institutions Rule: Institutional Arrangements and Economic Performance," *Public Choice* 139, no. 3–4. (2009): 371–387.

10 John Higley and Jan Pakulski, "Elite Theory versus Marxism: The Twentieth Century Verdict," in *Elites after State Socialism*, ed. John Higley and György Lengyel (Rowman & Littlefield Publishers, 2000), 229–243.

11 Ilonszki and Lengyel, "An Elite Divide."

back into the functioning of institutions.[12] In the conclusion, we construct a scheme that grasps the interplay of different factors—namely, policies, institutions, and perceptions—that contribute to economic performance.

Populism and state capture across CEE

The rise of populism is a worldwide phenomenon, observable beyond Central and Eastern Europe. It's enough to think, among many other factors, about the referendum that would force Britain to leave the European Union ("Brexit") or the extensive use of fake news in American politics and elsewhere. Eastern—and in some cases Central—European populism is different from its Western variants as the former seems to undermine basic democratic principles, and pluralistic media and society as well.[13] Populism has been mounting partly, but not exclusively, because of economic insecurity caused by the 2008 global financial and economic crisis.[14] Inglehart and Norris examined European countries and found more consistent evidence supporting the cultural backlash thesis versus the economic factors.[15] One conclusion is that disillusionment with liberal democracy is widespread among many countries in Europe.

Democratic backsliding throughout Central and Eastern Europe has been subject to vast academic and policy research in the past years.[16] In several countries, democracy seems to be emptying out and has become just procedural, focusing only on elections and on the rule of the majority.

---

[12] North, *Institutions, Institutional Change and Economic Performance.*

[13] Sławomir Sierakowski, "How Eastern European Populism is Different," *Project Syndicate*, January 31, 2018, https://www.project-syndicate.org/commentary/populism-stronger-in-eastern-europe-by-slawomir-sierakowski-2018-01?barrier=accesspaylog.

[14] Takis Pappas and Hanspeter Kreisi, "Populism in Europe During Crisis: An Introduction," in *European Populism in the Shadow of the Great Recession*, ed. Takis Pappas and Hanspeter Kreisi (Colchester: ECPR Press, 2015), 1–33.

[15] Ronald Inglehart and Pippa Norris, "Trump, Brexit and the Rise of Populism: Economic Have-Nots and Cultural Backlash," HKS Working Paper, no. RWP16-026, Harvard Kennedy School, Harvard University, Cambridge, MA, 2016.

[16] See, Transparency International Hungary, *Corruption Risks in Hungary. National Integrity Study* (Budapest–Berlin: Transparency International Hungary, 2011); János Kornai, "Hungary's U-turn," *Capitalism and Society* 10, issue 1, article 2 (2015): 1–24; idem., "The System Paradigm Revisited"; Martin, "Continuity or Disruption?"; Dimitrova, "The Uncertain Road to Sustainable Democracy."

Democratic norms—i.e., functioning checks and balances, the protection of minority rights, and active participation of citizens in the political process—are losing ground. Most CEE countries seem to be regressing, to use Douglass North's terms, from the previously established "free access order" towards "restricted access order."[17]

Dimitrova argues that, to better understand the relatively quick deterioration of democracy that appeared to be consolidated after the fall of the Berlin Wall until the Great Recession, it's not enough to focus excessively on formal institutions.[18] Democracy is not only about regulation, but also about enforcement and culture. To sustain democracy, the responsiveness of a given society seems to be indispensable. Democratic culture, however, has been weak in CEE. Unlike a number of Western European societies living in democracies over centuries, CEE states introduced capitalism by democratic design relatively swiftly after the *annus mirabilis* of 1989.[19] These developments were managed through short-term, top-down, elite-driven mechanisms aiming at a political desire,[20] namely "to catch up" with the West. The democratic and capitalist transition was a pre-designed normative process of establishing formal institutions in compliance with the Western concept of democracy, the rule of law, market economy, and by the adoption of European law. Through these elite-driven developments, a primary role was given to formal institutions under the presumption of a permissive consensus[21] by the population.

But the elites that established democratic rule, and intended to separate politics and economy, seem now prone to undermine this polity and its norms. Detecting and bestriding popular discontent, populist politicians across CEE have decided to undermine formal democratic institutions, and

17 North et al., *Violence and Social Orders.*

18 Dimitrova, "The Uncertain Road to Sustainable Democracy."

19 Claus Offe, "Capitalism by Democratic Design? Democratic Theory Facing the Triple Transition in East Central Europe," *Social Research* 58, no. 4 (Winter 1991): 865–892.

20 Péter Balázs, "Közeledés vagy távolodás?" [Convergence or divergence?], *Közgazdasági Szemle* 61 (2014): 350–362.

21 The term and its antithesis ("constraining dissensus") are mainly used in the European integration literature describing the role of the population in the integration process. See Liesbet Hooghe and Gary Marks, "A Postfunctionalist Theory of European Integration: From Permissive Consensus to Constraining Dissensus," *British Journal of Political Science* 39, no. 1 (2009): 1–23.

in one or another way have "captured" the state for the sake of long-lasting power and easy access to state resources.[22] The capture of the state by influential groups—i.e., the systematic downplaying of furtherance of commonweal in favor of making particularistic gains[23]—has become rather a rule than an exception across Central and Eastern Europe.[24] Formal institutions have a tendency to be hollowed out, while informality is gaining salience. Particularism, extractive institutions, and favoritism seem to be overcoming universalism, inclusiveness, and public integrity. State capture and particularism are manifested rather in enforcement and informal practices (e.g., staffing institutions with loyalists) than in formal institutions, which, in many cases, seem to comply with democratic principles.

Innes distinguished between an "oligarchical" and a "party" state capture.[25] In the former, business interests hijack public resources for private gain. In the latter, the ruling party captures the state in pursuit of a political monopoly, and then decides over the fate of oligarchs. Dimitrova fine-tunes this typology, differentiating between a "network-type dominant coalition" consisting of businessmen and politicians belonging to different parties, on one hand, and an "ideological party-type dominant coalition" consisting of politicians from one party and associated businessmen, on the other.[26] Péter Mihályi and Iván Szelényi put state capture in a broader context, distinguishing among three types of developments: market capture by political elites (e.g., in times of large-scale privatization), state capture by oligarchs (when business elites take over state institutions), and capture of oligarchs by autocratic leaders (in autocratic regimes).[27] This paper sophisticates these classifications by showing the specificities of the Hungarian case.

---

22 Transparency International Hungary, *Corruption Risks in Hungary*; Abby Innes, "The Political Economy of State Capture in Central Europe," *Journal of Common Market Studies* 52, no. 1 (2014): 88–104; Péter Mihályi and Iván Szelényi, "The Role of Rents in the Transition from Socialist Redistributive Economies to Market Capitalism," *Comparative Sociology* 16, no. 1 (2017): 13–38; Dimitrova, "The Uncertain Road to Sustainable Democracy."

23 Joel S. Hellman, Jones Geraint, and Daniel Kaufmann, "'Seize the State, Seize the Day.' State Capture, Corruption and Influence in Transition," Policy Research Working Paper, no. WPS2444, The World Bank, Washington, DC, September 2000.

24 Innes, "The Political Economy of State Capture in Central Europe."

25 Ibid.

26 Dimitrova, "The Uncertain Road to Sustainable Democracy."

27 Mihályi and Szelényi, "The Role of Rents."

Policy debacle and captured institutions in Hungary: two sides of the same coin?

After twenty years of a seemingly "consolidated" democracy, Fidesz—the right-wing party that governed from 1998 to 2002 under the leadership of Viktor Orbán, and then spent eight years in opposition starting in 2002—won the 2010 national election with a supermajority, i.e., two-thirds of the parliamentary mandates, and started to reshape the whole public arena to its own liking. The new government mutated the rules of the game while considering that elite change was more important than shaping established formal institutions. The endeavor has been to construct a new elite, a "national" bourgeoisie, and a middle class.[28] This attempt at elite change was supported through general discontent about the existing liberal democratic system before 2010. A 2010 Pew Research poll revealed that 77% of the Hungarian public was not satisfied with the "current state" of democracy in their country, and 72% responded that the country's economic situation had been better under "communism," i.e., before 1990, the highest numbers among CEE countries.[29]

After a landslide victory in 2010, Fidesz extended its power in ways unusual in liberal democracies and constructed a de facto "upper house" by appointing and staffing loyalists to public institutions nominally independent from executive power.[30] The party declared a new "System of National

---

[28] An unveiling reference in this respect is the statement given by András Lánczi in a newspaper interview in 2015. (At the time, Lánczi was the head of the Századvég Foundation, the most important pro-government think tank.) Lánczi said, "What [the critics of the Orbán regime] call corruption in practical terms is the most important policy goal of Fidesz. [...] The government puts forth such goals as the creation of a domestic entrepreneurial class, or the building of the pillars of a strong Hungary in agriculture and industry..." See Eva S. Balogh, "András Lánczi: What Others Call Corruption is the *Raison d'Être* of Fidesz," *Hungarian Spectrum*, May 18, 2016, http://hungarianspectrum.org/2016/05/18/andras-lanczi-what-others-call-corruption-is-the-raison-detre-of-fidesz/.

[29] Richard Wilke, "Hungary Dissatisfied with Democracy, but Not Its Ideals," *Pew Research*, April 10, 2010, http://www.pewglobal.org/2010/04/07/hungary-dissatisfied-with-democracy-but-not-its-ideals/. However, the same survey shows that Hungarians *in abstracto* support Western values and liberal democracy, and among the surveyed countries Hungary shows the biggest gap between the imagined and the real functioning of democracy.

[30] József Péter Martin and Miklós Ligeti, "Hungary," in *Lobbying in Europe: Public Affairs and the Lobbying Industry in 28 EU Countries*, ed. Alberto Bitonti and Phil Harris (London: Palgrave, 2017), 177–193.

Cooperation" in 2010; shortly afterward, the Fidesz-led government began systematically subordinating state organs—such as public prosecution, the central bank, the media authority, the State Audit Office, and others—under executive power. By 2019, democratic checks and balances characterizing Western-type democracies have been almost entirely eliminated. However, despite Fidesz nominating its loyalists to top posts in the judiciary, the functioning of individual courts has remained decentralized, and the judges have preserved their independence. Apart from this exemption, the institutions initially designed to control the government's endeavors have become instruments of the ruling elite. As Kornai observed, institutions change their functions according to the the main aim of keeping and strengthening power.[31] Fidesz unilaterally changed the constitution in 2011, and the electoral law was also transformed towards a more majoritarian (and less proportional) system. Some gerrymandering was introduced as well. As the "level playing field" shared among political players was distorted, the elections both in 2014 and 2018 could be considered free, but not fair.[32]

Seen against the general trend of populism and democratic backsliding in the region, the Hungarian case seems to be peculiar in Europe. In 2015, Kornai observed a clear "U-turn" in Hungary when it came to rule-of-law developments, the diminishing role of private property, and crackdowns on civil society.[33] The Hungarian regime has turned away from market coordination mechanisms[34] toward more bureaucratic mechanisms, a phenomenon described by Kornai as a "half-turn." Due to, in Kornai's language, the "obsession with centralization" of the ruling elite, the political system has become the most centralized one in the European Union. Nowhere else in Europe does the

---

31 Kornai, "The System Paradigm Revisited."

32 See, for example, reports by the Organization for Security and Cooperation in Europe (OSCE): OSCE, *Hungary, Parliamentary Elections, 6 April 2014: Statement of Preliminary Findings and Conclusions*, April 7, 2014, https://www.osce.org/odihr/elections/117205; and OSCE, *Hungary, Parliamentary Elections, 8 April 2018, Statement of Preliminary Findings and Conclusions*, April 9, 2018, https://www.osce.org/odihr/elections/hungary/377410.

33 Kornai, "Hungary's U-turn."

34 Kornai distinguished six coordination mechanisms: market, bureaucratic, ethical, municipal, familial and aggressive. See János Kornai, "Bürokratikus és piaci koordináció" [Bureaucratic and Market Coordination], in *Központosítás és piaci reform* [Centralization and Market Reform] (Bratislava: Kalligram, 1983); and idem., *The Socialist System: The Political Economy of Communism* (Princeton: Princeton University Press, 1992).

central government have such a tremendous regulatory and executive power. The redistribution rate, as an indicator to measure state interference in the economy, has been way above the other three Visegrád countries (i.e., Poland, the Czech Republic, and Slovakia) for decades.[35] In addition, under the Orbán regime, the disruption of the political system and the elimination of control powers created enormous space to deliver the government's endeavors.

Thus, the Hungarian case shows a unique case of state capture. An informal network of politicians and oligarchs has re-politicized the state in pursuit of a political monopoly. Contrary to Innes's notion,[36] the high officials of the governing party, as a formal entity, are not the subject of state capture, because these bailiffs have no weight in de facto decision-making. Fidesz has become a party with a huge concentration of power at the top,[37] so party officials serve just as passive executors in the power game designed by Prime Minister Orbán. But the nature of state capture is not oligarchical, either—by now, there have been no oligarchs who could challenge the government since the 2010 election.[38] An inner circle, composed of politicians, oligarchs, businessmen, and grey eminencies,[39] has been formed to pre-determine decisions

35 International Monetary Fund (IMF), "Country Report on Hungary," (2018): 24. By redistribution rate we mean government expenditures compared to GDP.

36 Innes, "The Political Economy of State Capture in Central Europe."

37 Lise Esther Herman, "Re-evaluating the Post-communist Success Story: Party Elite Loyalty, Citizen Mobilization and the Erosion of Hungarian Democracy," *European Political Science Review* 8, no. 2 (2016): 251–284; Zsolt Enyedi, "Populist Polarization and Party System Institutionalization: The Role of Party Politics in De-Democratization," *Problems of Post-Communism* 63, no. 4 (2016): 210–220.

38 The developments at the beginning of 2015 clearly showed the non-oligarchical nature of Hungarian state capture. Then, Orbán fell out with his former ally and best friend, Lajos Simicska. See Marton Dunai and Krisztina Than, "Hungary PM Faces Renewed Fire in Feud with Oligarch," *Reuters*, February 12, 2015, https://www.reuters.com/article/us-hungary-orban-oligarch/hungary-pm-faces-renewed-fire-in-feud-with-oligarch-idUSKBN0LG2BZ20150212. But Simicska, over the next three years, could not break away from Orbán's power, and eventually had to sell most of his businesses. See Anita Kőműves, "Ex Orban Friend is Selling all his Businesses," *Atlatszo*, July 17, 2018, https://english.atlatszo.hu/2018/07/17/ex-orban-friend-is-selling-all-his-businesses/.

39 One example of an obscure consultant is Árpád Habony, a mysterious speechwriter and advisor of PM Orbán, who is considered to be one of the most influential oligarchs around the PM, albeit lacking any formal position. See, Eva S. Balogh, "Orbán's Chief Advisor Árpád Habony and His Encounter with the Law," *Hungarian Spectrum*, March 4, 2013, http://hungarianspectrum.org/2013/03/04/orbans-chief-adviser-arpad-habony-and-his-encounter-with-the-law/.

while neglecting the pluralistic decision-making process, even though they are formally present. In the Hungarian model, the prime minister is the most powerful player. This mode of monopolizing state positions and resources can be labeled as "political" state capture. This regime is distinct from liberal democracy and dictatorship alike—rather, it is, as Kornai classifies it, an autocracy.[40]

Previously, I showed through detailed analysis that not only disruption prevailed after 2010, but also continuity from the turn of the millennium.[41] The World Bank's World Governance Indicators,[42] Transparency International's Corruption Perception Index,[43] and competitiveness rankings, such as that of the World Economic Forum, have all shown declining trends in Hungary at least in the past fifteen years according to their different indices.[44] In these proxy indicators, no major shifts or deviations have been observable, due either to the eruption of the global financial crisis in 2008, or to the change of government in 2010.

The growth potential of the Hungarian economy began to decline well before the global financial crisis. Then, the main source of economic insecurity was that Hungary pursued an extremely loose fiscal policy and plunged into "fiscal alcoholism" between 2001 and 2006.[45] In the two election years, in 2002 and 2006, and also in 2005, the budget deficit rose to 9%, the highest rate among all OECD countries when world markets were still liquid.[46]

The sources of economic insecurity were different before 2010 and after. Prior to 2010, mismanaged economic policy, i.e., excessive public spending, caused turbulence, and led to the loss of market confidence before the eruption of the 2008 crisis. In the Fidesz regime after 2010, however, the institu-

---

40 Kornai, however, refuses that his concept of autocracy would be somewhere in-between democracy and dictatorship with blurred boundaries but argues for using the term as a Weberian "ideal type." See Kornai, "The System Paradigm Revisited."

41 Martin, "Continuity or Disruption?"

42 World Bank, "Worldwide Governance Indicators," http://info.worldbank.org/governance/wgi/#home.

43 Transparency International, "Corruption Perceptions Index," https://www.transparency.org/research/cpi/overview.

44 World Economic Forum, *The Global Competitiveness Report, 2016–2017* (Geneva: World Economic Forum, 2016); see also WEF reports from 2001 onward.

45 György Kopits, "The Sickest Men of Europe," *The Wall Street Journal Europe*, September 21, 2006.

46 OECD, "General government deficit," OECD (2019), last updated September 9, 2019, https://data.oecd.org/gga/general-government-deficit.htm.

tional factors undermining the level playing field have emerged as potential sources of economic insecurity.

The general performance of the economy operationalized by GDP in a time series between 2005 and 2018 also reinforces the interpretation of a continuous sliding trend. In thirteen years after Hungary's accession to the EU, its economic performance became the poorest among all CEE member states to have joined the EU in the past decade (see Table 1). The differences are conspicuous: Polish and Slovak GDPs rose by 66% and 59%, respectively, while in Hungary it only grew by 22% over the same period. With these "lost" years, by 2017, once the eminent country of the region, Hungary rests at fourth from the bottom with 68%, above only Bulgaria (49%), Romania (63%), and Latvia (67%) in terms of GDP per capita compared to the EU average (100%) across the ten EU countries of Central and Eastern Europe.[47]

Table 1. Cumulate GDP growth in CEE countries by 2018 (2005=100)

	2005	2018
Hungary	100	122
Slovenia	100	126
Latvia	100	130
Estonia	100	133
Czech Republic	100	135
Lithuania	100	141
Bulgaria	100	142
Romania	100	155
Slovakia	100	159
Poland	100	166

Source: Eurostat[48]

[47] Eurostat, "GDP per Capita in PPS," last updated June 1, 2018, https://ec.europa.eu/eurostat/tgm/table.do?tab=table&init=1&language=en&pcode=tec00114&plugin=1.

[48] Eurostat, "Real GDP Growth Rate—Volume," last updated September 9, 2019, https://ec.europa.eu/eurostat/tgm/table.do?tab=table&init=1&language=en&pcode=tec00115&plugin=1.

The investment climate has shown signs of deterioration after 2010, and the investment rate has slightly eroded as well compared with the previous period. The rule of law proxy indicator published by the WGI pinpoints a moderate correlation with the investment rate between 2004 and 2017 (see Figure 1). If we take only private (business and household) investments, Hungary's rate was also modest in CEE in 2017 (see Table 2).

Figure 1. Rule of law and investments in Hungary

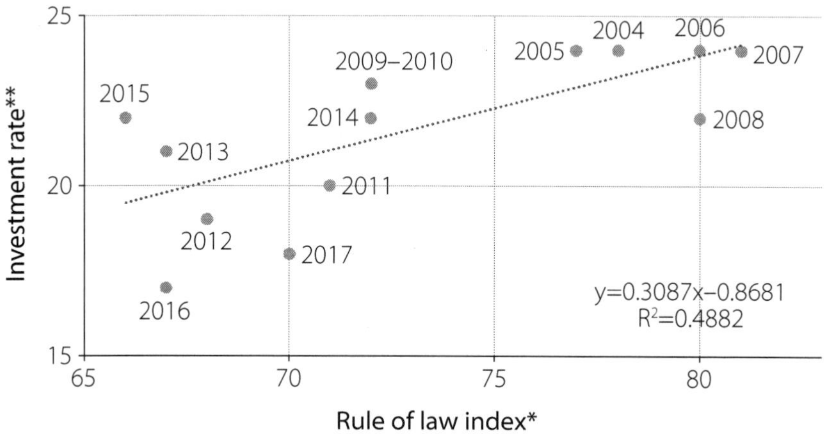

*On a scale ranging between 1 and 100 where 1 is the worst and 100 is the best performance
**Gross capital formation compared to GDP
Remark: The latest available data are from 2017
Source: Eurostat, World Bank, own calculations[49]

[49] Eurostat, "Gross Fixed Capital Formation (investments)," last updated September 9, 2019, http://ec.europa.eu/eurostat/tgm/refreshTableAction.do?tab=table&plugin=1&pcode=tec00011&language=en; and World Bank, "Worldwide Governance Indicators," http://info.worldbank.org/governance/wgi/index.aspx#reports.

Table 2. Private investments in CEE in 2017

	Private investment rate*
Czech Republic	21.4
Slovakia	19.9
Latvia	19.2
Romania	19
Lithuania	18.2
Hungary	17.7
Estonia	16.5
Bulgaria**	16
Poland**	16
Slovenia	15.4

*The sum of business and household investments compared to GDP
**The latest available data is from 2016
Source: Eurostat[50]

A deeper explanation of economic instability—whether of policy or of institutional origin prior to and after 2010, respectively—leads to an analysis of elite endeavors and moves.[51] In the first decade of the 2000s, the agreement of elites in formal institutions started to erode. After losing the national election in 2002, Fidesz questioned the legitimacy of the new government. As the government and the opposition did not recognize each other as reliable partners, the consensus concerning formal and informal institutions crumbled. Hungarian politics plunged into a vicious circle catalyzed by deep distrust fol-

---

[50] Eurostat, "Investment by Institutional Sectors," last updated July 26, 2019, http://ec.europa.eu/eurostat/tgm/refreshTableAction.do?tab=table&plugin=1&pcode=tec00132&language=en.

[51] György Lengyel, "Elites in Hard Times: The Hungarian Case in Comparative Conceptual Framework," *Comparative Sociology* 13, no. 1 (2014): 78–93; József Péter Martin, "Felzárkózás vagy bezárkózás? A magyar gazdaság teljesítménye és az euroszkepticizmus alakulása az EU-csatlakozás után, összehasonlító keretben" [Convergence or isolation? The performance of the economy and the development of Euroscepticism Following EU accession in Hungary, in a comparative framework], PhD diss., Corvinus University of Budapest, 2016.

lowing the leaked speech of then-Prime Minister Ferenc Gyurcsány in 2006.[52] In a climate of "cold civil war," the power game was played at any price, both in government and opposition. This might have been a logical explanation for why mismanaged fiscal policy until 2010 and institutional capture after 2010 were pursued even if they are supposed to be economically detrimental. Populistic manipulation emerged as a legitimate means of keeping or obtaining power. Excessive public spending was green-lighted by Hungarian elites, unlike in Poland where in the same period the implicit elite consensus of a pragmatic economic policy created favorable conditions for growth.[53] Eventually, the lack of any elite agreements made it easier for Fidesz to capture the state in 2010.

State-driven resource reallocation as a form of systemic corruption

Corruption in Hungary was already substantial and institutionalized prior to 2010, as central and local governments regularly abused power for private gain.[54] However, with the disruption of the institutional system in 2010, the scheme of corruption has significantly changed.

Just like the Hungarian political and economic system, corruption has also become centralized. The process of eliminating control institutions increased corruption risks—now, sanctioning the corrupt practices of govern-

---

[52] In a speech probably intended to be kept secret, Gyurcsány admitted to his party members that between 2004 and 2006 the Socialist-liberal coalition had lied and done nothing to win the next election. The leaked speech triggered a political crisis after which the government's popularity started freefalling. Ferenc Gyurcsány, of the Hungarian Socialist Party (MSZP), was prime minister of Hungary between 2004 and 2009 in a coalition with the liberal Alliance of Free Democrats (SZDSZ). See the full text in English at "Őszöd speech," *Wikipedia*, last edited August 13, 2019, https://en.wikipedia.org/wiki/%C5%90sz%C3%B6d_speech.

[53] Dóra Győrffy, "Bizalmatlanság és gazdaságpolitika. Hajlamok és ellenszerek" [Distrust and economic policy: inclinations and remedies], in *A bizalmatlanság hálójában. A magyar beteg* [In the net of distrust: the Hungarian patient], ed. László Muraközy (Budapest: Corvina, 2012), 56–82.

[54] Transparency International Hungary, *Korrupciós kockázatok az üzleti szektorban. A Transparency International Nemzeti Integritás Tanulmánya* [Corruption risks in the private sector: national integrity study of Transparency International] (Budapest: Transparency International, 2008).

ment-close actors has become unlikely. In a captured state, rent seekers are prone to look for the grace of government in forms of regulation, practices, or the judiciary system, instead of being involved in fair competition. The collusion of political and economic interests—or, in other words, officials and oligarchs—provides both groups with benefits and blurs the boundaries between economy and politics.[55] This particularistic way of money-making as a form of rent-seeking undermines the level playing field and disrupts some market mechanisms. In the short term, it can reduce transaction costs as loyalty crowds out investment-needy market performance. But, in the longer run, it results in suboptimal transactions through the misallocation of resources.[56]

State capture is often coupled with cronyism, which refers to a regime that allows for preferential regulations, rent-seeking, and favoritism. In other words, cronyism is when the state allocates its resources to individuals and groups closely related to the ruling elite.[57]

Under Fidesz's system, corruption happens not only in the forms of kickbacks, fraud, or bribery, but with a systemic and partial redistribution of resources. Corruption becomes part of the system instead of involving a system dysfunction. State actors unduly extract public money through intentionally designed and professionally managed channels to cronies and loyalists. Some of the formal institutions are designed for siphoning off public money to cronies. Entire mechanisms have been built by the government to reallocate these resources.[58]

[55] North et al., *Violence and Social Orders*; Dimitrova, "The Uncertain Road to Sustainable democracy."

[56] Kevin M. Murphy, Andrei Shleifer, and Robert W. Vishny, "Why is Rent-seeking so Costly to Growth?" *American Economic Review Papers and Proceedings* 83, no. 2 (1993): 409–414.

[57] Stephen Haber, "Introduction: The Political Economy of Crony Capitalism," in *Crony Capitalism and Economic Growth in Latin America: Theory and Evidence*, ed. Stephen Haber (Stanford, CA: Hoover Institution Press, 2002), xi–xxi.

[58] Some case studies show how state resources and public money have been funneled with the assistance and/or active participation of the government. Just to mention some, the case of "tobacco kiosk licenses," the "government residency bond" scheme, or the foundations established by the Hungarian Central Bank serve as vehicles of such resource reallocation. See Martin and Ligeti, "Hungary," 186–190; Martin, "Continuity or Disruption," 270–273; Transparency International Hungary, *Corruption in Hungary in 2010–2018* (Budapest: Transparency International Hungary, 2018), 12–18.

However, cronyism in Hungary is not only manifested in the public procurement practices often discussed in the literature,[59] but also in other forms of resource reallocation. We distinguish four groups of manifestations of cronyism: favoritism (including the public procurement system), wealth transformation, market manipulation, and displacement of foreign ownership (see Table 3).

The public procurement system works differently on paper than in practice. As far as regulation is concerned, the Hungarian Act on Public Procurement implements the European Directives on Public Procurement correctly, which is reflected in the fact that until the end of 2018, no infringement procedure was leveraged against Hungary related to public procurement regulation. The Hungarian Parliament also takes into account the case-law of the European Court of Justice on public procurement, and regularly aligns the regulation to this case-law. Despite formal compliance with EU law, the functioning of the public procurement system has become one of the biggest corruption risks; a feature of cronyism, as it extracts public money and hands it to politically loyal groups.[60]

In 2017, 9.4% of GDP was spent on public procurement by state organs, which is higher than in previous years when this share was 5.5% (in 2010) and 5.7% (2016).[61] Competition in public procurement is constrained. The ratio of one-bidder public procurement procedures has been mounting for several years. It has been steadily around 30% since 2009, which significantly exceeds

---

59 See, István János Tóth and Miklós Hajdu, *How does the Kleptocratic State Work in Hungary?* (Budapest: Corruption Research Center, 2018). Also, see European Semester country reports of the European Commission, e.g., European Commission, *Country Reports Hungary 2018* (Brussels: European Commission, 2018), 8, https://ec.europa.eu/info/sites/info/files/2018-european-semester-country-report-hungary-en.pdf.

60 Transparency International Hungary, *The Corruption Risks of EU Funds in Hungary* (Budapest: Transparency International Hungary, 2015); Tóth and Hajdu, *How does the Kleptocratic State Work in Hungary?*

61 See the chart of the share of total value of public procurement/GDP from 2007 to 2017 at Transparency International Hungary, *A Korrupció Érzékelési Index 2017-ben: Korrupció, jogállamiság és gazdasági teljesítmény Magyarországon, nemzetközi összehasonlításban* (Budapest: Transparency International Hungary, 2017), 10, https://transparency.hu/wp-content/uploads/2018/02/CPI-jelent%C3%A9s-2017.pdf. The author expresses kudos to the Head of Public Finance Programs in Transparency International Hungary, Gabriella Nagy for her initial description of the Hungarian public procurement system.

the average in the European Union. In 2016, in 36% of the bigger procedures above the "EU threshold," only one player submitted a bid. By contrast, in the European Union, this ratio was 17%. The ratio of procedures with no public announcement—i.e., contracts awarded without competition by intention—has been around 13% for several years, which is three times as high as the European Union average. In addition, the "four bids" public procurement procedure is a unique Hungarian scheme: the state entity does not announce open competition but rather sends an invitation for bids to four companies of its choice.

The complaint mechanism is relatively well-regulated. However, there are two serious shortcomings of implementation that significantly questions the system's effectiveness and impartiality: on one hand, the fee for legal remedy is high, especially for small and medium size enterprises, and, on the other hand, the market players might not trust the Public Procurement Authority since its independence is questionable.

The partial allocation of public procurement contracts contributed in a major way to the fabulous enrichment of some oligarchs. In 2016, the wealth of Lőrinc Mészáros—a politically built-up oligarch, former gas fitter, and a former mayor of Felcsút, birth town of PM Orbán—amounted to HUF 35 billion (€108 million), which earned him the 28th place on the Forbes list of richest Hungarians. In 2018 he became *the* wealthiest Hungarian, with a net worth of HUF 381 billion (€1.2 billion).[62] Various companies in which Mészáros holds a stake won public procurement contracts at a total value of HUF 476 billion (€1.5 billion, i.e., more than 10% of the total value of procurements) in 2017, and 83% of this sum was covered from European Union funds.[63] Another telling fact of cronyism is that Lajos Simicska, former best friend and political ally of PM Orbán, won an significant share of public procurement contracts until 2014, when his relationship with the prime minister

[62] Gergő Zsiborás, "Magyarország 50 leggazdagabb embere—már nem Csányi az első," *Forbes Hungary*, December 28, 2018, https://forbes.hu/a-magazin/magyarorszag-50-leggazdagabb-embere-mar-nem-csanyi-az-elso/.

[63] The data can be accessed from Public Procurement Authority and was compiled by *Átlátszó.hu*, an investigative reporting news portal, at https://docs.google.com/spreadsheets/d/1TsJJ3n3ytQavWnFgU9vi9jxULd0h_gWzQPiqkq2TN9Y/edit#gid=0. The portal processed data in this piece: "Túlnyomórészt uniós forrásokból gazdagodtak Mészáros Lőrinc családi cégei az elmúlt hét évben," *Átlátszó.hu*, January 15, 2018, https://atlatszo.hu/2018/01/15/tulnyomoreszt-unios-forrasokbol-gazdagodtak-meszaros-lorinc-csaladi-cegei-az-elmult-het-evben/.

soured considerably. From that point until the present, the former oligarch has been awarded of hardly any contracts.[64]

Table 3. Manifest forms of cronyism in Hungary

	Sectors /areas
Favoritism	The functioning of public procurement system
	Distribution of EU Funds
	Individual government decisions to support big companies across sectors
	National Bank of Hungary's foundations' support to loyalists
	Strategic partnership agreement as an unusual form of lobbying
Wealth transformation	Nationalization and then redistribution of licenses of tobacco retail
	Nationalization and then redistribution of casinos
	Distribution of lands
	Nationalization and then redistribution in banking sector: saving cooperatives, MKB Bank, Budapest Bank
Market manipulation	Media: advertising market distorted towards crony media companies
	Sport: tax exempts to those supporting sport in a non-transparent scheme
Displacement of foreign ownership	Banking: lowering the share of the foreign ownership though still in majority
	Media: only one big international player remained
	Energy: in majority Hungarian ownership
	Retail: in majority Hungarian ownership

Favoritism as a form of cronyism and resource reallocation entails several other areas. The partiality of public procurement system, and that of the distribution of EU funds, partly overlap—60% of the latter are distributed through public procurements. The corruption rent looks huge: on average, a rate of 25% overpricing, compared to the market price, was observed in 90% of projects funded by the EU.[65]

[64] The share of public contracts won by Simicska's companies was estimated to 10% in 2014. See Corruption Research Center, Budapest, "Versenyerősség és családi gazdaság" [Competition strength and family economy], May 30, 2015, https://crcb.atlatszo.hu/2017/05/30/versenyerosseg-es-csaladi-gazdasag/.

[65] Transparency International Hungary, *The Corruption Risks of EU Funds in Hungary*.

As another form of favoritism, the Fidesz government, after 2010, provided HUF 256 billion, twice as much as the previous governments between 2002 and 2010, to big companies in the form of tax exemptions.[66] In addition, the foundations established by the National Bank of Hungary funneled public money to cronies and relatives in 2014 and 2015.[67] After 2012, Strategic Partnership Agreements as special deals have been established between the government and private companies, which provided a communication and political tool without any legal obligation, and allowed the government to differentiate between "good" and "bad" companies.[68]

According to a suggested classification, the next manifest form of cronyism is wealth transformation. The government nationalizes some state assets, and then redistributes them to loyalists. This happened in the tobacco retail sector, the casino market,[69] the banking sector, and also in land redistribution.[70] In the case of the redistribution of tobacco retail licenses, thousands of tobacco owners lost their property.[71] In the past four years, three banks (or saving cooperatives) underwent or are still undergoing the same method. That was the case with the saving cooperatives and its "umbrella bank," Takarék-Bank[72] and MKB Bank.[73]

When it comes to a third type of cronyism, market manipulation, the media market is one of the best examples. Funneling a huge amount of public money in the form of advertisements by the government and state-owned

---

[66] The data source is the Ministry of Foreign Affairs and Trade. See Tamás Wiedemann, "Kétszer annyi pénzt adott a multiknak a Fidesz, mint az MSZP," *G7.hu*, February 1, 2018, https://g7.24.hu/allam/20180201/ketszer-annyi-penzt-adott-a-multiknak-a-fidesz-mint-az-mszp/.

[67] Martin, "Continuity or Disruption," 272–273.

[68] Transparency International Hungary, *Transparency International Hungary, Lifting The Lid on Lobbying: National Report of Hungary Lobbying in an Uncertain Business and Regulatory Environment* (Budapest: Transparency International Hungary, 2014).

[69] CSD, "5 milliárdot keresett a kaszinómonopóliumán Andy Vajna," *Index.hu*, May 31, 2017, https://index.hu/gazdasag/2017/05/31/5_milliardot_keresett_a_kaszino-monopoliuman_andy_vajna/.

[70] Népszava, "Fideszes haveroknak játszották ki az állami földeket". *Nepszava.hu*, July 1, 2016, https://nepszava.hu/1098697_fideszes-haveroknak-jatszottak-ki-az-allami-foldeket.

[71] Martin, "Continuity or Disruption," 270–272.

[72] Martin and Ligeti, "Hungary," 188–189.

[73] Transparency International Hungary, *Corruption in Hungary in 2010–2018*, 46.

enterprises has been revealed in recent years. More than 90% of state advertisements are directed toward pro-government outlets.[74]

The system of corporate donations to team sports (ice hockey, handball, basketball, soccer, water polo, and volleyball) gives an insight into a non-transparent lobbying for state resources. This system, devised in 2011, aims to channel large sums of corporate tax funds to sports clubs and associations. Corporations deduct the amount of donations from their profit before tax. This way, between 2011 and 2018, HUF 522 billion (approx. €1.7 billion) were diverted from the state to sports clubs.[75] For a long time, the government would not reveal the donors, claiming that these donations were private. However, the European Commission concluded that the sports donation system was state aid.[76] At the end of a multi-year series of court procedures, Transparency International Hungary won in the final instance, and the highest law court ordered that it was public money, and that donor corporations' names, the amount of their donations, and names of the recipient organizations should be disclosed.[77]

Political aspects play an important role when making a decision on sports donations. Nothing else can reasonably explain why some sports organizations—i.e., those with good political connections—absorbed a larger amount in donations than more successful sports clubs. The absolute champion with the highest rate of absorption has been the soccer club of Felcsút, hometown of PM Orbán.[78] This system of tax-exempt corporate donations might give businesses the opportunity to secretly divert large sums of public money to sports team, thus showing their political loyalty.

---

[74] Ágnes Urbán and Gábor Győri, "State Advertising 2006–2017," Mértékblog, *Atlatszo.hu*, last modified February 25, 2018, https://mertek.atlatszo.hu/state-advertising-2006-2017/.

[75] Dániel Bita and Péter Pető, "Őrült összeg, 522 milliárd forint ment Orbán szívügyére," *24.hu*, April 4, 2018, https://24.hu/belfold/2018/04/04/tao-felcsut-sport-tamogatas/.

[76] European Commission, *SA.31722—Hungary: Supporting the Hungarian Sport Sector via Tax Benefit Scheme*, Report no. C(2011)7287, Article 65, November 9, 2011, http://ec.europa.eu/competition/state_aid/cases/240466/240466_1271180_52_3.pdf.

[77] FüHü, "Financing of Hungarian Sports: Court Rules it must be Transparent," *Fuhu.hu*, November 19, 2017, https://fuhu.hu/financing-hungarian-sports-court-rules-must-transparent/.

[78] Transparency International Hungary, *Corruption Risks in Hungarian Sport Financing* (Budapest: Transparency International Hungary, 2015).

And finally, we find some sectors in which the explicit government policy was to displace foreign owners. It happened this way in the banking, media, energy, and retail sectors. The share of foreign ownership in the banking sector decreased from 75% in 2010 to 68% in 2015.[79] In the media sector, apart from RTL Klub, no big foreign player remained, although prior to 2010, the majority of the media market was controlled by foreign owners.[80] After 2010, in the energy sector, domestic ownership increased from 48% in 2010 to 64% in 2015; in the retail sector, from 47% in 2010 to 53% in 2015.

A glass half full or half empty? The ambiguous economic situation

Institutions function according to perceptions of societal actors.[81] Actors implicitly compare their beliefs about reality with their normative presumptions and make decisions as functions of the perceived consequences. Formal institutions, as well as policy-making itself, are influenced by these perceptions.

Under the Fidesz regime, the government echoes that the "Hungarian economy performs better"[82] and draws a rosy picture about it. There has been ground for these assessments, since the economy has been growing at a significant pace since 2013. Since 2011, public finances have been kept under control. The budget deficit has not exceeded the 3% ceiling of GDP since 2011, and the rate of indebtedness has also been decreasing. The gross external debt, compared to GDP, has declined from its peak of 149% in 2009 to 84% by the end of 2017. The inflation until 2017 proved to be not significant. There has been a significant surplus in trade and on the current

[79] For these cases, see Bence Stubnya, "Már rég teljesült Orbán álma," *Index.hu*, October 10, 2016, https://index.hu/gazdasag/2016/10/10/orban_multi_hazai_ceg_bankszektor_kiskereskedelem_energia_media/.

[80] Gábor Polyák, ed. "Nyilvánosság helyett propaganda. Lágy cenzúra a magyar médiában" [Soft censorship in Hungary: when propaganda rules public discourse], *Mérték Füzetek*, May 13–21, 2017. https://mertek.eu/wp-content/uploads/2017/05/MertekFuzetek11-2.pdf.

[81] North, *Institutions, Institutional Change and Economic Performance.*

[82] Éva Nagy, "Government Spent $3.6 Billion on 'Hungary is Performing Better' Campaign in 2013," *Budapest Beacon*, January 2, 2014, https://budapestbeacon.com/hungary-is-performing-better-campaign-cost-government-3-6-million-in-2013/.

account balance for more than five years.[83] Despite PM Orbán's populistic and Eurosceptic rhetoric, the government has subscribed to a prudent and stable economic policy.[84] That should be an explanation why the GKI confidence index[85] showed a historically high peak in the business segment and a 15-year record in the consumer segment at the end of 2017.

But, on the other hand, state capture and institutional deficiencies led to slight decreases in the investment rate and a relatively low level of private investments after 2010, as described earlier. Productivity also remained feeble, signaling structural problems in the economy,[86] a lack of internal resources to boost growth, and relying heavily on foreign funding.

The exposure to foreign resources is not a new development. Between 2002 and 2010, under left-wing governments, the excessive budget deficit and rate of indebtedness soared due to the lack of domestic triggers for growth. Under the Fidesz regime, the government uses European Union funds to boost growth. In the financial period of 2007–2013, they constituted on average 3.9% of the annual GDP, which rose to 4.7% between 2014 and 2020.[87]

---

[83] See 2018's country report of the International Monetary Fund on Hungary: International Monetary Fund, European Dept., *Hungary: 2018 Article IV Consultation—Press Release and Staff Report*, Country Report No. 18/252, August 3, 2018, https://www.imf.org/en/Publications/CR/Issues/2018/08/03/Hungary-2018-Article-IV-Consultation-Press-Release-and-Staff-Report-46151.

[84] József Péter Martin, "Pragmatizmus, ideológia, szkepszis. A magyar politikai elit és a közvélemény viszonyulása az Európai Unióhoz" [Pragmatism, ideology, skepticism: the attachment of the Hungarian political elite and public opinion vis-a-vis the European Union], in *Nemzet és Európa* [The nation and Europe], edited by Ágnes Széchenyi and Géza Buzinkay (Eger: Líceum, 2014), 161–179.

[85] GKI is an independent think tank. See trends of economic sentiment indexes here: BBJ, "GKI: Economic Sentiment at Historic Peak," *Budapest Business Journal*, December 18, 2017, https://bbj.hu/analysis/gki-economic-sentiment-at-historic-peak-_143114; in Hungarian, "Új történelmi csúcson a GKI konjunktúraindexe," *GKI*, December 18, 2017, http://www.gki.hu/wp-content/uploads/2017/12/GKI_konj_1712.pdf.

[86] European Commission, *Country Report Hungary 2018*, March 7, 2018 (Brussels, European Commission, 2018), https://ec.europa.eu/info/sites/info/files/2018-european-semester-country-report-hungary-en.pdf; BBJ, "Hungarian Economy Weakened by low Productivity," *Budapest Business Journal*, September 8, 2017, https://bbj.hu/economy/hungarian-economy-weakened-by-low-productivity_138475.

[87] European Commission, European Structural and Investment Funds, Data, "Country Data for: Hungary," https://cohesiondata.ec.europa.eu/countries/HU.

In addition, some one-off measures helped to sustain the development pace in the short term. For example, the administrative decrease in public utility fees payed by the population have undermined companies' profits and the long-term viability of energy networks. Another example: the nationalization of a private pension scheme back in 2011—funneling as much as HUF 3200 billion (around 10% of the 2011 GDP) into the national budget—contributed to growth.

The bleak picture depicted on competitiveness reinforces longer-term concerns about the Hungarian economy. According to World Economic Forum (WEF) data, based partly on hard indicators and perceptions, Hungary's competitiveness has been nosediving for more than fifteen years.[88] Hungary was the 28th most competitive economy in the world in 2001, but it only ranked 60th in 2017. Hungary's competitiveness as well as institutional performance has been deviating not only from the EU but also from the CEE average. The main trigger of the slide of competitiveness has been the poor performance of state institutions. In the rankings of "institutional efficiency"—that is, the extent to which institutions can enhance economic development—Hungary's position has been sliding since the beginning of the millennium, positioned at 26th in 2001 and dropping to 101st by 2017. These factors suggest that this two-faced performance might look similar to a Potemkin-economy: appearing genuine from the outside, but hollow on the inside.

The ambiguity of business perceptions is reflected in a qualitative study (based on structured interviews) made by Transparency International Hungary in 2017.[89] The organization asked businessmen to underline "recent positive tendencies," such as the macro-stability, in the economy. They pointed out that during the Great Recession, "the Hungarian economy was heading towards a disaster," and extraordinary measures had to be adopted to cover the budget deficit. The interviewees emphasized that, since then, Hungary has become a predictable country with a moderate budget deficit. On the other hand, businessmen have warned about institutional perfor-

[88] See WEF reports from 2001 to present, in particular, see World Economic Forum, *The Global Competitiveness Report, 2016–2017*.

[89] Transparency International Hungary, *Democratic Backsliding and Economic Performance in Hungary: Country Report* (Budapest: Transparency International Hungary, 2017).

mance, describing governmental measures "rather tailored to the political narrative created by the government than to the real needs of economy and society." The study concludes that politics in Hungary seems to be "radically centralized"—people with powerful relationships can influence authorities, courts, or law enforcement bodies.

While business perceptions are ambiguous, the population's assessments show a steeply improving trend. Growth has rebounded after 2013, as did positive perceptions toward the economy (figure 2). In 2006, 18% of Hungarians had a positive image of the economy; amidst the financial global crisis in 2009, only 4%. Yet, by 2012, this number crept up to 7.5%. Most, in 2018, this share increased to 54%. This perception might have been influenced partly by media bias, partly by a recent huge real wage increase recently despite a moderate rise in income inequality. Hungary's real gross disposable household income per capita rose by 13% between 2014 and 2017 and, although the inequalities have significantly grown since 2010, its level measured by the Gini coefficient has stayed below the average EU level as of 2018.[90] These factors might have contributed to the persisting popularity of the government underpinning a trade-off argument: citizens in autocratic regimes might support governments that are capable of delivering economic outcomes—even if they are corrupt.[91]

90 Eurostat, "The Real Gross Disposable Income of Households per Capita," last updated August 2, 2019, https://ec.europa.eu/eurostat/tgm/table.do?tab=table&init=1&plugin=1&pcode=tepsr_wc310&language=en; Eurostat, "Gini Coefficient of Equivalized Disposable Income—EU-SILC Survey," last updated August 30, 2019, https://appsso.eurostat.ec.europa.eu/nui/show.do?dataset=ilc_di12&lang=en.

91 Guillermo Rosas and Luigi Manzetti, "Reassessing the Trade-off Hypothesis: How Misery Drives the Corruption Effect on Presidential Approval," *Electoral Studies* 39 (September 2015): 26–38.

Figure 2. Growth rate of and perceptions about the Hungarian economy (2006–2018)

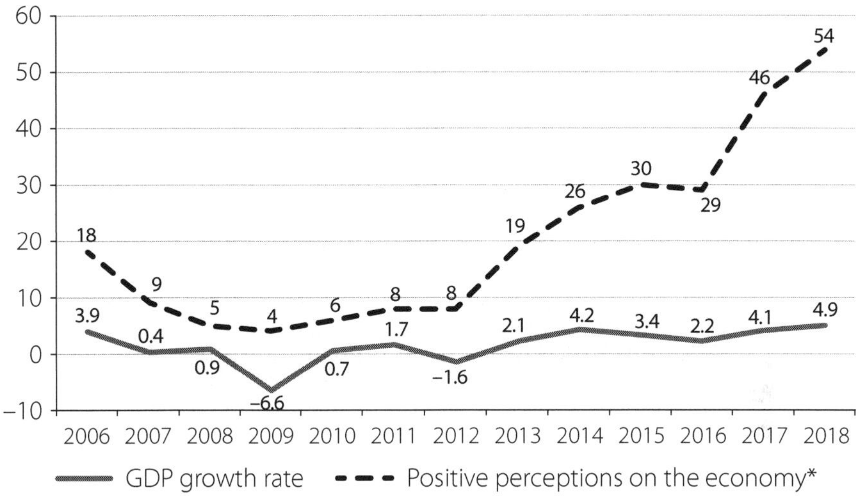

*The share of those who think that the situation of the national economy is "good" or "very "good."
Source: Eurostat, Eurobarometer, own calculations.[92]
Remark: Spring and Fall Eurobarometer data per year were averaged

A scheme of interplay and concluding remarks

In this paper, I analyzed the disruptive nature of the Hungarian regime built by the incumbent party after 2010, pointing out its extremely centralized nature, which has, in turn, entailed state capture and cronyism. Four specific forms of resource reallocation have been identified: favoritism, wealth transformation, market manipulation, and displacement of foreign ownership. We also pointed out the mismanagement of economic policy prior to 2010. Crumbled consensus and deep distrust among elites contributed to rising

92 Eurostat, "Real GDP Growth Rate—Volume," last updated September 9, 2019, http://ec.europa.eu/eurostat/tgm/table.do?tab=table&init=1&language=en&pcode=tec00115&plugin=1; European Commission, "Public Opinion—How Would you Judge the Current Situation in each of the Following? The Situation of the (NATIONALITY) Economy," last updated June 2019, http://ec.europa.eu/commfrontoffice/publicopinion/index.cfm/Chart/getChart/themeKy/27/groupKy/229.

populism and democratic backsliding. After 2010, the established system produced two-faced economic performance with promising short-term, but challenging long-term, indicators. Perceptions of Hungarians on the economy have improved radically in the recent decade. However, business perceptions measured and interpreted in a longer time series—such as perceptions of corruption, institutional efficiency, or competitiveness—have been rather bleak. Based on these factors, a scheme of the interplay of the described factors can be constructed (Figure 3).

Figure 3. The interplay of institutions, policies, and perceptions in Hungary

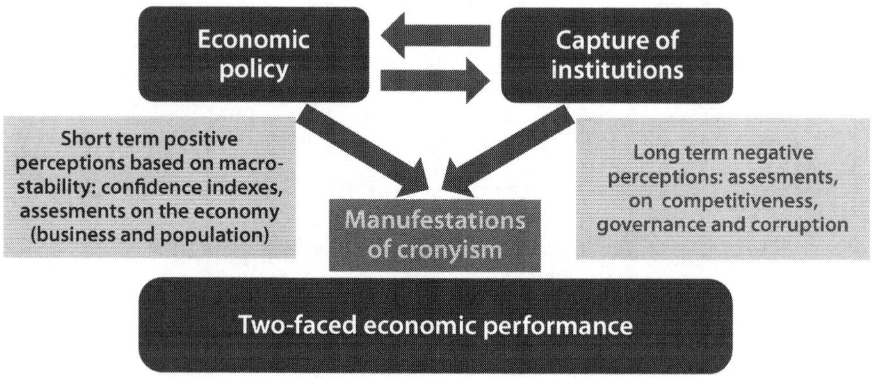

On one hand, the ruling party's economic policy has granted stability and has improved most basic economic indicators. On the other hand, its economic policy was prone to serve the captured state and crony system, providing means for resource reallocation. Due to these ambiguities in short- and long-term facts and perceptions, the economic performance is two-faced. This characterization doubts the inherent sustainability of the system.

References

Acemoglu, Daron, Simon Johnson, and James A. Robinson. "Institutions as the Fundamental Cause of Long-Run Growth." NBER Working Paper Series, no. 10481, National Bureau of Economic Research, Washington, DC, May 2004.

Acemoglu, Daron, and James A. Robinson. *Why Nations Fail: The Origins of Power, Prosperity, and Poverty.* Boston: Harvard University Press, 2012.

Balázs, Péter. "Közeledés vagy távolodás?" [Convergence or divergence?] *Közgazdasági Szemle* 61 (2014): 350–362.

Dimitrova, Antoaneta L. "The Uncertain Road to Sustainable Democracy: Elite Coalitions, Citizen Protests and the Prospects of Democracy in Central and Eastern Europe." *East European Politics* 34, no. 3 (2018): 257–275.

Enyedi, Zsolt. "Populist Polarization and Party System Institutionalization: The Role of Party Politics in De-Democratization." *Problems of Post-Communism* 63, no. 4 (2016): 210–220.

Győrffy, Dóra. "Bizalmatlanság és gazdaságpolitika. Hajlamok és ellenszerek" [Distrust and economic policy: inclinations and remedies]. In *A bizalmatlanság hálójában. A magyar beteg* [In the net of distrust: the Hungarian patient], edited by László Muraközy, 56–82. Budapest: Corvina, 2012.

Haber, Stephen. "Introduction: The Political Economy of Crony Capitalism." In *Crony Capitalism and Economic Growth in Latin America: Theory and Evidence*, edited by S. Haber, xi–xxi. Stanford, CA: Hoover Institution Press, 2002.

Hellman, Joel S., Jones Geraint, and Daniel Kaufmann. "'Seize the State, Seize the Day.' State Capture, Corruption and Influence in Transition." Policy Research Working Paper, no. WPS2444, The World Bank, Washington, DC, September 2000.

Herman, Lise Esther. "Re-evaluating the Post-communist Success Story: Party Elite Loyalty, Citizen Mobilization and the Erosion of Hungarian Democracy." *European Political Science Review* 8, no. 2 (2016): 251–284.

Higley, John, and Jan Pakulski. "Elite Theory versus Marxism: The Twentieth Century Verdict." In *Elites after State Socialism*, edited by John Higley and György Lengyel, 229–243. Rowman & Littlefield Publishers, 2000.

Hooghe, Liesbet, and Gary Marks. "A Postfunctionalist Theory of European Integration: From Permissive Consensus to Constraining Dissensus." *British Journal of Political Science* 39, no. 1 (2009): 1–23.

Ilonszki, Gabriella, and György Lengyel. "An Elite Divide: Irresponsible Elites in Opposition and in Government." Conference paper, presented at the conference "Farewell to the Elites?" Jena, Germany, September 25–26, 2014.

Inglehart, Ronald, and Pippa Norris. "Trump, Brexit and the Rise of Populism: Economic Have-Nots and Cultural Backlash." HKS Working Paper, no. RWP16-026, Harvard Kennedy School, Harvard University, Cambridge, MA, 2016.

Innes, Abby. "The Political Economy of State Capture in Central Europe." *Journal of Common Market Studies* 52, no. 1 (2014): 88–104.

International Monetary Fund (IMF), "Country Report on Hungary," (2018): 24.

Kopits, György. "The Sickest Men of Europe." *The Wall Street Journal Europe*, September 21, 2006.

Kornai, János. "Bürokratikus és piaci koordináció" [Bureaucratic and market coordination]. In *Központosítás és piaci reform* [Centralization and market reform]. Bratislava: Kalligram, 1983.

———. *The Socialist System: The Political Economy of Communism*. Princeton: Princeton University Press, 1992.

———. "The System Paradigm." In *Paradigms of Social Change*, edited by Waltraud Schelkle, Wolf-Hagen Krauth, Martin Kohli, and Georg Elwert, 111–134. Frankfurt: Campus Verlag; New York: St. Martin's, 2000.

———. "Hungary's U-turn." *Capitalism and Society* 10, issue 1, article 2 (2015): 1-24.

———. "The System Paradigm Revisited: Clarification and Additions in the Light of Experiences in the Post-Socialist Region." *Acta Oeconomica* 66, no. 4 (2016): 547–596.

Lengyel, György. "Elites in Hard Times: The Hungarian Case in Comparative Conceptual Framework." *Comparative Sociology* 13, no. 1 (2014): 78–93.

Martin, József Péter. "Pragmatizmus, ideológia, szkepszis. A magyar politikai elit és a közvélemény viszonyulása az Európai Unióhoz" [Pragmatism, ideology, skepticism: the attachment of the Hungarian political elite and public opinion vis-a-vis the European Union]. In *Nemzet és Európa* [The nation and Europe], edited by Ágnes Széchenyi and Géza Buzinkay, 161–179. Eger: Líceum, 2014.

———. "Felzárkózás vagy bezárkózás? A magyar gazdaság teljesítménye és az euroszkepticizmus alakulása az EU-csatlakozás után, összehasonlító keretben" [Convergence or isolation? The performance of the economy and the development of Euroscepticism following EU accession in Hungary, in a comparative framework]. PhD diss., Corvinus University of Budapest, 2016.

———, and Miklós Ligeti. "Hungary." In *Lobbying in Europe: Public Affairs and the Lobbying Industry in 28 EU Countries*, edited by Alberto Bitonti and Phil Harris, 177–193. London: Palgrave, 2017.

———. "Continuity or Disruption? Changing Elites and the Emergence of Cronyism after the Great Recession—The Case of Hungary." *Corvinus Journal of Sociology and Social Policy* 8 (2017): 255–281.

Mihályi, Péter, and Iván Szelényi. "The Role of Rents in the Transition from Socialist Redistributive Economies to Market Capitalism." *Comparative Sociology* 16, no. 1 (2017): 13–38.

Mungiu-Pippidi, Alina. *The Quest for Good Governance: How Societies Develop Control of Corruption.* Cambridge: Cambridge University Press, 2015.

Murphy, Kevin M., Andrei Shleifer, and Robert W. Vishny. "Why is Rent-seeking so Costly to Growth?" *American Economic Review Papers and Proceedings* 83, no. 2 (1993): 409–414.

North, Douglass. *Institutions, Institutional Change and Economic Performance.* Cambridge: Cambridge University Press, 1990.

———. *Understanding the Process of Economic Change.* Princeton: Princeton University Press, 2005.

———. J. J. Wallis, and B. J. Weingast. *Violence and Social Orders.* Cambridge: Cambridge University Press, 2009.

Offe, Claus. "Capitalism by Democratic Design? Democratic Theory Facing the Triple Transition in East Central Europe." *Social Research* 58, no. 4 (Winter 1991): 865–892.

Pappas, Takis, and Hanspeter Kreisi. "Populism in Europe During Crisis: An Introduction." In *European Populism in the Shadow of the Great Recession*, edited by Takis Pappas and Hanspeter Kreisi, 1–33. Colchester: ECPR Press, 2015.

Polyák, Gábor, ed. "Nyilvánosság helyett propaganda. Lágy cenzúra a magyar médiában" [Soft censorship in Hungary: when propaganda rules public discourse]. *Mérték Füzetek*, May 13–21, 2017. https://mertek.eu/wp-content/uploads/2017/05/MertekFuzetek11-2.pdf.

Rodrik, Dani, Arvind Subramanian, and Francesco Trebbi. "Institutions Rule: The Primacy of Institutions Over Geography and Integration in Economic Development." NBER Working Paper, no. 9305, National Bureau of Economic Research, Washington, DC, October 2002.

Rodrik, Dani. "The Past, Present, and Future of Economic Growth." Global Citizen Foundation Working Paper, no. 1, Global Citizen Foundation, Isle of Man, UK, 2013.

Rosas, Guillermo, and Luigi Manzetti. "Reassessing the Trade-off Hypothesis: How Misery Drives the Corruption Effect on Presidential Approval." *Electoral Studies* 39 (September 2015): 26–38.

Tilly, Charles. "Democracy is a Lake." In *The Social Construction of Democracy*, edited by George Reid Andrews and Herrick Chapman, 365–366. New York: New York University Press; Basingstoke: Macmillan, 1995.

Tóth, István János, and Miklós Hajdu. *How does the Kleptocratic State Work in Hungary?* Budapest: Corruption Research Center, 2018.

Transparency International Hungary. *Korrupciós kockázatok az üzleti szektorban. A Transparency International Nemzeti Integritás Tanulmánya* [Corruption risks in the private sector: national integrity study of Transparency International]. Budapest: Transparency International, 2008.

———. *Corruption Risks in Hungary: National Integrity Study.* Budapest–Berlin: Transparency International Hungary, 2011.

———. *Transparency International Hungary, Lifting The Lid on Lobbying: National Report of Hungary Lobbying in an Uncertain Business and Regulatory Environment.* Budapest: Transparency International Hungary, 2014.

———. *The Corruption Risks of EU Funds in Hungary.* Budapest: Transparency International Hungary, 2015.

———. *Corruption Risks in Hungarian Sport Financing.* Budapest: Transparency International Hungary, 2015.

———. *Democratic Backsliding and Economic Performance in Hungary: Country Report.* Budapest: Transparency International Hungary, 2017.

———. *Corruption in Hungary in 2010–2018.* Budapest: Transparency International Hungary, 2018.

Urbán, Ágnes, and Gábor Győri. 2018. "State Advertising 2006–2017." Mértékblog, *Atlatszo.hu*. Last modified February 25, 2018. https://mertek.atlatszo.hu/state-advertising-2006-2017/.

Weber, Max. *Economy and Society*, vols. 1–2, edited by Günther Roth and Claus Wittich. Berkeley: University of California Press, 1978 [1921].

Williamson, Claudia. "Informal Institutions Rule: Institutional Arrangements and Economic Performance." *Public Choice* 139, no. 3–4. (2009): 371–387.

World Bank. *Building Institutions for Markets: World Development Reports.* Washington, DC: World Bank, 2002.

World Economic Forum. *The Global Competitiveness Report, 2016–2017.* Geneva: World Economic Forum, 2016.

About the Value of Democracy and Other Challenging Research Topics[1]

Closing Remarks at the Conference on February 22, 2018

János Kornai

Dear Friends,

Our chairman has just said that I will say a few words. I will say more than a few words, if you forgive me.

I would like to thank the organizers; they did a fantastic job. The first expression of gratitude goes to Miklós Rosta, who was the main engine of the whole process, and who really kept rigorous centralization. He personally did a huge part of the organizational tasks, and devoted much time to that. Also, I'm very happy to thank the team who gathered around him, who, for weeks and weeks—or maybe I can say for several months—has worked on bringing all these people together, and this wonderful collection of interesting lectures and interesting debates. And when I say these words, I think not only of the February conference, but of all the other events which were related to my birthday. It started in January with another extremely interesting conference, and there is also an exhibition, and—what I must mention—there are two journals, *Közgazdaság* and *Acta Oeconomica*, which devoted whole special issues to discussing the impact of my work or thoughts related to my work. Also, a paper in *Közgazdasági Szemle* by László Csaba; an important article. Behind the papers, there is also the work of editors, and of course all the authors of the papers. I have to thank all of you who made contributions to these collections of works.

---

[1] The transcript was made by Eszter Mohácsi. The above text is consistent in its content with the spoken text, only minimal changes to facilitate understanding and to avoid misinterpretation have been made. First published as "About the Value of Democracy and other Challenging Research Topics: Closing Remarks at the Conference on February 22, 2018," *Köz-gazdaság* 13, no. 8 (2018): 59–63.

Here, I could end my closing words, saying that I am grateful for all that. Personally, for me, it was a great, great pleasure to attend—but I don't want to finish here. I got a lot of praise, and everybody knows from his or her own experience that to be praised is a pleasant feeling, and usually people don't reject laudations. But I recognized that it is not only praise which I got, but one or two, or three, or maybe more people included criticism and disagreement, and criticism of or disagreement over important issues. So, instead of resting on my laurels, which is a comfortable position, I can promise you that I am not going to do that. And the first thing that I want to do is to read everything that was presented. I tried to listen to many of the presentations, but I didn't attend, for instance, debates in this conference section. Due to health problems, I cannot sit here from early morning till late in the evening. I am, by the way, more of a reading type, who perceives ideas better by reading than listening. So, for the next few months—I need one or two or maybe more months for the reading process, since, in the meantime, other obligations will certainly appear. If possible, I will react to some papers in publications of my own, or I will send a letter to some people. I also hope that with at least a few of those who are residing in Budapest I will have personal conversations.

For me, reading the conference material is a learning process. And this is not the first time in my life that I start to learn from the reactions to my contributions. I have spent much of my time in the world of academia, learning. From the very first day until today, I proceeded with learning. Let me be a bit more specific about learning. In my first book on overcentralization, I already touched upon the problem of shortages. If anyone reads this first book of mine again, they will discover that I already had the feeling that it is one of the central problems of an economy, especially of a socialist economy. And then, throughout my life, that problem has excited me. And each period led to new experiences. I got rejections after the overcentralization book. Part of the disagreement was expressed in a rather harsh way by firing me from my workplace. Later on, there were not so rude, but more civilized voices of disagreement. A part of the later discussions were fruitful, and I was ready to revise my ideas. I repeatedly altered the wording, the labels of the non-equilibrium situations. But that is not the most important part of the revision process. I tried to refine the analytical methods, the way to study the phenomena of market disequilibria. At a rather early stage in research on equilibria, I became interested in comparing capitalism and socialism. What kinds of departures from Walrasian equilibria exist in these two types of systems?

Are excess demand or excess supply only random fluctuations, or is there something systemic? Is there some kind of a fixed point in a dynamic system, characteristic of a special type of system? Does some kind of normal shortage or normal surplus exist in various socio-economic systems?

My most recent research results on this subject are summarized in my latest book, *Dynamism, Rivalry, and the Surplus Economy.* My feeling today is somewhat similar to that of a student when he gets grades for his work. This conference meant to me some kind of grading of my performance by checking the impact. And I see that this part of my work has had much less impact than, for instance, the soft budget constraint issue. It's somehow less fashionable. Or people are not interested in the shortage versus surplus contrast since most economists are living in a market economy. People are used to a surplus economy and find it self-evident that everything is available on the supply side. But I have had a long life, and lived through long decades of a shortage economy, so for me it is not self-evident that today the situation is the opposite one. And while I have many co-workers in other subjects, I feel—and I regard this as a failure of my own work—that I was not able to motivate others to work seriously on the non-Walrasian equilibria theme. There are exceptions, luckily. At this conference, an exception was Yingyi Qian's talk. I'm not saying that I'm alone in this direction of research: I have a few allies. However, I would like to see more work on the subject.

Now let me move on to research on the soft budget constraint. For me, it was not simply a kind of discovery, but it was from the first day onwards a learning process. I gave my first talk on that—I remember the day, it was at the Stockholm School of Economics, where I gave a course on socialism. I explained this idea of the soft budget constraint, and then two of the graduate students who attended the course came to me and told me: "That sounds very interesting." Both graduate students have made great careers since then. But that was a crude first approximation. When I realized that people misunderstood me, I felt that I'd have to write it again, and explain it better. Then to my great fortune along came Erik Maskin, and produced a game theoretical model together with Mathias Dewatripont on this phenomenon. Their model, by the way, captured only one aspect of it; soft budget constraint is a richer concept. Then came many empirical studies; all of these efforts are very instructive, and I tried to learn from them. Today's panel, just this afternoon, was a very insightful event. Here, the Chinese participants were not satisfied to consider concepts of private ownership, or public ownership, or market, or bureaucracy, exclusively at an abstract level. Let's look at the facts! I would like to learn from experience. I don't think that now the problem of the soft budget is solved, and it's time to close research on soft budget constraint. On the contrary, I feel that we are, of course, not at the beginning, but we are in the middle of the way, and a lot of work has to be done in the future, also in pure theory, because there are many aspects of the problem which require pure theory. Serious further research should be done in the empirical field as well. And what is missing very much is an attempt to unify these two lines of thought, the soft budget constraint and persisting, non-Walrasian equilibria. There is certainly a relationship between them. For instance, Chengang Xu and Yingyi Qian, and perhaps other friends and colleagues, started to work on this issue. I tried, but up to now I haven't succeeded. I will continue my personal efforts, but I must be realistic. You came to my ninetieth birthday. Age ninety is not the time to complete such a tremendously difficult task, which we all, who are interested in the subject, didn't get through yet. So, I rather want to encourage at least those who are here, or those who will join us, to work on that. And maybe I'm biased, but I think a unification of these two theories would be an extremely exciting task for a whole generation to come.

There is also a third subject deserving special attention. I'm sorry, but maybe it is a sign of lack of gratitude that I mention problems where I didn't get satisfaction at this conference, nevertheless, I just feel I must say it. The third theme is related to politics and values. True, somebody who studies a large part of my life-work seriously could draw the following conclusion. Our job is description, analysis, understanding in a positive way. I use here this term "positive" as it is used in the philosophy of science. Positive knowledge means understanding the real world, and that's it—we may abstain from normative thinking and from value judgements. Everyone has the right to do that. And I especially don't urge anyone to go on the barricades with a flag and announce his political program, or give suggestions for the next government. I understand people who don't do that. But everyone has a mirror at home and can look in the mirror, and check his own conscience. He or she may speak to himself, or speak to his wife or husband confidentially. And think over the relationship between ultimate ethical values, social values, politics on the one hand, and the economy and economic policy on the other. At least in our thoughts, we must not evade this problem. And that is a very, very timely warning.

Let's come back—it was a favorite subject during the whole conference—to our thinking about China. Making judgements about China's performance, one cannot sidestep serious consideration of fundamental ethical issues. China has produced quite incredible performance in growth. That can be shown in tables and graphs, and everyone will be impressed. I'm always impressed too. And not only impressed, but in my modest way I tried to exert a certain influence on Chinese policy-makers to promote an economic institutional framework that is favorable for growth. But now, after we see this giant China, we have to consider what China will do in the future. Two of our Chinese friends here at this table a few minutes ago tried to guess whether it can maintain a six percent growth rate, or it will slow down. I want to be quite frank: my main concern is what China is going to do as one of the giant powers of world politics. The question is not only intellectually exciting. Simply as a citizen, and as a father, and grandfather, and great-grandfather, I am worried what will happen in a world where China is becoming one of the great players. Of course, it's already a great player, and will keep becoming even greater and even more powerful, a country with a peculiar ideology. Ideology—again an issue not discussed sufficiently at this conference, or at the earlier conference, or in the papers. The official Chinese ideology is very much influenced by nationalistic ideas. Now, if China were the only nationalist power in the world, then one can think about isolation. But that is not the case. There are other giants, which are also nationalist. There is the USA, where the president is announcing "America First." Not the globe first, not the international community, not the future of the international community first, but America first. And then we have Russia, where the leadership again is explicitly and emphatically nationalistic.

I always thought that I was talking and writing about political economy. My book *The Socialist System* has the subtitle *Political Economy,* and when I gave it this subtitle, I didn't think about Marxian "politecon" as it was taught in the classes of, say, the old Karl Marx University. I was always interested in the relationship between politics, ideology, economy, and the whole society. And for me it's important to emphasize in these closing remarks that at least people who have no limitations on the expression of their views—because there are countries where it is not so easy to do that, I know that very well: I know from past experience that there is such a thing as the limitation of free speech and free writing—but at least those who don't suffer from these limitations have to think about the interconnections between politics, ideology, and economy.

This train of thought leads to some kind of ordering or ranking of values. It is always an individual choice what kind of value system you regard as your own. I don't accept a simple trade-off, saying that an X-thousand-dollar increment in growth is equivalent to the imprisonment of a freedom fighter. That is not acceptable for me. I do have a ranking, or more specifically, a lexicographic ranking, where my top priority goes to freedom, liberties, liberty of speech, liberty of free expression of thoughts, liberty of the press, autonomy for the individual, and for voluntary communities, democracy, state of law. That is a group of values which are very strongly interconnected. I didn't arbitrarily select these desiderata. In my political ethics, this group of values has a higher priority than the increase of the growth rate.

It's not mandatory to share my value system. Other people have other value systems. I must confess that for a long while I didn't think over this dilemma with all its implications. And I was just looking in amazement at the Chinese miracle. And I didn't think with sufficient depth about the contradiction, that the political system basically didn't change in parallel with the economic miracle. True, there were changes. It shifted for a while from a brutally repressive system to a less brutal, somewhat milder repressive system. Of course, that's important. I don't deny that the degree of the brutality of repression matters. Whether there is torture in prisons, or whether there is no torture. That matters a lot. But it's still basically the same system. And here I use the term "system" in my own interpretation. Repression in that society is systemic.

The formation of my order of ethical and political preferences was strongly influenced by lessons I learnt in Hungary. We know from research in behavioral economics that gaining something is not identical with losing something. Behavioral economists can rigorously prove that a hundred-dollar gain brings more utility to the individual, or a more intense feeling of well-being, than the same hundred-dollar loss from a given level. Now, China has never experienced democracy, and therefore they don't know from personal experience what the value of democracy is.

Eastern Europeans got democracy mainly as a gift. There was a fight for democracy, and I have genuine respect for people like János Kis and Adam Michnik, who talked here two days ago, and who, taking serious risks, fought for freedom and democracy. But even they admitted that their fight was only one of the contributing factors, and there were many other contributing factors. So, it's not an exaggeration to say that to a large extent we got democracy almost as an additional gift when the transition to a free market started. We, the citizens of Eastern Europe, immediately adjusted to that, and started to be discontent with all the imperfections of democracy and began to say nasty words about all politicians. The historical period of democracy started with a certain disappointment in democracy. And it is only now, in the last few years, when we are losing democracy, that at least a part of the Hungarian population has started to feel what the genuine value of freedom is. Therefore, I suggest that everyone who is not Eastern European should study the recent Eastern European experience, should study what is going on in Hungary, what is going on in Poland. These are two remarkable countries, which could serve as laboratories demonstrating the procedure for liquidating the great achievements of democracy.

In any case, even if you are working in other fields of economic analysis, at least in your way of thinking don't become apolitical. At least in the back of our minds, all of us should be political economists. And in that capacity it is our never-ending task to think about the complex dilemmas of choosing fundamental values. That is not simply a suggestion for others, it is also an ambition of my own. I feel that I didn't succeed in convincing my colleagues to do that. I tried, but in practice my words reach very few people. I wouldn't say that all of those whom my words reach are here, but still, it is a small group. It would be interesting to know what these people are teaching in their classrooms and to hear how much of my message is getting through in their teaching. So, there are a lot of things to do. I promise you that as long as I can, I will not rest on my laurels, but try to continue: the work is still far from completion.

Thank you again for coming to the conference, and thank you for giving me further tasks.

Notes on the Contributors

Bruno Dallago, PhD, is Professor of Economics at the Department of Economics and Management, University of Trento, Italy. His research interests include the European Union, comparative economics, the transforming economies of Central and East Europe, SMEs and entrepreneurship, local development. He is the author and editor of several scholarly books and journal articles. He was visiting professor at various international universities, President of the European Association for Comparative Economic Studies (1995–1996), consultant to international organizations and a member of the International Advisory Board of the Institute of Economics of the Hungarian Academy of Sciences.

Geoffrey M. Hodgson is Professor in Management at Loughborough University London. He is the author of over 20 books including *Is Socialism Feasible?* (2019), *Is There a Future for Heterodox Economics?* (2019) and *Conceptualizing Capitalism* (2015 – winner of the Schumpeter Prize). He has published over 150 articles in refereed academic journals. He is Editor-in-Chief of the *Journal of Institutional Economics* and Secretary of the World Interdisciplinary Network for Institutional Research (WINIR).

László Jankovics received his PhD in Economics from the University of Debrecen (UD) in 2007. From 1999 to 2005, he worked for the Economics Department of UD as an assistant professor. In 2006, he joined the European Commission (EC) as an economic analyst, where the functioning of independent fiscal institutions has recently become his main dossier. In 2009 and 2010, while on unpaid leave from the EC, he served as director for fiscal analysis at the Office of the Fiscal Council in Hungary. His research interests include fiscal governance and economic policy issues. He is author of several publications related to these topics.

Éva Krenyácz, PhD, is Assistant Professor at Corvinus University of Budapest. For the past nearly 15 years she worked in organizations of the health care sector as controller, accountant, manager, and consultant.

József Péter Martin is senior lecturer of the Department of Comparative and Institutional Economics at Corvinus University of Budapest and has been managing director of Transparency International Hungary since 2013. His research field is the political economy of corruption, governance and European Union focusing on institutional triggers of development. Previously, he worked as an economic journalist and was editor-in-chief of Hungarian business magazine *Figyelő*.

Péter Mihályi started his career as a researcher of the UN Economic Commission for Europe in Geneva in 1983. After returning to his native country, he served—inter alia—as Deputy Government Commissioner for Privatization in 1994–95 and played a major role in the largest transactions in energy and banking. In 1997–98 he was promoted to Deputy State Secretary in the Ministry of Finance. Currently he is full professor of Corvinus University and the Central European University in Budapest. Since 2012, he is Editor-in-Chief of *Acta Oeconomica*, an English language academic quarterly.

Dora Piroska holds a PhD in Political Science from the Central European University. She has been a Lecturer at the Department of Government at the University of Texas at Austin, an Associate Professor at the Corvinus University of Budapest and currently a Visiting Professor at the CEU. She is a political economist with a special interest in the Central and Eastern European region. Recently she has published on the macroprudential turn in bank regulation, the Banking Union's perception in Eastern member states, the competing crisis management approaches of the Troika, and the impact of EU banking governance on Slovenian democracy. Her publications appear in *New Political Economy, Journal of Common Market Studies, Third World Thematics,*

Competition and Change, edited volumes by Oxford University Press, Routledge and in several Hungarian outlets.

Gérard Roland is the E. Morris Cox Professor of Economics and Professor of Political Pcience at the University of California Berkeley where he has been since 2001. He has received many honors including an honorary professorship from the Renmin University of China in Beijing in 2002. He is the author of over 150 journal articles, chapters in books, and books; and has been published in leading economics journals on topics of transition, political economy, culture and comparative economics. He wrote the leading graduate textbook *Transition and Economics* (2000, MIT Press), which has been translated into various languages, including Chinese and Russian. He co-organized with Olivier Blanchard a Nobel symposium on the transition economics in 1999. In recent years, his research has broadened to developing economies in general with special emphasis on the role of institutions and culture. He wrote the undergraduate textbook *Development Economics* (2013, Pearson Addison-Wesley).

Miklós Rosta received his PhD in Economics in 2012. Currently, he is the head of the Department of Comparative and Institutional Economics and Director of the Center of Central Asia Research at Corvinus University of Budapest. His main research interests include issues connected to institutional economics and public management studies. He serves as editor of the *Hungarian Economic Review (Közgazdasági Szemle)*. His publications appeared in *Administration & Society*, *International Studies of Management and Organization* and *Society & Economy*. He published a monograph titled *Innovation, Adaptation or Imitation: the New Public Management* in 2012. In 2019, he received a Bolyai research grant from the Hungarian Academy of Science.

Ivan Szelényi is a Hungarian-American sociologist. He is William Graham Sumner Emeritus Professor of Sociology and Political Science, Yale University and Max Weber Emeritus Professor of Social Sciences, NYUAD. He is the author or co-author of several monographs, including *Urban Inequalities under State Socialism* (1983), *The Intellectuals on the Road to Class Power* (1979), *Making Capitalism without Capitalists* (1998) and most recently *Rentseekers, Profits, Wages and Inequalities: The Top 20 Percent* (2019) and *Varieties of Post-communist Capitalism* (2020). He is a fellow of American Academy of Arts and Sciences and an ordinary member of the Hungarian Academy of Sciences.

Index